PACIFIC OCEAN

NEW IRELAND

NEW GUINEA

Wewak

GAZELLE
PENINSULA

CAPE
GLOUCESTER

NEW
BRITAIN

Mt. Hagen

Goroka • Kainantu

PAPUA

Okapa

Lae

SOLOMON SEA

Wau

N

Port Moresby

AUSTRALIA

CORAL SEA

• Towns
_ _ _ Administrative Districts
1 Western Highlands
2 Southern Highlands
3 Eastern Highlands
4 Morobe
5 Sepik

Laughing Death

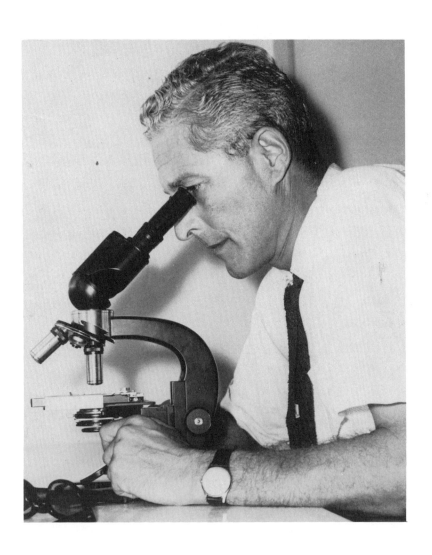

Laughing Death

The Untold Story of Kuru

by

Vincent Zigas

Foreword by

D. Carleton Gajdusek

Humana Press • Clifton, New Jersey

To
Sir John Gunther

With amiable gratitude and unbounded affection

Library of Congress Cataloging-in-Publication Data:

Zigas, Vincent.
    Laughing death.

    1. Zigas, Vincent. 2. Microbiologists—Biography. 3. Physicians—Biography. 4. Kuru—Research—History.
I. Title.
QR31.Z47A3 1990   610.92 [B]   89-24706
ISBN 0-89603-111-X

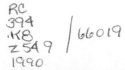

Foreword

Also the task is to evaluate and assess, and to decide whether the work is a novel, or a book of memoirs, or a parody, or a lampoon, or a variation on imaginative themes, or psychological study; and to establish its predominant characteristics; whether the whole thing is a joke, or whether its importance lies in its deeper meaning, or whether it is just irony, sarcasm, ridicule...

Witold Gombrowicz
in *Ferdeydurke*

After procrastinating for over two years since Vin's death on the writing of this Foreword for his second autobiographical work, I finally begin using the above quotation from Witold Gombrowicz.

Vin Zigas was a genius; he was a romatic, he was a physician with compassion, he was a scientist with penetrating curiosity, he was an actor, and he was a loyal friend. He was fundamentally a stylist. Many who knew him compared him to Don Quixote; the younger generation compared him to Danny Kaye, not only in his appearance, but in his speech, movements, and actions. In his first autobiographical essay, *Auscultation of Two Worlds*, Vin surprised many of his friends by the flamboyant accounts of his dramatic life. I was hard pressed to comment on this first work, either to Vin himself or to our mutual friends. Everyone, after all, recognized me as his "mentor" in those passages, as they did most of his other thinly disguised characters. After much thought, I praised the work as the best example I could imagine of

v

an original prose form of "abstract expressionist ironical parody in the form of a historical and biographical novel." Having so categorized the work I could see its genius and alleviate the misgivings of many of Vin's friends who were saddened by what appeared to them as frank errors in fact and chronology, severe lapses in memory or ingenuous admission of strange prejudices.

Vin's first work was a work of imagination, more a novel than a biography, and in it all those who knew him could recognize the sensitive showman and raconteur in the extravagances and hyperbole and embellishment. So it is here in his second work where he presents the history of Kuru research as he recalled it. He shows, as we all do and jokingly recognized early in our involvement, "The disease everyone catches from working on Kuru."

I disagree with Vin on many of the "facts" and many of his judgments—we always did! He has disarmed my criticism by the undocumented style of presentation he has chosen. I cannot quibble with historical fiction—Vin has taken the liberties of imaginative creative writing and protects his "truths" with the ambiguities of poetry.

Was Vin writing under exquisite control, as I have implied he was, when he copied paragraphs from later works of others, used them with minor modifications, out of context, for his own purposes, and altered their time and content to suit himself...as would a Jonathan Swift in his parodies? My uncertain verdict is that he has written the most remarkable work in existence of abstract expressionistic ironical parody, his own style of biography. One hopes he wrote with more humor than bitterness.

D. Carleton Gajdusek

Contents

List of Illustrations

Front cover: Kuru victim

Endpapers: Map of Papua New Guinea

Frontispiece: **Vincent Zigas**

Plates

1. Top left, Children free of Kuru; top right, Afflicted child with symptoms; bottom, Village scene
2. Top, Men about to roast wild boar; bottom, Men and children feasting on the freshly roasted meat
3. Top left, Adult Kuru victim; top right, Zigas and child Kuru victim; bottom, Males with typical personal and war shields
4. Top, Doctor and patient; bottom, The author in his office

Author's Note

This book is written especially for those who took pleasure in my first book devoted to the Green Dwelling of My Desires, my island— *Auscultation of Two Worlds*— and have continued to show an interest in its various exotic landscapes, not only for their geographic form, but for the living communities that inhabit them.

I was away from civilization for such a long time that my friends, hostages of technology, abandoned hope of seeing me again. Although I kept notes at the time, it has taken me all these years to arrive at the actual writing. But now that a partial retirement has freed me from the grimmer aspects of my profession, I have nothing to lose by referring to my research as an avocation. Largely it has been concerned with a carefully selected set of observations made in a rather unknown field.

It has been a difficult, sometimes painful, story to tell in its entirety, but I have done my best to be accurate both in facts and in dates, for I feel that I owe the truth to the many who have become valued acquaintances, and sometimes friends. All these have constantly requested more news of my "Green Dwelling" and my discovery of a fatal neurological disease previously unknown to Western medicine. This book is for them, in lieu of letters that I ought to have written and did not.

It is also my concern to produce innocent amusement, unrestricted by canon or precedent, for those who require some relaxation from the fatigue generated by so many parasitic forms of life in this less than perfect world.

My peers, the medical scientists, who read this will realize that this book is neither a scientific treatise, nor a balance-sheet of all the achievements and failures of medical science, but a presentation of the major implications of the factors that continually determine our medical ethics—including some of the less prizeworthy drawbacks.

Any narrative that is personal is bound to be eclectic; if it were not, it would not be personal. No doubt, therefore, the persons concerned would tell a different tale from mine; they would remember what I have forgotten and forget what I have remembered.

Whence the following...

Vincent Zigas

The Island and I

Bird-shaped island, with secretive bird voices,
Land of apocalypse, where the earth dances,
The mountains speak, the doors of the spirit open,
And men are shaken by obscure trances.
                                        —*James McCauley*

It was not through destiny or fate that I landed on this tropical wonder that is New Guinea. Destiny for me is not a matter of chance, but often a matter of choice; it is not something to be waited for, but something to be achieved.

My fate is determined, and I have determined it. I, and nobody else, have made this choice.

I have often been asked why this green island took such strong hold of me. I too ponder this sometimes—why is it that I'm so enchanted by new Guinea and its people?

I am a man of the Old World, the product of a metropolitan center, yet I prefer to live here, among contemporary preliterate society, isolated from the neoteric world. Why indeed?

I can only guess the whys and wherefores: Was it because I was looking to evade the fearful new battle I saw looming in my Vaterland, the battle between the star-spangled banner and the hammer-sickled emblem? Or was I seeking a place of tranquility where I could study humanity, people close to nature, and offer my services to help fight disease and its incapacities? Or was it perhaps because of my desire to study the people—the people of yesteryear: Were they the slaves of our gain, or children of contentment? I know that there are many other possible reasons, but let the above suffice.

Yes, I wonder why, thirty years later, this island still claims a unique place in my overstocked memory. Even now, the natives remain—etched with such sharp delineation—as the chief attraction and focus of my whimsical memory, while often those who were far more important in my life are merely dim ghosts.

• • •

Silently, slowly the moon rose near the Southern Cross, softly illuminating the exposed coral shores of an island dense with tall and shapely palms. The old ocean liner Bulolo cleaved the South Pacific waters, then leisurely turned the corner of the island to drop anchor in the middle of Port Moresby harbor—a natural bay named after the British Captain John Moresby, its late nineteenth century discoverer.

As we came in, the sun began to open the day. And the gulls rose with it, unfolding their wings to kite upon the sky—waltzing across the firmament, wheeling and curving, softly inscribing salaams on the blue paper of the air. Now the liner once again moved gracefully towards the wharf, where she was firmly secured by ropes to the stone platform. We went ashore.

It was in the Year of Our Lord Nineteen Hundred and Fifty that I made my entrance into the eastern tropical islands under Australian administration, following a four-month course at the Australian School of Pacific Administration in Sydney. There I was indoctrinated with everything then known about this new frontier, a world beyond sight and almost beyond imagination, an unexplored terrain, both interior and exterior, where many so-called stone age voices were still speaking with undiminished echoes of their past.

That special course was given by two scholars: Camilla Wedgewood, the anthropologist, and James McCauley, an expert in colonial administration. Their patient efforts constituted my sole training in the often arcane arts of anthropological and sociopolitical observation, efforts for which I am even now grateful.

Camilla had learned nearly everything there was to know about New Guinea, where she had spent a considerable time during the war. She was extremely individualistic: the age, size, and shape of her were all variables. Sometimes she appeared a fragile little woman of middle age or so, with nostalgic eyes, especially when she was talking about "her people" of Manam Island. But when she was on the subject of "cultural relativism," in the sense of blending Western culture with the natives' traditional beliefs and customs, she appeared a young, vigorous intellectual. Her legacy to me in her last letter was: Disarm your Vaterland's prejudice and look upon these 'savages' with fresh eyes. They are whole people and not little bits of some fragmented society.

McCauley, too, was not a mere man of the world. A quite extraordinary person, he had been endowed with many uncommon talents. He was a superb scholar and a far-ranging critic with impeccable standing and deep feeling; one of a few Australian intellectuals with a reputation as a liberal right-thinker. He was active in politics and New Guinea affairs and visited our island frequently, almost every year, sometimes staying for up to several weeks. According to one of his close friends, "he fell under the spell of its traditional, premodern society where the facts of life and death, the inexorable, organic rhythms are insistent." McCauley wrote numerous articles about New Guinea and its future in the professional journals of decolonization.

His views on many subjects were delivered as cleanly as well-done amputations. Most were published in the magazine *Quadrant*, a masterful combination of scientific scholarship and poetic insight that he edited.

He was a seeker—from nihilism to "harmonizers"— with a basic desire to find a universal explanation, a key to everything. But above all, McCauley was one of Australia's most distinguished poets.

I was privileged to accompany him on one of his New Guinean "hunting expeditions," where he talked to people of different tribes about their fundamental values and ambitions, their customs and beliefs. We walked from the mountains to the coast, some hundred miles of jungle, probably more, over rough tracks, rocks, and mountain ridges covered with a dense forest canopy of leaves and rotten tree roots, infested with leeches and snakes; we crossed many flooded rivers, beset by crocodiles. Once, while resting between one of his recurring attacks of malaria, he looked at me with his grey-green eyes and, in a voice exactly pitched to reach the edge of the crowd and not a breath beyond, he poured the full tide of traditionalist questions.

Has the West anything to offer its colonies but the ideal of economic growth, which, despite an ever-increasing productivity, has been accompanied by unprecedented human slaughter and cruelty? Is the West's own disintegrating civilization a model for so-called backward countries? Are we undermining a traditional society and replacing it with a culturally sterile modern state that will probably collapse in disorder? May we not suspect that the devaluation of traditional cultures will produce profound psychic dislocation among these peoples, with evil consequences to bedevil us all for many generations?

When I compared the present technical aid from the colonial government with that from the Christian missionary activities of earlier times, McCauley reflected in his typically imagistic fashion: "I believe they have the same apostolic zeal, the same moral justification; the same paternalistic touch and naiveté about economic and political realities; the same basic subservience to, and lack of critical appraisal of, the system of domination itself." On the doctrinal basis of missionary work he summed up:

"A critic, not necessarily unsympathetic, might feel justified in saying to Christians: You claim to have a universal religion, but do not the facts suggest that your religion is merely a religion of the West and of some outlying areas, mainly territories formerly lacking a civilized religion and culture? And in remolding humankind in the name of a romantic vision, are there not one or more hidden considerations, such as power and politics?"

I responded that my father was of Teutonic origin, and my mother from a gentle Finno-Ugric family, and that I thus had to call myself a plain mongrel. McCauley rejoicingly commented: We are all mongrels and we have been mongrels for a long time.

On the whole his philosophical and religious worldview attracted strong advocates—and equally strong detractors. He was a person of my own taste.

It was very gratifying to me later to become a member of his warmly knit family as Godfather to his son, Timothy.

• • •

To understand the significance of New Guinea, it is essential to delve into its history, flora, fauna, and people.

This beautiful but outlandish island, from time immemorial, has had a sinister reputation. Its massacres, its cannibalism, and the fearlessness of its warriors had all created an aura so full of dread that the redoubtable Captain Bligh, desperate as he was for food and water after the mutiny on the "Bounty," had steered past it.

New Guinea is an island greater in size than any other in the world except for the bare and barren stretches of Greenland.

The great island of New Guinea, shaped in outline like a giant primeval bird with its neck outstretched, and its claws resting at the tip of Australia, is known to us today in a way never dreamed of by the men who discovered and explored it.

The New Guinea land mass, with an area of about 350,000 square miles, is politically divided—the western half being the Indonesian province of Irian Jaya, and the Eastern half belonging to the Papua New Guinea government, which not long ago became an independent nation and a very young member of the United Nations.

Unlike other large islands, New Guinea is little more than a name on a map, or a postage note in a diary, to millions. Most Europeans know the Pacific area only on the "world atlas" scale, with the result that many people in Europe are inclined to regard the island as a small one. But a crow's flight from west to east across New Guinea is something like 1500 miles—farther than the mass of Europe stretching from the Baltic Sea to the toe of Italy; and it is more than three times as large as Great Britain.

New Guinea's historical records begin with exciting accounts of the perils and adventures of the many navigators and explorers who had taken home the collected records of their observations and findings. But the massive island seemed nonetheless to remain closed and aloof.

It was a great, untamed heathen land that beckoned; and yet it put up fearsome barriers, was rife with unknown dangers. Tropical wonders and tropical horrors occurred side by side, and such was its reputation that no nation took definitive steps to claim the baffling country as a colony for some centuries.

There are, however, some features of the discovery and exploration of this "tropical wonderland" that are quite unusual. Explorers and navigators from many nations—Portugal, Spain, Russia, Holland, England, and France—had a part in the discovery of the "exotic gem" over a period of more than 300 years. In fact, some historians think it probable that the island was known to the Malays and Chinese still earlier, before there were written records.

There is a belief that during the early Egyptian dynasties, several thousand years ago, a flourishing trade route existed between present West New Guinea and Egypt. Scarabs and ancient Egyptian pottery have been unearthed at various places along this route, which also appears to have touched at what is now Darwin in the Northern Territory of Australia. The main purpose of the trading was to bring spices and Bird of Paradise plumes to the Egyptian royal court. The plumes, which were sacred, and hence reserved solely for the use of the Pharaohs, arrived in Egypt packed in leaves gummed together with sandalwood resin. The latter was used as incense.

There is a theory that the legend of the phoenix rising from the flames was inspired by a glimpse of the divine Pharaoh, clad only in this gorgeous plumage, and sitting amid a cloud of fragrant smoke.

Strange to say, it was "some unknown Portuguese" —now believed to have been Antonio D'Abreu—who about 1511 discovered the existence of this terra firma.

Nothing further seems to have been recorded, however, until 1572, when Jorge de Meneses, a Portuguese colonial governor, unexpectedly came to its western shores. He was on a voyage from the Spice Islands and was forced by wild and stormy weather to take shelter in the lee of an island at the extreme northerly tip.

A year or so later a Spanish sailor, Alvar de Saavedra, coasted along the northern shores and was much impressed by its bold outlines. Finding traces of gold there, he named it "Isla del Oro"—Island of Gold. But it was Ynigo Ortez de Retez, another Spanish navigator, who sailed along the coast in 1546 and gave it the name:

"New Guinea."

Who was really first to discover New Guinea has been asked from time to time, and it seems likely that the honors may be shared equally by Portugal and Spain. The exploration of New Guinea in modern times has often been so gradual that it cannot be tabulated or fully appreciated.

There have been many instances in history where adventurers have braved terrible dangers, unknowingly stopping just short of some important discovery. The tracks in the jungles could tell of multitudinous bitter disappointments. But it is well to realize that so much hard endeavor, enthusiasm, and plodding often add a sense of infinite value to the grand total of any such achievement.

The extensive discoveries made in New Guinea over the last few decades reflect the incredible toughness that seems to characterize the islands. The very exploration of New Guinea's coastline was completed less than eighty years ago, with the interior of this great tropical region yielding to exploration only still more recently. Fresh discoveries continue to be made— often by accident— even into the present. Information, until recently, was very limited, but so was any real interest until the great island itself sprang to life and demanded attention.

It is hard to describe the island generally. It lies at a rather peculiar map angle, so that North, South, East, and West are not easily defined in stating the position of various places. To say there are mountains is as inadequate as saying there is water in the sea.

High mountains—higher than any in Australia—dominate its shape and its central chain, dividing the country like a backbone, runs almost the entire length of the island. Dense forests and jungles clothe most of its surface. There are many broad valleys with waterfalls dropping hundreds of feet—some are hidden in the deep and inaccessible clefts in the mountains, and one may only hear their solemn thundering and see the steam-like spray rising out of the dark jungle background. The valleys are more or less open in appearance, gently undulating, with stands of primary forest punctuated by neatly molded gardens, swamps, and grassland.

The pattern is similar on the outlying islands, where the mountains and ranges rise steeply and, in some places, almost vertically, from the narrow valley floors, creating difficult terrain for human settlement.

Other important geographical features include the rivers and swamps, many of which are formidable obstacles to human communication and settlement. The New Guinea Plain, a trapped-river area, is one of the largest and most sparsely populated swamplands in the world. The island is a constituent part of the Pacific "ring of fire," an area of volcanic activity and earthquake disturbance that encircles the Pacific Ocean.

The climate is no less an insuperable obstacle to human well-being. It is, in fact, more reminiscent of Hades than of Eden, with its unbearable combination of heat and humidity. However, the climate patterns vary from one place to another, determined by seasonal shifts of wind directions. The temperature of the highland valley is many degrees cooler than that of the lowlands.

Then there are the waterspouts, the hurricanes, and even the rain, which transform paths into rivers of mud and streams into impassable torrents. New Guinea, prophetically named the Island of Gold, is one of the few islands also blessed with a miracle of nature: The island's feathered fauna rival those of any part of the world. There are known to be over six hundred species and more than a thousand subspecies of birds on the mainland and the adjacent islands; no doubt this number will grow when the opportunity for further research eventually arises.

Thus, New Guinea is an immense tropical aviary with birds of brilliant colors and of soft pastel shades, birds with strange habits and weird notes, birds of exquisite carriage. The cassowary of nursery-rhyme fame is the largest. The black and glossy "running bird," is kin to the emu and the ostrich, and is only to be found in New Guinea and Australia. The most famous is the Bird of Paradise, of which there are more than fifty species. In the breeding season the male bird wears a dress of extraordinary beauty. Probably the most strikingly picturesque of all New Guinea birds is the garden bower-bird, which not only builds large playhouses, but also creates gardens in front of them. Parrots come in all colors and sizes, from tiny parakeets to the well-known cockatoo with its sulfur crest, to the large cockatoo.

Birds of prey, such as eagles, hawks, and owls, share this island home with its mixture of forest, mountain and crag, jungle, fertile plateau, swamps, and unusual coastline. Herons, ducks, ibises, and others live in the marshes or on the shoreline, and quails inhabit the grass regions.

Some of the most fully crowned pigeons in the world are to be found in New Guinea, and other pigeons and doves are plentiful.

In short, New Guinea is one of the world's richest islands in its variety of animal life. At the same time, however, it is one of the world's poorest areas in mammalian fauna. Here one finds such marsupials as the tree kangaroo and various species of wallaby. Other animals are the spiny anteaters, gliders, bandicoots, cus-cus, native cats, wild dogs or dingos, bats, rats, pouched mice, opossums, and wild pigs.

An account of the flora of New Guinea—which many know simply as "tropical vegetation"—would fill volumes if the knowledge were available.

Parts of the New Guinea landscape look very similar to Australia. One reason, of course, is the presence of the "gum" or eucalyptus tree that grows naturally only in Australia and on a few of the islands to the north, together with the phyllodinious species of Acacia or Wattle. In addition to these, there are almost fifty families of plants common to both Australia and New Guinea, particularly on the coastal and lower mountain regions.

The evergreen true oak, which we invariably associate with the northern hemisphere, makes its appearance even in fairly low areas in New Guinea. Ferns grow in profusion, from tiny mossy fronds to the tall tree fern. Many of the creepers and climbing plants display great beauty and grace, especially the various Mucuna Lianas, the Ecoma, and the lovely waxy Hoya.

The most surprising of all New Guinea flowers is the magnificent Nelumbo waterlily, a unique combination of beauty and utility. It can definitely be called a food plant, for its stalks make an excellent vegetable and its numerous seeds compare favorably with almonds. It grows in isolated parts of the island, but there appears to be no reason why it could not be transplanted elsewhere. Several other kinds of waterlily may be seen, also beautiful, but unfortunately not edible.

It has been said that New Guinea displays more species of the orchid family than are found anywhere else; the number estimated to be found there is in excess of two thousand. This profusion is understandable, and very likely extends to other plant families as well. Nowhere else is there an island whose long axis approximately parallels the equator, and is also very close to it. From the forest areas that overhang the beaches up to New Guinea's highest peaks one can find extremely colorful orchids. Most are related to the shower or antelope orchids and are characterized by a profusion of flowering stems that tend to fall in graceful curves from the leafy shoots. Each flower has two long horns (sepals) above, much like the horns of an antelope. Though the basic pattern is standard, the variegated minor structure and coloring is almost inexhaustible.

Orchids have attracted botanical collectors to New Guinea from the days of the earliest expeditions. Soon living plants were reaching Europe, and numerous species, previously quite unknown to the scientific world, had produced flowers in England and Germany, and thence were named.

Of all flowers of New Guinea, however, the most representative is the brilliant scarlet hibiscus, a rare gift of nature that is often taken by the natives with pride and tucked in the hair as an adornment.

Even the insects are a strangely varied family. Exquisite butterflies and moths share the exotic, natural glory of the island with its birds and brilliant flowers. The butterflies of the day and sunlight, and the moths with their nocturnal habits, literally merit study by day and night. To describe a butterfly seldom conveys any real idea of its wonder; that can only be known by seeing it. Quite apart from their entrancing colors and markings, there is surely no other living creature so gentle in movement, so amazingly fragile, and yet so much aquiver with the essence of life.

Indeed, because of the size and beauty of its native species, New Guinea has become a Mecca for insect collectors. The largest known butterfly in the world (the *Ornithoptera alexandrae*) can be found there, along with one of the largest moths (*Casinocera hercules*), some of the most elongate stick insects, and the largest known grasshopper (*Siliquofera grandis*).

To complete this striking picture I must not neglect marine treasures that include the pearl, pearlshell, trochus shell, and bêche-de-mer. Fish are plentiful; some of the most exquisitely colored and some of the most hideous types known are to be found in the New Guinea waters. The dolphin and dugong—sometimes called "sea cow"—must be included along with the starfish, exquisite sea urchins, and other natural marvels; even the coral that fringes the reefs and river estuaries.

One of the many surprises is that, although they are so geographically close, the natives of New Guinea are not related to the Australian aborigine. They are physically and culturally quite separate types. The early explorers were often mystified by the variation in appearance, customs, and behavior of the natives, and it has since been established that three definite types exist. There is the tall, light-skinned, curly-haired native of the south coast; the pygmy of the mountainous region— probably the earliest inhabitant; and the lighter-skinned, wavy-haired native of the southeast coast.

Although they have freely intermarried, it can be said that the Melanesian type is found mostly along the coastal regions. This was an immigrant race of seafaring people who wandered the Pacific and no doubt reached New Guinea's shores by means of the outrigger canoe.

The island is the home of manhunters and artists, of farmers rather than fishermen. One would expect that a people who live surrounded by the sea would quite naturally be fishing folk. Paradoxically, this is not the case, although everything seems arranged by nature to enable them to live from and in the sea. The shores and banks are broad and easily accessible, the waters are warm and abundant with fishes and mollusks. Yet, the larger number of Melanesians seem to have deliberately rejected this proffered abundance. They have turned their backs on the sea and withdrawn into the mountains and jungles, where everything seems designed to assault humanity.

The intense religious zeal of the people is an important factor in their culture. This is a land characterized by many magical practices, by a supernatural approach to agriculture, by communication with the hereafter—and by intimacy with the dead.

The language difficulties are more than just a nuisance; they have immense national significance. For in this sparsely populated island, some seven hundred different languages—not just dialects, but completely separate tongues, as dissimilar as English is to Russian—are spoken by people from over four hundred different cultural groups.

New Guinea is not a poor land. By today's standards, or the immediate yesterday's, it is wealthy, and the people are potentially rich. Each native male holds, on the average, one hundred times as many broadacres as an Australian.

The natives of New Guinea are a Stone Age humanity, though. Their tools are the stone adze, the bow and arrow, the bone dagger, the stone axe, the spear, and the ground-digging sticks. They have no metals, nor do they have the wheel.

But they are masters of hunting, using their primeval weapons with deadly accuracy. They are also agriculturists who employ a slash and burn technique, and who give much time to the cultivation of the sago palm, along with yam, taro, sweet potatoes, breadfruit, beans, tapioca, and of course coconut and banana.

The people themselves are of outstanding and surprising quality—intensely and sincerely affectionate among themselves, in their homes, and with the other members of their tribe. If one is in trouble, the whole village is often upset over the misfortune.

They have innumerable ravishing stories, legends, and laws. They recognize only two worlds; the world they inhabit and the world to come. The youngsters have a deep-felt respect for their elders, who govern aided by the physical fear induced by their witchcraft. Before government came magic; before Premier or President came the Chief; and ruling him still was the witch doctor, the sorcerer, the fakir, the holy man—the power behind the throne.

A naturally warlike people raised from childhood to use the bow and arrow and spear, the main pastime of these warriors past and present is battle. They delight in skirmishes.

They are, in short, just people, though among the first Europeans there was a disturbing tendency to regard them as intelligent animals of a lesser genus, as subjects for the study of anthropology, or as museum pieces. Those students who earnestly put these "primitives" and their reactions under the microcope have been variously concerned with establishing their racial "genesis." The resultant theories, however—here based upon a turn of language, there upon blood groups and types—place this "genesis" almost anywhere in the known world.

Not all the natives are gentle, not all have discovered the arts, nor do all have grace and beauty. They are, as I discovered, also the plainest, most down-to-earth, average persons: the man in the street, the man in the jungle. We all know an occasional person who is both average and different—and whose little differences make life more interesting. Differences from Western customs lead us in our role as "Everyman" to believe that the New Guineans are "primitive" or "barbaric," though like all of us, these barbarians are descended from a line of heroes, from the "Great Men of Yore."

I was assigned—as first medico to the Goilala cultural group—to the remote, forested, snake infested, and rugged mountainous region. Its inhabitants were known for being thick-skinned, rough, and earthy, with a savagely inflammable spirit. Any death demanded revenge by "payback"—mostly by decapitation.

As I began, our main medical objective in New Guinea was to find a more effective chemotherapeutic agent against granuloma venereum, a destructive ulcerative disease of the genitalia of both sexes that had a high incidence among the local people.

Three years later, and only after assiduous effort, we were finally successful in eliminating this plague, and the region, which had previously been under quarantine, was consequently reopened for labor recruitment.

As a result of this initial success, my immediate superior—whose Teutonic name shared that in the Nibelungen epic, Gunther—made me an offer of Australian citizenship. This would allow me to become a permanent civil servant with the Department of Public Health. His proposal was promptly accepted.

I believed sincerely in the Australians' cultivated myth of "Fair Go"—that one is accepted as a citizen, though not by birth, with all rights, free of words and deed, and entitled to all of the privileges of the Australian-born citizen. Alas! Not long afterward I discovered that "civis," that most honorable name among Romans, did not apply to naturalized citizens. It soon became obvious that only persons of kindred stock could be unqualified citizens of this vast continent. The rest were regarded as merely more "bloody wogs," according to Australian terminology.

After almost five years among the "savage flock," I was transferred to the large mountainous region of the Central Highlands of New Guinea. This territory had been described to me as comprising majestic vastnesses— range after range of stretched cloud-capped mountains— wooded, grassed, rock-faced, and red or green glinting limestone—several hundred thousand indigenous dwellers of many distinct languages, cultures, and intrinsic differences from Western modes of thought. They were huddled in their round, smoke-filled huts, tenaciously guarded by evil spirits and the destructive weapon of disease.

So my first appointment was over, and the second at hand.

The Threshold

It was early afternoon and the plane banked lazily in a cloudy sky over the Highlands of New Guinea. The pilot chuckled as he swiveled to peer back into the dim cavern of the plane's cabin. He had a full load, and the cabin reeked of its many cargoes: tools, tractor parts, grub, kerosene drums, and three sheep secured in crates.

I sat on oil-stained sacks piled on the floor with my back to the fuselage as it wallowed in air turbulence over the heaven-brushing peaks. I squirmed in discomfort and viewed my surroundings with distaste, subdued somewhat by the roar of the engine.

Up front, in the cockpit of the fluttering air freighter, the skipper worked hard with the stick and rudder to fly through the turbulence as nonviolently as possible. He was actually aware that his single two-legged passenger sat alone in the cabin with no seat belt—in fact, without even a seat. The pilot, Peter Manson, who in later years became my "partner" in medical emergency mercy flights, was not worried about getting lost in the maze of mountains and valleys. He had traversed the skies of this wild country many times and could recognize its craggy features like a familiar face.

I tried to forget my unhappy situation by thinking of the territory assigned to me and its inhabitants. Are they really "like children, with no thought for the future; euphoric from malnutrition—the less protein one eats, the greater the potbelly and the lightheaded feeling of being gay," as I was told by one of the labor recruiters—or live headhunters?

In my flight of fancy, they were muffled, ragged people shuffling along invisible jungle trails; living in small coop-like hovels scooped within dark grass huts; a flare of kindling wood gliding a broad-nosed face with pig tusk pierced through septum. I felt this was by no means Shangri-la, but merely another morbid place untouched by modern medicine. Sanitation was nonexistent and disease rife, with scraggy dogs and filth, fat pigs, and marasmic children abounding.

All this was to be expected, entrapped in the work of "progress." I was determined to do something to change things.

But at that moment I knew only that I was in touch with myself again—alive, aware, and wanting to help. And then the clouds parted. The monoplane glided, and below lay a tumultuous land with narrow-crested hills strung as a tangle of beads, coiling in knots, dovetailing and twisting, melting into each other. Bewildered crests and contorted gullies and narrow valleys, a heaving and restless landscape, as if these mountains were still moving, like ocean waves. Clouds again, and the airplane shadow rainbowed upon them; another gap and below, the rolling grassland of a lovely valley bathed by sunshine, the green basin of the valley skylined by rugged mountains topped with fleecy clouds against vivid blue.

All this enlivened my somewhat mopish mood.

Peter pulled at a cluster of throttle knobs. The thunder of our powerful engine diminished and the broad-winged monoplane glided toward the mountain-locked airstrip. The thrilling ride soon ended, and there I was, among "cannibalistic savages living in a Stone Age culture," as newspapers and magazines described them.

When I arrived at the hospital, I was horrified at the filthy conditions. The walls were so thick with dirt and vivid crimson splashes of betel nut juice that it took three applications of caustic soda in boiling water to obtain a semblance of cleanliness. After a few weeks of arduous work, the hospital was clean, but still quite rudimentary.

There was a large population in the area, chiefly in the center of the region. About three hundred Europeans, including traders, planters, missionaries, government servants, a constant thin sprinkling of anthropologists forever investigating the life of the indigenes, and an unknown number of native Highlanders. The latter were continually coming and going, so no one could say how many of them were in the government settlement at any time; perhaps several thousands.

I was the only medical officer in the densely populated region, and had been assured that another doctor, when available, would soon assist me. It had always been difficult to obtain doctors from Australia for service in New Guinea because of the extremely isolated life. The isolation caused many who made the journey to become addicted to alcohol or drugs. So, meanwhile, I had to go it mostly alone. If not for two Australians, Harry and Des, former army medical orderlies, and an ex-army nurse, Joyce, coined by me the "indispensable triune" for their great mine of experience, all of my attempts in the fight against invalidism would have been trivial.

After exploring the hospital, I found it wanting in many respects beyond cleanliness. I observed native nurses, male and female, handling dangerous medicines of which they scarcely knew anything. They made diagnoses such as "feverish," "bad foot," and "bad blood." Many other diagnoses were equally vague. "Bellyache," I told one nurse, was just not good enough. I wanted to know the exact position of the pain and whether the patient was constipated or suffering from diarrhea. I was rewarded next month when a patient was reported as having a "bellyache west of the navel with no sign of stool on the backside."

One afternoon I was urgently called to the hospital. One of the nurses, I was told, had poisoned a patient. I dashed up and asked to see the bottle of poison, and was relieved to find that it contained only a strong chlorohydrate solution, which could do no harm beyond making the patient sleep. I nevertheless put on a grave expression and asked the nurse what had happened. He said he had gone to the usual shelf to get a cough mixture, and had given the patient a dose. The patient promptly protested that the taste was not that of his usual mixture. They argued for some time, then the patient started to lose consciousness and accused the nurse of poisoning him. Only then had the nurse read the label. He saw to his horror that it was indeed an unknown substance. Although he was terrified, I didn't change my mournful expression, conveying that there was no chance of recovery. By this time the nurse was nearly in a state of collapse, looking as shaky and pale as a native can. So I relented and told him that the patient would be all right. I never again had to face similar accidents.

The elderly natives have a natural dignity and courtesy that is often quite wonderful. The nurses, however, with their abecedarian education, were often apt to forget the respect due to age. One bossy but inexperienced nurse had ordered around a very old man in the hospital, until one day he decided he had had enough. He called the nurse to his bedside, looked him straight in the face, then very slowly and deliberately said, "Young man, be careful! I ate your grandfather!" Horrified, the now very subdued nurse rushed to his father for comfort. The father admitted that, in his youth, the old man had indeed done what he had said.

A doctor can experience no more exciting adventure than to teach, train, and explore such a community, hitherto completely isolated from all contact with Western medicine—to tabulate the indigenous diseases and experiment with methods devised against their ravages.

Teaching the people to take an interest in their own health problems was a fundamental intent. I was encouraged by the sanguine expectation that a school for training local youths in nursing would be erected in the Highlands. It would produce a number of medical personnel who already know the local customs, languages, and superstitions of their own people, who would live among them permanently, or at least for a prolonged period, who would have the interest of the country at heart, and who would do the job at a cost the government could sustain. I felt that here was a unique opportunity for the people to absorb the necessary knowledge.

Nurturing the hope of a future school of nursing, I took the first step toward forming a preliminary basic training program. In this rugged country, a single doctor with a trained skeleton staff could not hope to meet all of its medical needs. I desperately needed nurses trained to handle the ordinary medical and surgical cases, and particularly, to cope with preventive medicine. With trained personnel stationed at strategic places in the region and the base hospital in the center, along with a good line of communication, I felt it would be possible to bring efficient service to this mountainous region—or at least part of it. The plan was based on past experience. My method was to provide a thorough technical training, then put the trainees into a position of practical responsibility and leadership in which they in turn would train others. However, it proved to be more complex than I had experienced in the past.

It was much like unraveling a Gordian knot to make the transition from teaching in my home country to teaching and training in New Guinea. A recent entry must first adjust to remarkable cultural differences all at once. It may not be very long before one will have to abandon fixed views on how best to teach one's own subject. Training local nurses and other health workers could not possibly follow the pattern set in Australian, English, or American training centers.

I observed in the first year of training that the native youths lacked the basic drive to delve deeply into theoretical considerations. At first the students were eager and responsive to the fundamental knowledge of bacteriology and elementary anatomy and physiology, but in the next few months this began to wear thin. Lethargy and inadvertance crept in. Was this just the product of the enervating tropical climate? Or was it the result of the dietary history of the students? Or was it emotional and psychological? Nobody seemed to know.

I doubt exceedingly that the students were unwilling to think for themselves and expected everything served to them on a platter, and that because they have been spoonfed for so long, they were now unwilling to show any initiative.

Rather, I personally believe that the problem is a result of disturbances characteristic of the local scene itself. For instance, lack of initiative affects the learning capacity of students. They often do not know where they are heading, and even if they do know, their studies seem unrelated to this aim. This lack of initiative may be caused by the difficulty the student has in seeing where such new knowledge is leading. One of the chief factors affecting initiative, I believe, is rooted in the cultural background of most New Guinean Highlanders, where failure is not likely to prove an irretrievable disaster. There is always the village to fall back on. There a villager is relieved of most of the unwelcome pressures of modern life. Beautiful nature will provide nearly all that is needed, with a minimum of human effort, and most of the hard work will be done by the women of the village. There is an endless succession of identical tomorrows to take care of what is not done today. To what end, then, is all the frenzied pressure of study, especially when the ultimate goal is so remote and nebulous?

During the first months of training, I gave up teaching half a dozen times as a result of an overdose of failure. But each time I crept back. Without persistence there would be no change, I thought. It was like exerting the willpower to quit smoking. So I maintained my course, changing only the techniques, drilling the students in every medical subject until the drill became automatic. I repeated the drills, using visual aids, over and over whether or not the drill's raison d'etre was understood. After all, supremely important to their well being was professional satisfaction of learning, I believed.

My first demonstration of the ubiquity of microorganisms was of mixed success. To prove my point I opened the mouth of one of the students, took a scraping from his gum, and prepared a microscopic slide. The gum is always a fertile breeding ground for a flora of spirochetes and other organisms, and the sight of these moving on the slide horrified the student nurses. They immediately looked on the subject-student as a pariah.

When the formal lectures ceased, the teaching became entirely clinical. I tried each day to show the students a patient with an interesting condition, so we could discuss all aspects of practical anatomy, physiology, and treatment. A large part of the nursing work consisted of giving injections, and it was important that the nurses be trained to do so correctly and painlessly. It was explained to them that the nerve endings responsible for pain are in the skin, not under it. Therefore, the faster the needle penetrates the skin, the less the pain. The new trainees practiced on a pillow, and were urged to put the needle in faster and faster. When a nurse seemed to develop a knack, an unsuspecting outpatient due for an injection would be selected as a guinea pig. All too often a trainee's needle would bounce off the skin, and the wretched victim would gaze up at the tormentor in reproach.

One of the most important aspects of medical work is that of midwifery; and for this, fortunately, nearly all female nurses showed a natural talent. Before the introduction of midwife training, I was frequently called in to assist a complicated childbirth. Normally when a woman was having a baby, all men were excluded from the site. The woman delivered the baby herself, often aided by another woman, in a rough shelter in the bush specially built by her husband. They would never bring an expectant mother to the hospital; if they sent for me I could be sure something had gone wrong. Resignation to death in childbirth was general, and was blamed on a malign spell. The witch doctor would usually be called to cast a good spell over the woman. If that did not work, I was sent for.

To my great relief, a second Australian qualified nurse was appointed to the hospital, and before long assumed responsibility for midwifery practice and training. Sister Kerry skillfully taught young women child care and the finer points of nursing, a subject about which I knew almost nothing.

There had been no practical teaching in obstetrics in my medical school in Germany during World War II, and no maternity beds in the hospital. We learned by attending women in their homes for one month. During my month, a fellow student and I had twenty cases of labor. The resident obstetric officer was supposed to accompany the student on the first "case" to show how babies are born and instruct in the simple management of labor. I, however, did not have much luck with my introduction, and had to attend my first case alone. I found an untidy little room smelling of sauerkraut, with one double bed covered by a worn blanket. A wooden box served as a cot for the last baby, probably one year old, and a coal stove and some rickety chairs completed the decor. The midwife in attendance was a fat old woman from the old school of training, with no elementary knowledge of antiseptics. Her chief duties were to provide a supply of boiled water to which she added lysol as an antiseptic, to keep the pot of ersatz coffee hot on the stove, to rub the mother's back, and to constantly call out exhortations such as "once more, dear," "you are doing fine," "just a few more pushes like that and it will pop out," and so on.

One of my duties was to give the mother an enema, which I did with rather conspicuous success, splashing only a few specks of malsmelling substance on the face of Fieldmarshall Goering, whose picture was printed on the official newspaper, "Das Reich." Many sheets of this newspaper were spread on the bed to serve as protection against soiling the mattress. No rubber or waterproof sheets were available. As the critical minutes arrived, I stood two or three feet from the bed, having no clear idea of what to do, and watched nature's remarkable process of birth with amazement. The appearance of the yelling baby on the bed seemed to signal the finish of my work, so I began to pack up to leave when the midwife called out, "Herr Doctor, what about the afterbirth?" Fortunately it soon appeared and was placed on a newspaper on the floor. Then, while I was in the process of opening the door, there was a sudden rush and a swoop—the cat had disappeared with the placenta. I went back to my quarters leaving the midwife plying the new mother with coffee. As I went down the rickety stairs I heard the husband, who was downstairs drinking beer with his pals, say, "You know, it's the experience that counts."

Most of our time in training had been spent learning about communicable diseases, such as cholera, smallpox, typhus, and the like, as well as performing war surgery. Although I had been qualified for less than two years, most of my time had been spent on the front lines where I gained wide experience in surgery, from skull and brain to feet. In the obstetrical field, however, I developed only a smattering of knowledge. Only much later, in New Guinea, did I learn the fundamental procedures of midwifery by gleaning textbooks. Under the guidance of Nature, I made considerable progress in instrumental deliveries and the manual removal of retained placentas, which were the most common emergencies in the Highlands. A retained placenta can result in two severe complications—bleeding and infection. Normally, following the birth of both baby and placenta, the womb contracts firmly and the bleeding stops. With a retained placenta, the womb is unable to fully contract.

The manual removal of the retained placenta is rather simple. The patient is anesthetized and the physician places a hand in the vagina, through the neck of the womb, and peels the placenta gently off the wall of the womb; all is over in a few minutes. Things were not that simple, however, in my Highlands region. I will illustrate one of the common cases. The patient lived in the hills, two days' journey from the hospital. Five days before I saw her, the womenfolk of her village had attended her during the delivery of her first baby, a little girl, and the afterbirth had failed to come away. She was carried to us by several of her relatives, having suffered a very severe hemorrhage. Usually on admission these patients are in truly desperate condition. Hemoglobin is often a mere three percent. The umbilical cord is sometimes still visible, protruding from the vagina, with an odorous vaginal discharge. In addition, this patient had bilateral pneumonia, one of the leading causes of morbidity and mortality in New Guinea. Sometimes I succeeded in finding compatible blood. Anesthesia in many such cases would hardly work, for the lungs were so full of infected sputum that the gases would simply not cross into the blood. The patient had a torn cervix from an unskilled attempt to remove the placenta. The bladder was full of urine, and the rectum full of feces. Before I could examine her I had to use a catheter to empty her bladder, then to remove the feces with my fingers. In these cases I had great difficulty in removing the afterbirth. I could get only two fingers through the cervical canal, so with a pair of forceps, normally designed to remove a fetus after an early abortion, I excised the placenta piece by piece. Every time I removed a piece the patient bled, blood which I knew she could ill afford to lose. It was a slow, tedious procedure.

I am a rather profane Christian and tend to pray to God only in those circumstances in which I desperately need help. This seemed to be quite often in the Highlands.

As I have said, all midwifery was soon in the hands of Sister Kerry with her trained local nurses. I now only rarely had to interfere in that field of medicine, and could rely on her special skill when faced with fetal malpresentation or a difficult removal of placenta. With no exception all malpresentations were corrected, and the small hands and sensitive fingers of the nurses made a better job of placenta removal than I could have managed.

On many occasions I had to perform craniectomies, an operation to reduce the size of the fetal head by cutting or breaking it up and removing strips or pieces of the cranial bones when delivery was otherwise impossible. I was deeply anxious to find the cause of these frequent incidents because I had an intense aversion to craniectomies, and regarded them as most abhorrent. To me this kind of operation was worse than butchery, to be performed in invisible dark—feeling, probing, crushing, decapitating the fetus, and extricating it piece by piece and placing them on a stainless steel tray for a final count of missing parts of the delicate, pulpy body.

One day Sister Kerry asked me shyly for my consent to carry out induced labor on an expectant mother. This meant that, while the patient was under sedation, one passed a sterile, gloved finger through the cervix, swept the membrane off the lower part of the womb, and finally, by applying an artery forceps to these membranes and giving a little tug, rupturing them. The pressure would then be released and labor usually commenced.

I never liked performing inductions, believing that nature is far superior at judging when labor should commence than I will ever be. So I asked her off-handedly for her reason. She looked at me sheepishly and replied, "You see, Doc, in the last four months you have had to perform three craniectomies, which I observed you to do rather reluctantly." She persevered, "Those three cases were issue from incompatible matings; namely, all three mothers' mating partners happen to be big Australian blokes, and thus..." She had to stop here, for I interrupted her hastily by asking what she meant by incompatibility and "big Australian blokes," since I failed to see any correlation. Furthermore, I was disturbed she might spell out the names of those three "husky chaps," because this would put me into jeopardy with the Public Service Commission. According to the Government directive, "Native Women's Protection Ordinance" (dubbed "Black Velvet" by the junior officers), all government officials were prohibited from close (sexual) relationships with native women. Native males were not included. We, as department heads, received frequent circulars on this subject, requesting us to report all "offenders." The circulars were always marked "strictly confidential," but most of us pinned them on the notice board as if to say "Fellows, take heed at your peril. Don't let yourself be sacked or dressed down." Sister Kerry was well aware of this newly imposed legislation, and I was concerned that she might ask me to denounce the "debauchable malfeasors."

She faced me once again and, as if reading my thoughts, commented, "Look here, Doc, I personally couldn't care less about these chaps' love affairs with native women. My deep concern is how to prevent some girls from the tragic consequences that are witnessed by yourself. Furthermore, what will we do about bastardy?" She took a momentary look at the small skeleton's model in my office and resumed her elaborate task.

"Surely you know the average weight of the newborn native baby?" I was startled by the tone of the question. Surely there is something amiss when someone can create a panic-like sensation by asking catechized questions of those who refuse to confess their ignorance then and there. In my case, I was unwilling to admit to her that the weight of the newborn natives was outside of my knowledge, so I dared to mutter, "Yeah."

Mistaking my brooding for concentration, she warmed to her subject. "The average weight of a native full term baby is just over four pounds, which by European standards is considered far too small and regarded as premature," she announced proudly. "Surely you have observed the unusually narrow, boyish-like hips of the native women. Haven't you?"

I had to admit my complete ignorance of this important observation by the open-eyed nurse. According to her, male and female chromosomes, apart from controlling the offspring's resemblance to either parent and determining sex, also play an important role in weight and size. Thus, from her point of view, there may be some correlation between size and cross-fertilization of two "foreign" chromosomes—the White man's and the Black woman's. She had a premonition that in some instances a cross-fertilization begets a much larger fetus, disproportioned to the native female's slender waistline, thus clogging up the parturition.

Her intended "induction" for the native women impregnated by the White man's spermatazoa, a month or so earlier than expected, was to me capricious. But what could I say? I felt there was no way to change her thinking, so reluctantly I gave the go-ahead. Sister Kerry's induction, which entailed introduction of a thick catheter into the cervix and tightly packing the vagina with long strips of sterile gauze, proved surprisingly effective in eliminating the need for the craniectomies that were so repugnant to me.

How she managed the other matter of bastardy I was never able to find out. I only knew that all the children of mixed race that were born in our hospital under the tender care of Sister Kerry had three-figure accounts in the bank for their future education, and some were happily adopted by European settlers. I can only guess that some kind of "pressure," perhaps a gentle sort of blackmail, was used by her on the fathers. There were, however, no complaints directed to me about her tactics. On occasion some of the fathers would remark to me, "Doc, you have there a bloody smart Sis," accompanied by a good natured smile and a wink.

Less successful was my "drill" to banish the belief in sorcery from the nurses' minds. By now I had hoped they understood the causes of sickness, and at first it seemed well resolved. Most nurses had the details of health conditions implanted in their memories for life, but confusion would creep in.

One day I asked one of the senior nurses, "What do you think makes people sick?"

"Germs," she proudly answered.

"Do your people in the village understand that?"

"No, I tried to explain, but they say 'We can't see germs.'"

"What do they think makes people sick?" I inquired.

"They think some kind of sorcery, something like that."

"Do you think that sorcery can make people sick?"

"I don't think it can. My people only pretend that they are using sorcery, but instead they use poison."

"And you think it's poison that makes people sick?" I kept on.

"Yes." She added, "They use some sort of poison."

"Tell me this," I finally asked her, "Have you known magic to make people better?"

"Yes, but it is a different sort of magic."

It was thus revealed to me that the old ways in which the natives had been brought up will almost surely abide for many generations to come. I ended the interview on this sensitive subject because I saw signs of distress and did not think it right to probe.

I had been advised before my assignment to the Central Highlands that my work would be mostly in clinical medicine and that surgery would be almost nonexistent. Experience soon showed otherwise.

The conditions under which I had to perform surgical operations may sound rather pathetic, but they were far superior to those of my wartime experiences. Only a month after my arrival a native woman was brought in with a strangulated hernia of five days. I then did my first resection of a gangrenous bowel. There was little else I could do. Peritonitis was already advanced and the woman died the next day.

A boy about five years old was carried to the hospital suffering from terrible burns. Not one square inch of his skin had escaped. Practically moribund on arrival, he was past screaming, and was now simply whimpering. Within seconds we took him into the operating theater. My scalpel slid through the charred flesh of his right groin to expose the end of the longest vein in the body. Through this vein I infused a mixture of saline and dextrose. The infusion was his only hope, though I knew it was almost certain to prove a futile attempt to save his life. His skin had been too badly burnt, and the surface blood vessels had also been destroyed. The odds were insurmountable. When his heart stopped, I immediately placed my hands over his breast bone, pressing rapidly on his chest to jerk his heart back to life. My assistant, Des, passed a tube through the small windpipe and pumped in oxygen under pressure. It was all to no avail; the gentle heart would not beat again.

This was not a good beginning for me, and it was some time before patients could be persuaded to come for surgery at the first signs of trouble, rather than await some magical cure.

The tragedy of these cases was typical of how the Highlanders suffered from lack of medical aid in the more remote regions. Even when available, it could take days of trekking across the mountains to reach help.

In time the situation altered, and the people began to realize that the white man's magic meant that conditions formerly regarded as hopeless could now be cured. This feeling of hopelessness in the face of illness or accidental injury was clearly brought home to me by the condition of an old woman in an outlying village. She was gravely ill and dying, according to the word that reached her son, who was one of the hospital orderlies. The son traveled to the village to find her grave already dug and the mourners assembled for the funeral feast. In spite of opposition, he succeeded in persuading some of his relatives to carry her over the mountains to the hospital. There I examined her and found that she was suffering from a large subcutaneous abscess of the abdominal wall. These abscesses, probably caused by thorn punctures, were quite common in the Highlands. They could grow to an enormous size, and could yield pints of pus when incised.

I asked the relatives to place her on the table in the dispensary that was used for "dirty surgery." As I sprayed ethyl chloride onto a mask over her face, scores of eyes watched every move I made. The woman's breathing became quieter and quieter, and finally her moans died away. Then came the moment of temporary cessation of breathing that always comes with this anesthetic, and I heard the murmur passing through the crowd, "She is dead."

It took only a moment to incise and drain the abscess. I then dressed it and turned away, going on to other work

in the dispensary. When a person has been in great pain
and has probably had little sleep, passing into natural
sleep from anesthesia proceeds smoothly. I knew that it
would be so in this case, and continuing my work with
other patients, I watched out of the corner of my eye until
the woman was clearly in a natural sleep. I then walked
over to the table and lightly slapped her cheek. The crowd
was aware that something was about to happen. I said, in
a loud voice, "Get up." My patient groaned, opened her
eyes, lifted her head, and slowly got up. There was a hiss
of indrawn breath from the crowd and, open mouthed,
they cast their bewildered looks from the woman to me as
they saw her apparently rising from the dead.

I knew too well that this "miracle" would not banish
the superstitious fears from their minds. I was just another sorcerer in their eyes, the white one with more
magical power than their own.

By now my surgical work covered a large area and I
eventually became used to dealing with anything from
accident surgery, which was a major part of my program,
to the extraction of teeth. There were all sorts of injuries
that required surgical treatment: patients who had fallen
out of pandanus trees, or been crushed by tree trunks
while preparing garden grounds, or pierced by arrows,
or, worst of all, gored by wild pigs. This last mishap could
produce really shocking injuries; the savagely sharp tusk
of the pig can rip an abdomen from end to end, leaving a
tangled mass of intestine and perhaps a torn liver or
spleen. Burns, too, were frequent, generally the result of
open fires in the grass huts.

The reasons surgery is so safe today, compared with
thirty years ago, are the new anesthetics, the skill of the
anesthesiologist, and the availability of antibiotics and
blood. It is not solely the advanced skills of the surgeons.

Here in the Highlands I had the necessary anesthetic agents, but lacked a qualified anesthesiologist. There was also a sufficient supply of antibiotics, but what made my work so extraordinarily tiresome was the lack of blood. My "blood bank" consisted of several meager pints generously donated by white settlers—and my own, which was safely stored in my body. A few pints that I kept under strict security for emergency cases was O-negative, which can be safely given to nearly anyone. Cross-typing blood by using serum against cells on a glass slide was a primitive technique compared with today's accurate work, but better than some. Without exception, no native would donate blood for transfusion, even to his or her own child, father, mother, wife, or husband.

To illustrate a common occurrence, a man was attacked by a wild boar. Only after several days, when it became apparent that he urgently needed help, did his relatives bring him to the village. He entered the hospital in a grave condition. A lot of blood had been lost and many muscles were badly torn. His guts could be seen protruding from the torn abdomen. I tried to explain to his relatives that there was little chance of saving his life unless one of them gave blood. That time I didn't care about the compatibility of blood. A quiet hubbub arose from the relatives and they were off at once, leaving their dying relative in my hands. I had to supply the blood from my limited reserve in the "blood bank" and operated on him on the same day. The next day, however, to my great surprise, the relatives returned to see one of my orderlies. With them they brought two live chickens.

"Ask the white 'dokta' to kill these and use the blood for our relative," they gravely requested.

"I am sorry, this is not good enough," answered the medical orderly. Overhearing this, I felt that he should have accepted the chickens. Through a misunderstanding of "not good enough," they returned the following day, this time with a sizable piglet. "This has much more blood," they told my orderly. "Surely this is good enough." I had to intervene, and took the wretched piglet. Quite undaunted, they departed. The piglet was barbecued that weekend and shared with the hospital staff.

I was amazed by the natives' astonishing resistance to most of the ordinary germs, and their impressive feats of endurance. On one occasion when I was making a brief field trip to nearby villages, I was asked to see a woman in the women's house (the men slept in separate huts). I was told she had had a baby the week before and was now unable to get up. I ducked down through the doghouse-like door of the grass hut, full of smoke, and barely made out the figure of a young woman sitting on the dirt floor. Between her legs I could see the fundus of a completely inverted uterus touching the ground and crawling with flies. Having no equipment, I asked for water and thoroughly washed her uterus with soap, then doused it with about two gallons of water while I reinverted it manually. The woman had a perfectly uneventful convalescence and was back in the garden within a few days. I was, and still am, at a loss to understand this phenomenon: Is it a genetic or an acquired immunity?

One of my earliest accident patients, Koya by name, stayed in the hospital for many months after recovery and became known as "the mascot of the hospital." Koya was a young man from a distant tribe. He was discovered by me, a passerby, lying in a river bed where he was pinned down by a large boulder that had fallen and crushed his leg. When he was picked up, after three days of lying in agony, he was in a bad way. The tibia and fibula were fractured and sticking through a gaping wound. He was carried to the hospital. With the patient under spinal anesthetic, I thoroughly cleaned the wound of putrefying tissue, restored the two fractured bones to their proper place, packed the leg with vaseline gauze, and enclosed it in a plaster cast.

After a month the cast was reopened. The smell was most repulsive and I had to praise my assistants for their perseverance in staying and helping. However, when all the slough was swabbed out, I found healthy pink granulations underneath.

After many months and many changes of plaster cast and dressings, his wound gradually healed. During this time Koya became rather unpopular with the nursing staff because of his olfactory presence. One day he asked me to remove the cast and look at what was moving underneath it. I carefully explained that such a feeling was probably caused by the leg getting better and, jokingly, tapped sharply on his plaster to demonstrate to this skeptic that there was nothing there. To my bewilderment a large maggot shot out from under the plaster cast. I cut off the cast and could see that the entire wound was infested with them. How anyone could have put up with the intolerable itch is beyond me.

The curious and amazing observation of all those who worked under these conditions was that, when a wound was infested by maggots, infections would disappear and good healing would follow. Presumably the maggots fed on the infecting microbes, thereby cleaning the wound. Later I cultivated the "surgical maggot," and often introduced them into septic wounds or bed sores as "antiseptic maggot therapy" with dramatic results.

Another memorable experience with these crawling creatures occurred in a case of acute abdomen (an abdominal condition requiring a prompt operation).

When the patient was brought to the hospital, she was literally skin and bones, with a large mass extending across her abdomen so clearly visible that palpation was not necessary. As my fingers gently tapped her abdomen, she whimpered. Next I listened with my stethoscope for a few minutes to the grossly distended abdomen in front of me. I didn't hear a single bowel movement during that time. This meant that the guts were paralyzed. I was in a great dilemma—perform a laparotomy immediately (the operation of cutting into the abdominal cavity), or build her up first by giving her a blood transfusion and plasma and then continuing to provide transfusion fluids to make her as strong as possible. I had only two pints of blood, though there was ample saline-dextrose solution. I felt that time was against me. I decided to perform the laparotomy.

With the patient under spinal anesthesia I opened the abdomen and there, to my utter dismay, was something I had never expected. Chronic intestinal obstruction, some three feet of swollen gut, appeared like a gigantic sausage. It had stuck to all surrounding tissues. Innumerable round worms in her intestine had caused her trouble—perforation and mechanical obstruction. What was I to do? If I milked out the worms through the incised cavity, there was a risk the intestinal fluid that collects when the guts are paralyzed would spill into her already infected peritoneal cavity, making the infection even more serious. I therefore had to extract the worms manually. They were enormous, some up to six inches in length and still feebly writhing, and it took some time to free the intestines of these noxious parasites. I lost count of them, but there was nearly half a bucketful when the operation was done. I succeeded in separating the diseased intestines and sutured the two open ends of the gut together.

She lived, not so much because of my surgical "magic," but through the goodly guardian spirits of her ancestors—call it Nature or God.

As a result of this episode with ascariasis (round worm infestation), I lost my fondness for spaghetti.

Later I learned from my invaluable collegue and friend, Roger Rodrigue, who coached my on-the-job training course in parasitology, that severe infestations of round worms, with their clinical complications, were not uncommon in the Highlands. He suspected all "acute abdomen" cases were caused by ascariasis.

These Highland people were extraordinarily hardy indeed. On another occasion I recall asking my native assistant to bring me a few ampules of local anesthetic.

"What do you want that for, Doctor?" he asked

"There is a fellow who wants a tooth pulled," I replied.

"You don't need an anesthetic for that," he said bluntly, "just pull it out."

To me, with my effete Western ideas, this seemed a barbarous practice, but when the patient obligingly opened his mouth, I located the offending tooth, rocked it a few times, and pulled. Out it came, without a murmur from the victim. Holding his bloody mouth with two hands and nodding as if to say, "it was a good pull," he disappeared.

I found that the natives of the government settlement did not lie with malice, but rather as children do—to bluff. At first they had little comprehension of the essential purpose behind the innumerable instructions that they had to carry out. They fulfilled their duties mainly by rote. I witnessed this when an Australian planter ordered his "house boy" to serve a few drinks. The boy was clumsy and dropped a glass on the cement floor. "That's right," shouted the planter, "now drop the bloody bottles too." The boy obeyed him.

I enjoyed playing the fascinating game of trying to outwit them.

"There are rats here," I said sternly to my hospital storeman.

"It is impossible," he replied stoutly.

"Oh yes there are."

"No, Doctor, there are no rats," he stubbornly maintained.

"What's that right under the roof?" I asked, pointing to a dark object on the top of the wall.

"That is just some old rag I put up there."

But I knew that a rag could not move by itself. "You get it," I ordered sternly.

"I do not have a ladder," he retorted.

Before my entrance to the bulk store I had noticed a ladder lying on the ground outside. I told him to bring it. He gingerly climbed up the rungs, and the animated rag quivered as he approached. The storeman hesitated.

"Bring it down," I ordered him.

He reached over and the rat, who could retreat no further, bit him savagely. He uttered a blood curdling yell.

"Are there any rats in here?" I demanded inexorably.

This was the only time I ever won the game.

There were periods of weeks at a time when there was no surgery, and little clinical medicine, which proved ample time for relaxation and diversion from the routine functions of the hospital. During these periods I would visit surrounding villages, or camp on the river bank in the sand in which specks of mica shone like gold. On these outings I was escorted by my loyal and trustworthy dark-skinned young companion, Sinoko. Whenever I left for the villages he would come along and on many occasions, rescued me from embarrassment. Or, again, when I would swim naked in the river, he would warn away the women at work in the nearby gardens, guarding my clothes on the bank, studiously looking in the opposite direction. He, like the rest of the Highlanders, was very shy of absolute nudity.

What most impressed me while visiting their homesteads was their oratory, which was looked upon as an art requiring special training. They endeavored to discourage amateurs from engaging in their festival speeches.

During one of my visits to a village, I had to make a speech. I told the chief and his villagers that I had come to look after them and that if they had any problems, such as a shortage of food or medicine, they were to come and tell me. I would always be happy to help them. In the meantime, I expected him to keep his village clean. That was the limit of my thoughts, so I stopped speaking. After the speech, complete silence, as dense as a monsoon rain, fell. The natives looked at me and I looked at them, near to panic, wondering what was expected of me next. My reliable Sinoko rescued me by prompting, "Master, you look at the village."

Relieved, I marched with my procession round the main street. I never went into the houses unless I was invited. Since I did not allow them to come into my house unless I asked them in, I felt that this was fair. So I just walked around and looked. Everything was swept clean.

Another impression of the area under exploration was that it was a land of unfinished churches. Every one of eight villages within two hours of walking distance had one or more. In some villages of two or three hundred inhabitants, Catholic, Seventh Day Adventist, Methodist, Lutheran, and a number of other western religious denominations would vie for favor. It often happened that while one church was under construction, another village would erect a bigger one, and the first village would tear down what it already had constructed and start all over again on an even larger scale. After the church was finally erected, the establishment of a school would commence and the capture of pagan souls was pursued with vigor.

I once met a disconsolate looking old Highlander sitting by the roadside. He looked so absolutely wretched that I stopped and asked, "What is the matter?"

"I feel so bad," he answered.

"Why, tell me about it."

"Oh, Bishop Smith is coming tomorrow."

"He is a nice man," I said reassuringly.

"Oh yes. I like him also."

"Then what is wrong?"

"When he was here last time he gave me a hat and I became an Episcopalian."

"That's fine. It is a good religion."

"Well, a little later a Catholic priest came along and gave me a pair of shorts, and I became a Catholic."

"Catholicism is also a fine religion," I assured him.

"But what is Bishop Smith going to say? I don't want to make him angry."

"Well, which are you going to choose?" I asked him finally.

Bringing up some phlegm in his throat, he spat with a loud hawking noise and said, "I think I'll give the Bishop back his hat and the priest his shorts and just be a Highlander again."

As far as I could observe, the missionaries, with few exceptions, had a tendency to descend on these pagans, tear their beliefs and customs apart, and compel them to believe in the missionaries' superiority. The anthropo-

centric aim of Western religion seemed to entitle mission-
ers to look down upon people who care only about the
soul, as Westerners did nine centuries ago. It is always
easy to condemn a whole people by calling them this or
that when, as a matter of fact, the adjective may only be
partly true. Highlanders have been termed by white settlers as a "lazy bunch." Australians found it difficult to appreciate the leisureliness of the Highlanders who, for example, measure distance by the time it takes to smoke
cigarets rolled in newspaper. The Highlander, on the
other hand, fails utterly to comprehend the importance of
time as viewed by Westerners. To an Australian an
appointment at ten o'clock means ten o'clock, but to a
Highlander it means the time at which they leave the
house; he may arrive at the meeting place at noon, even
later afternoon. To them time and space are nonentities.

I once witnessed an incident that dramatically dem-
onstrated how oblivious the natives are to duration and
distance. One siesta, while asleep, I was awakened by
Sinoko, who said there was a girl outside asking urgently
to see me. A small girl was standing timidly on the porch.
She said that her father had had an accident. Would the
"dokta" come to make him well? I collected my medicine
bag, asked where the girl came from, and she said, "Not
far, Dokta, not far." She lead the way south and east
across the river, down a jungle track, and after we had
walked for about two hours I asked, "How far now?" The
girl said, encouragingly, "Not far, Dokta, not far." After
more than five hours of brisk walking, our expedition of
mercy arrived at the village, which was on the top of a
steep stony cliff.

The girl's "not far" was not an illuminating reply. It
was a figurative location that could mean anything from
an hour's walk to several days of steady marching.

The Highlanders have no measures for time and space. After a while one knows how to interpret their descriptions, the five main ones being: really far away—anything from one day's walk upward; small distance—about six or eight hours; not too far—three or four hours; fairly near—one or two hours; right near—less than an hour. The journey that day with the girl was between "not too far" and "fairly near." Or to speak precisely, a fair bit.

Their customary greeting, a standing embrace in which both men and women handle each other's genitals, was an unfailing source of sniggering amusement to white settlers. It appeared that they were in need of continual exposure to the possessiveness that characterized their relationships by direct physical contact with other people. Even in the villages, among people who saw one another every day, hands were continually reaching out to caress a thigh, arms, and searching mouths hung over a child's lips or nuzzled a baby's penis. Once I witnessed a rather whimsical scene. An Australian VIP landed at Goroka, the capital of the Central Highlands. He was met by the District Officer and several indigenous chiefs. One of the chiefs came to him, full of admiration, and put his hand, palm down, on the VIP's manhood. A black sooty fat imprint of a hand remained on the white pants of a very red-faced VIP.

On the days when there was not much doing to keep me in the hospital, I would be invited by John Colman, the young magistrate, known here as Patrol Officer, to hear court cases in distant villages.

I recollect one of those hearings on the "circuit." The court house was erected in no time. Grass roof, supported by shaky thin poles, and walls of nipa palm leaves comprised the complete construction of the court. The Australian national flag was also hoisted, to give as much majesty to the law as could be introduced in such an unlikely place. John ordered the portable field table moved so that he sat facing the entrance, trying to defy nature by looking magisterial and weighty.

Native policemen stood beside him and others acted as court ushers. He put an empty kerosene can by the entrance into which the litigants were made to spit their betel nut before coming into the "courtroom." A policeman inspected their mouths with his finger and thumped them on the head to make them spit as they came in. Nobody was going to be allowed to chew and foam at the mouth in court. John wanted to create a judicial atmosphere so that they felt they were in a serious place.

A husky policeman spoke to the first customer for justice. He said that a man from a neighboring village wanted to bring a charge of adultery with one of his wives against a young man of the village. Would the Master Magistrate hear the case? John indicated that he would. The husky policeman returned with the injured husband, then took the plaintiff by both hands, pried open his mouth, took out the mass of betel nut leaf, areca nut, and lime, and threw it into the tin. Procedure in the court was basic. The magistrate commenced by asking the name. The plaintiff and the rest of the court looked at the Magistrate blankly, so he loudly repeated the question. One could have heard a gobbet of betel nut drop. Nobody stirred. When he recited the formula a third time, his interpreter recognized it, beamed with pleasure, and said, "Oh, Master, I am going outside to ask one of his friends what his name is." The interpreter returned and gave the defendant's name as Gipo. The Magistrate wrote it down. What was the name of the village, and what was the complaint? The plaintiff explained in gross detail, with gestures, precisely how one performs fornication. From his graphic description, I understood that the copulation was not of the "missionary position." The Magistrate then sent for the accused; he gave the evidence, as garbled by the interpreter, "This woman Guma, she say we make love; she say her husband long, long way; she say her husband is old and 'too small' for her; she want me copulate with her, so we copulate." The Magistrate wrote this down and made the accused scratch his cross of affirmation underneath.

Guma then gave considerable evidence negating the man's statement, her tongue unable to keep pace with the rush of expressive, highly descriptive endearments as she extended her hands in squeezing gestures of appreciation. There was shrewdness in her lively eyes, evident delight in creating an effect, a willingness to play humorously on her own infirmities, calculating the effect of her exaggeration, deliberately working for the tolerant, involuntary smiles that would gain the sympathy she wanted.

All this was apparent to me as the case proceeded. There she was, pointing at the breasts engorged with colostrum and to the belly that would give birth to an unwanted creature. There she was, guiltless party of sexual congress, graphically moaning in recollection of the pain caused by Gipo's "big like yam" penetration. There she stood, unwilling performer, with her rolling eyes, tongue tripping through the wrongs she had to bear. How her knees quaked and her poor back ached from Gipo's "load," which she supported. She blamed her husband; had he not been "long, long way" she would not have had to suffer this treatment. When you are young and able to bear children, many men care about you. What can a young, lonely woman do to protect herself?

And there on the opposite side of the courtroom was
Gipo, impassive, standing on his right to show his manli-
ness. Whatever the provocation, he should have offered
some self-defense, I thought. He surely knew the jungle's
law: that an adultress is killed, for all women are Circes,
enticing men to casual dalliance, initiating affairs to satisfy their own desires. He certainly knew and believed,
like his people, that to impregnate a woman one must
have many fornications, for a fetus must be "made" over
a period of time—he couldn't impregnate by a single act
of intercourse. Yet he kept his mouth sealed.

The Magistrate found Gipo guilty of adultery, and
wrote on the bottom of the form, "Sentenced to serve a
period of three months of hard labor at Goroka jail."

John dealt with cases involving pride, price, pigs,
and land disputes. Most of them, however, were matters
of adultery, which seemed to be endemic in this region.

In more recent years the term "jail" has been abol-
ished and replaced by "corrective institution." There is
thus no ex-convict stigma attached to a man after his release; in fact he becomes an influential man in his village.
In prison he learns the elementary principles of hygiene
and sanitation, the value of discipline, and, if the term is
long enough, he sometimes learns a useful trade. It must
be said that the prisoners are well looked after medically
and are fed a well-balanced diet. He comes home almost
unrecognizable; healthy, with shiny skin, and a gain in
weight. Very often he becomes a trustworthy government servant, and even a constable.

I myself was served loyally and helpfully for nine
long years by an ex-convict—a cold-blooded murderer by
the definition of Western society. Bless his soul, he was
killed—knocked down by a Western innovation, the
Land Rover.

The months went by. It was now the end of 1954.
Medical progress in the Highland region was forging
ahead. The Health Department, with additional doctors
and auxiliary staff, was running smoothly by this time.

Then, during a restless night, I felt impelled to "Get
out of the routine business of the hospital." This was not
a wholly new idea—lately I had begun to feel a feebleness
and lack of any real work, except for the hospital clinic. I
was growing more and more depressed. Death had become both a tragedy and a release from tremendous tension. I had spent hours and hours, day and night, days on
end, trying desperately to keep patients alive, and in the
end had been so physically and mentally exhausted that
the patient's death had often come as a relief. "How many
lives have been saved through my professional skill?" I
asked myself. Just a handful. "And how many more people were in need of relief from burdens caused by sickness and death?" An immense number of them.

Ultimately I decided to do the obvious—my time
would be spent not on curing individual cases, but rather
on the prevention of unobstructive, devastating diseases,
so that native people could compete on equal terms with
races not so handicapped. I set myself the goal of trying
to save not a handful, but a thousand, lives a year.

By now I realized that treating patients had been, for
me, much less interesting than dealing with social problems, such as mass disease. Indeed, many patients present no problems at all. But every member of a clan, I felt,
has a personality and is a specimen of humanity that may
be dull and stupid, quick and intelligent, or just ordinary.

For weeks I stuck to my resolve, making a conscious
effort to start my journey into the interior of this region.
The interior where people live, people who drink water
from streams in their cupped hands, who don't know

what a wheel is, and who regard a knife made of bamboo
and an axe made of stone as the last word in man's technical equipment. But somehow I couldn't put my intent
into action. I staved it off as I would going to the dentist.

And then, as a result of a particular night's event, I
made my start. The night was breezeless, cool, and bright,
and the rays of the full moon glittered on the mountain
tops and flowed like quicksilver over the motionless bamboo leaves of the valley. I had finally gone to sleep
drenched in sweat, flattened by my recurrent malarial
fever. Suddenly sharp cries and shrill voices brought me
from blissful unconsciousness. I got up and went out to
my narrow veranda. Leaning over the railing I saw on the
ground of the nurses' quarters no more than fifty yards
away waving lights, fleeting shadows. There was something going on over there. As a substitute for a dressing
gown, I pulled an old worn raincoat over sweat-soaked
pajamas, grabbed my electric torch, and ran to see what
unimaginable catastrophe had occurred.

The spectacle I saw on arrival was more than unusual. A vituperative senior nurse was standing in the middle of a group of shapely, brown, trainee girls, unrefined
enough to be "topless." "Oh Doctor," she wailed, "this
brute sneaked into our chicken run and swallowed at
least two of our hens. But the others gave the alarm. I
woke some girls up, we came running down, and then I
saw it. There were two of them, one a little bigger. I gave
it a sharp blow with the bush knife and you can see it's
been properly punished," she exclaimed.

In the diffused light of the storm lanterns held by the
girls, I saw, to my disgust, a long knife in one of her bony
hands; the body of the "brute" lay on the ground like a
large embellishing tube, except that the tube was disfig-
ured in places by large hernia-like protrusions.

"I'm sure there's another in the henhouse," the nurse went on. "Here Doc, take this knife and have a look while, I fetch our hens from the belly of this creeper."

I bent and stared down at the head of the boa. It was my Kiki, my pet. But where was Miki, the smaller one?

And here lay Kiki's dark, shiny, and slender body still feebly wriggling on the ground. Two pairs of eyes, one of the serpent and one of the man, came together. I leaned closer over Kiki's head. That was when I saw the eyes properly—wide open, enormous. They seemed to me as a dead man's, not bright yellow—that would be an injustice—but the color of molten copper, even more flaming, but dark green and black. Their look sent out lightning flashes that betrayed no evil, hatred, or fury. There I could see only an indescribable need for survival.

Suddenly I noticed I had instinctively come to a halt, gazing into those glaring eyes. I tried to move, but it was impossible. I was as if paralyzed. My eye's were glued to the serpent's and could not leave them. The strange thing was that I was perfectly conscious of my situation, but my body no longer obeyed my will. I was hypnotized.

Doubts have been expressed whether snakes have the power to hypnotize. The accepted explanation is that the fear of the prey paralyzes it to inactivity while the snake advances on it. But I was not afraid; the beautiful creature was my pet and it was dead. No, I was well and truly hypnotized and realized it. In my heart of hearts, furious at being dominated by a snake's eyes, I swore to myself, "Goddamn it, don't be an idiot. It is bloody stupid. Move! Turn your head, imbecile." I summoned all my willpower to turn my eyes away at least. No use. The snake did not blink, for it had no eyelids, and although I did, I too could no longer blink. How long did this struggle last? I cannot say—a minute, perhaps only a few seconds. I must have made a last despairing effort of will for I finally managed to lower my eyelids. Freed, and slightly ashamed of my behavior, trembling and sweating, I left the place of execution. Under the vigilance of wide-eyed girls and the nurse, I went to the hennery in the hope of finding Miki. The hens had gone back to sleep peacefully; only the cock was obstreperous, trying to hail a nonexistent dawn. I found her coiled around one of the rafters. With no hesitation, she uncoiled herself and slid into my outstretched arms. Then she wriggled under my raincoat and wrapped her slender body around my clammy torso.

Upon leaving, the first object I saw was the decapitated body of Kiki and the senior nurse slitting the whole length of the snake and taking out the two chickens that lay inside intact, but dead, their feathers simply ruffled and moistened. I heard her say, "Tomorrow we have them for lunch, cooked with brown rice."

Miki and I proceeded to our home. Demoralized by the grim night's incident I fell into troubled slumber, occasionally interrupted by vivid recollections of the day I first came across Miki and Kiki.

It had happened less than two years ago. On my arrival here I found them in my house as lodgers, two boas of the type known as carpet snakes because of the colored pattern like a Persian carpet that decorates their backs. They had taken up residence among the joists of the house, and when I first saw them I had quite a start. But, taking a second look, I realized that they were perfectly harmless carpet snakes. I began to whistle gently to charm them. The two boas, snugly wrapped around one of the rafters, took no notice of my musical efforts. At the time I did not know that most snakes have no acoustic cavity. The flute used by Indian snake charmers on cobras only helps the magician to charm the snake by rocking his head and holding its attention by means of rhythmic movement.

I was annoyed that my snakes paid no attention to my variation of Mozart's "Eine Kleine Nachtmusik," which came to the same thing as far as they and I were concerned. Then I decided to sacrifice a tin of condensed milk to them. I poured all of its content into the plate and placed it exactly below the snakes; I then began to whistle again. This time I gave an accompaniment of my soldiering days song "Lily Marlene," tapping the back of the empty milk tin and nodding my head rhythmically. It was a hit. Slowly the two boas raised their heads, slowly they unfolded their coils and stretched out their pretty jaws, then their bodies, thick cables that gleamed like precious satin. Finally they flopped to the floor. They let themselves fall completely. There they made a few respectful gestures, sniffing from side to side, looking at me in search of approval, or so it seemed; then without further ado they began to lap the milk. Like cats, but noiselessly; and without showing any flash of a tongue.

After this treat we became "ménage à trois." They were a more than content couple, Kiki and Miki; they were an alluring twain, smitten with a self-complaisance and simplicity. I saw them often, after their banquet of milk, facing each other in an almost upright position, embracing each other then letting go, leaping and jumping and performing a fantastic ballet in the middle of the room. And then, both with modesty and prudence, gracefully retreating to the nook above.

The scenario of the previous night was still imprinted in my mind as I woke up. I shakily blinked back my tears at not finding Miki; she was gone with no "adios," to an unknown destination, leaving her milk untouched.

I commenced my journey into the interior of this mountainous region where human beings were more authentic, the jungle thicker, and the rivers more dangerous. I began my entry into the largest natural museum any where on earth.

Martial People
with Dignity

The melody of New Guinea's waters is for me a tune rising from every rock, root, and rapids. This melody of the rivers and cascades is audible to every ear, but there is another music in the jungle's mountains, by no means audible to all. To hear even a few notes of it, one must live here for a long time and know the speech of this mountainous domain. Then on still nights when the campfire is low and the moon amid Aurora Australis has climbed above the rimrocks, one needs to sit quietly and listen for a distant beat of drums and the wailing cry of bamboo flutes, and think hard of everything one has seen and tried to understand. Then you may hear it—a vast undulatory harmony; the score inscribed on a thousand hills and mountains, its notes like the life and death of humanity, is this imaginative culture's sole improvisor, its rhythms spanning the seconds and the centuries.

There I was among martial people no one knew: this people, unscarred by civilization, capable of inhabiting a natural realm without disturbing the harmony of its life. They lived in thousands on the mountains and in the valleys, on little plots of soil that are gardens, subirrigated by the showers that fell endlessly across the steep adjoining slopes.

At first this spacious region appeared to my eye as hard and snaggy land, full of cruel slopes and cliffs; its trees too gnarled for post or sawlog; its ranges too steep for pasturage. Later, much later, I learned by experience that it was a land of flowery sufficiency. That these twisted trees and junipers each year bear a crop of plentiful human nutriment. That the tall golden grasses conceal under their waving plumes a subterranean garden of bulbs and tubers, an open crop for fat possums and hogs, a gastronomic feast for the people.

And here I stood aloof, the first white aesculapius and neophyte ethnologist, environed by the hunter's wandering moons.

Having been blinded and made halt of mind by the cruel doctrine of racial prejudice and xenophobia of my former Vaterland's Führer and his henchmen, I initially looked upon these jungle dwellers as a most inferior race.

So much time has gone by since then, time during which I became aware of the misconception of the word "race" that had for me been conventional in many of its connotations. Without any deliberate and systematic study of race and races, I feel I have nonetheless gained insight from living among and observing the individual lives of these preliterate beings. And I have learned to narrow my focus to specific investigations, even while trying not to lose the connection with the whole.

My belief has become that this is the most illuminating approach to the study of any community. To carry it out, one must furnish one's mind with comprehensive impressions of the nature of the individual, in both its wholeness and its growth. To create a portrait emphasizing only the helplessness, inhibitions, and the use of defense mechanisms by these people distorts the picture of them severely.

To study a Stone Age culture should indeed be a personal experience rather than a merely intellectual encounter with books of life histories. Many of the well known figures of anthropological literature, especially those who venture to write without comment or interpretation, have contributed considerably to our knowledge of personal life in the "primitive" socie ties. However, the effort to find deeper meaning within the known seems far more worthwhile than simply reading a book about it. No book can replace the personal effort at understanding that comes from living and sharing the materials of actual lives. Today I've come to the personal conclusion that, aside from the major groups—Caucasian, Mongoloid, and Negroid—there are no such things as races. There are communities, there are ethnic or cultural groups, but they blend into one another to such an extent that the terms race and subspecies, as normally defined in zoology, are meaningless when applied anthropologically. There are no obvious differences in the mental abilities of such groups, nor are there genetic racial capacities for intellectual or emotional development; it does not hold true that one group is superior or inferior to another in intelligence. Intelligence involves brightness, cleverness, reasoning power, and the ability to solve problems. Every person possesses these characteristics that we call "intelligence." Some appear extremely "bright," some appear extremely "dull," and the vast majority fall somewhere between. There is a continuous gradation of mental ability from one extreme to the other, from idiot to genius, regardless of "race." Just as we see a continuous gradation of differences in other characteristics of humans, such as physical stature, so too is there a gradation of differences in intellectual ability.

The question why people differ in intelligence has been asked for centuries, but a scientifically acceptable answer is still not wholly possible. The layperson usually asks, "Is intelligence influenced by heredity or environment?" One school of thought would say "heredity," whereas another believes it is "environment." And yet another would promptly answer "Both—but the environment outweighs the effects of genes."

There are in fact only anthropomorphic differences —in terms of linguistic, behavioral, and physical characteristics—between the races. One does not have to be an anthropologist to recognize that a Chinese, a German, and a New Guinean do not look alike. They will not think alike either, but that is a question of culture and not genetics. So out with all talk of races. On with unsullied folk, not wholly known...

Certain foreigners from the New and Old Worlds still view the inhabitants of remote jungles of New Guinea as "people in isolation." There are no longer "people in isolation" or tribal societies unaware of the existence of the so-called civilized world; the passage overhead of airplanes and the appearance of manufactured items via natural trade routes have already brought an awareness of the cosmopolitan world to every band of hunter-gatherers, to all hoe and digging-stick agriculturalists who may previously have been truly isolated.

I recollect a day about twenty years ago, while wandering among these remote people of the mountains, when I came across an old bow-and-arrow hunter who had just shot a fast-leaping wallaby. He was frightened at seeing me. My two native companions put him at ease. It was obvious that the man had never been in contact with white people and lived in a remote hamlet high in the mountains. Through the good offices of my companions as interpreters, I learned that he had nonetheless heard about white men coming into this area. Even as we were praising him for his skillful kill, in the sky high above, a two-engine plane was flying over and my new acquaintance told me that this kind of iron bird flew over very often. Curious, he asked if one could sit in the iron bird and how many people it could carry. I told him that there were seats in the plane and that it could carry many people, almost half of his village. I also told him that in front of this iron bird was a man who could boss the plane. He nodded in agreement.

"Can one eat in a plane?" he then asked. I assured him that one could not only eat but also drink. Pensively he nodded and asked then if one could stand up in a plane, to which I nodded and added that a plane was much larger than his hut. The next question kind of staggered me, when he asked if one could relieve the call of nature in the plane, or as he expressed in the local lingua franca, "pek pek na pis pis." When I answered in the affirmative, a smile could be seen in his eyes and he shook his head saying, "That's impossible." "Why is that impossible?" I asked him. "Because I and my people would have felt it when it falls down." It was my turn to show a glimmer in my eyes as I explained to him about the box in a little room in the iron bird used to stop the fall of "pek pek na pis pis" on people's heads. He shook his head once again, but finally accepted my explanation. After a bit more talk we went our ways, with our own individual thoughts—mine of the "man in isolation."

To some foreigners these mountainous folk of the Central Highlands have an effect akin to conversion. The elements of that harsh, sunstruck place are so stark, so boned down, its inhabitants so separated and durable, its rituals so essential and so graceful, that being here feels like purification. In the more remote parts of the country, the quality the people have of being able to do with much less, of wearing lack with a kind of grace, often seems to more sophisticated eyes a positive and proud resistance to the trappings of civilization—the cosmic shrug and the stoic proverb take on the aura of nobility. But for foreigners to assume the Central Highlander's identity is something of a romantic indulgence; for the Highlander it is fate, and that fatefulness is hard to feel, let alone enter.

I think this is the real allure of the New Guineans, their attitude of almost mystical attachment to the land, to their village, a fervent engagement they appear to feel with an intensity and tenacity that other people are no longer capable of. To the outsider's eye, their experience seems at first like a simple devotion to be envied; only time and experience can reveal how much torment lies beneath that bare, taciturn surface.

If one were a writer, one would soon be tantalized by a multitude of contradictions. Committed to making sense of the Highlander, one discovers that the whole cloth has a most complicated weave, that all conclusions are likely to be paradoxes, that being illiterate is less typical in this folk than the polarities of their minds. As paradoxes flesh out, one learns that "sickness" is to be forever divided against oneself; one learns to be loyal to opposites, to be a fatalist who is simultaneously an anarchist of the will, and to cultivate death as the clarifier of life. Pride and resignation are one, less simple than defiant. The people know what they must do, without necessarily understanding why. To the observer, the "understanding" is necessary, though often incalculable, and the outsider's last resort is to impose order on these people, to make them over in the outsider's own image. In consequence, much is written about "people of the jungle"— some of it perceptive. But for anyone attempting to put mountainous jungles into words, there is always the baffling feeling that the experience itself will escape either explanation or incarnation, that the jungles and their peoples will remain no more than a setting, a backdrop forever out of reach.

The people of the Highlands reside in villages that contain two or more residential compounds, or wards. Usually one hut among the group of dwellings forming a ward is considerably bigger than all the others. This is the men's house, a special domicile for men and boys old enough to have been initiated. Women and uninitiated boys live in much smaller huts, each of which usually houses a number of pigs. The residents of a men's house constitute a unified political and ritual community, which is the principal war-making unit.

From an anthropological perspective, any kind of war is generally a system of the absence, inadequacy, or breakdown of other procedures that aim at neither territorial gains and the conquest of resources nor at the suppression of one political or religious ideology.

In all societies, some individuals wield more influence over the affairs of their fellows than most. In the Highlands, a man gains such a position of authority— which never extends much beyond the immediate kin group—through the acquisition of an esoteric knowledge of rituals and the clever management of livestock to the benefit of his relatives. Every important event demands the exchange of pigs to solemnify or legitimize the creation of a new status or to settle a conflict. Most disputes are over women, pigs, or gardens, and any may well generate enough political enmity to cause armed conflict.

In every Highland war, one person on either side, called the "man-at-the-root-of-the-arrow," is held responsible for the outbreak of hostilities. These are the parties to the original dispute, which ultimately escalates into armed combat. Being the "man-at-the-root-of-the-arrow" carries the responsibility of providing compensation for all injuries and deaths suffered by supporters on the battlefield, as well as all others—including women and children—victimized in clandestine revenge raids. This responsibility acts as a built-in force favoring an early end to hostilities.

At the time I understood little of the political realities of this society, where neither formal government nor forensic institutions existed for the settlement of conflicts. Later, when I understood one of the languages, I began to comprehend the conditions that make military action the inevitable consequence when there is no effective system of political control.

Throughout their remembered past up to the present, the Highlanders have fought among themselves. According to myth, the black-palm bow was one of the first creations. Every youth learns to use the bow and every able-bodied man is expected to actively defend his own interests. People esteem successful warriors; the most admired men are brave and daring.

Apart from a few mountain tribes, the Highlanders have no idea of "lex talionis." A man simply tries to inflict a greater injury of his enemy than that which he has suffered. Moreover, the people who suffer as a result of vengeance do not accept their injuries as just or appropriate; they too seek countervengeance, and so the chain of conflict is unending. Even men who fight as allies fight about the indemnities for casualties. Each conflict, however it may be resolved, breeds new problems.

Most Highland wars originate not from traditional hostilities between groups, but from personal disputes between individuals. Longstanding injuries may prompt an individual to exact vengeance against a particular man, but this does not involve groups in permanently hostile relations. Groups that are enemies on one occasion may be allies on another.

Among a few tribes there are "traditional enmities," which are permanent unchanging political relations between particular clan-oriented parishes. Every male has an equal obligation to maintain and perpetuate hostility toward the traditional enemy, seeking opportunities to kill any member of the group he may encounter.

A war requires no elaborate preparation and a man can be ready to fight at short notice. A Highlander ordinarily carries a bow and arrow whenever he travels beyond the borders of his own gardens. He also carries a stone (now steel) axe, a bamboo pipe with tobacco, and a day's supply of sweet potatoes.

Many fights break out unexpectedly, but men intent on vengeance make advance arrangements, send word to friendly allies, discuss when and where to attack, and see the women, children, and pigs off to safety. Some of the aggressors are bound to have affine or cognate ties with the enemy, and they send superstitious warnings. Before a fight, a man performs rites of protective magic or incants spells to ensure that his arrows will find their target.

The bow is the Highlander's most important weapon. From about the age of twelve a boy learns marksmanship and develops skill by hunting possums and birds. After passing the first stage of initiation, an adolescent receives his first black-palm bow; henceforth he will fight alongside the men.

Bowmen use four kinds of arrows. For long-range shooting they employ plain hardwood-tipped arrows; for close fire they select one that is razor sharp with a bamboo tip. To make certain of a kill, a man uses a barbed arrow that cannot be removed by the victim without aggravating the wound. An arrow tipped with a cassowary claw is also used for close fighting. There are no poisoned arrows, for Highlanders believe their bespelled arrows to be magically potent. The arrows have little penetrating power over one hundred yards distance. The maximum effective range is about fifty yards. At this distance a skilled bowman can hit a stationary man-sized target three times out of four.

Other Highland weapons include the wooden fighting pick and the stone axe. Men who fight with the wooden pick or axe in hand-to-hand battle also carry a bark-faced shield; but this is mainly used in defense, being too heavy to carry in attack.

During traditional fights, bowmen exchange volleys of arrows at a distance of about one hundred yards. Since this distance is beyond the bow's effective range, many casualties are in fact accidental. During a skirmish, the warriors insult and abuse each other, usually by reciting a standard piece in the repertoire. A typical verse goes like this:

> *Your women bake only tiny potatoes for you*
> *Your mothers too bake only the end of potatoes for you*
> *Our women and mothers bake big potatoes for us*
> *You are weak like babies, we are strong like wild pigs.*

The reply from a hostile group may sometimes be raucous and obscene: "We make you eat woman's vulva," or "We make you to eat our shit and drink our piss." The larger the fighting groups, the harsher the insult. In the course of the insolence, at a given signal and still shouting, they let fly a volley of hundreds of arrows. Then there would be charges and flanking movements and attempts at infiltration by small groups. Prominent warriors have some influence in controlling the attack, but they are often disobeyed. In prolonged fights different men may lead the groups for periods of a few weeks at a time.

When two clans are at war with each other, periods of daily combat are interrupted by short "cease fires" during which the warriors attend to the more mundane tasks of garden work and hunting, but they are always prepared to counter a surprise attack launched by the enemy. After weeks of discontinuous fighting, however, the threat of famine caused by the prolonged neglect of proper cultivation induces the belligerents to maintain an informal and precarious truce.

There are no permanent battlefields, and fighting takes place anywhere in open country, often near the boundaries of the parish or territory. Tactics are in part determined by the terrain. Deep drainage ditches bordered by cane-grass are used for protection to conceal movement. In the level country that predominates, defensive fighting is difficult. Most battles occur during the day; at night the leaders post guards at strategic points, and the main body retires. At dawn the fighting resumes.

I was intrigued to learn that in the course of a battle, kinsmen and affines often fight on opposing sides; friends, "in-laws," and even blood relatives may meet as "enemies." To avoid killing one's own maternal uncle, wife's brother, or best friend, one fights at the edge of the battlefield; but if they do meet, there is a recognized method of mutual protection. One runs up to the other, shouting to his fellow warriors, "This is my relative. Don't shoot him." The latter usually respects this request.

A man who kills in war exchanges his bow for another in order to baffle the victim's vengeful ghost. He also stays awake on the first night to repeat spells. The next morning he rubs his body with dew and drinks bespelled water as a magical protection against the ghost.

He then plants a magical bog-iris for additional protection. When he returns to the men's house he announces the killing, but without directly naming the victim. Boys in particular are not told the identity of a war victim, for they may unwittingly repeat the name and thereby endanger both the killer and themselves. To utter your own name is also a strict taboo, and on many occasions it was time-consuming to learn the name of a native. When asked his name, rather than bring bad luck upon his head, he would turn to a friend and ask, "What is my name?"

I once asked a middle-aged man, "What is your name?" "Mutmut," he replied. "And what's yours?" I asked the man's companion. "Mitmit" was the answer. "Mutmut and Mitmit! Are these your true names?" The man shrugged and grinned, "Yes, our true names." But I knew they had given false names lest they put their spirits under the power of an evil foe.

The whole parish mourns for a person killed in battle. The victim's brothers daub the corpse with red ochre as a reminder to avenge the death. In the course of the mourning, dancing, and singing, if the mood so moves the Highlander, a poetically gifted man may introduce a new song. If the lyrics appeal to others, it becomes a routine verse for that particular clan.

On one occasion I had an opportunity to record one of the men's mourning songs. The singer sings of how his brother had led the dancing on proud ceremonial occasions before his death. Now he is being given as a "present" to the earth. In the last lines he wonders what he will do without his brother and whether to take revenge:

> *My brother, he was*
> *At the head of the dance*
> *Now he is presented*
> *To the clay.*

My brother man,
What shall I do?
My brother man,
What shall I do?

I was fortunate enough to be an onlooker at one of the aforementioned battles. During one of my earlier field trips, our party lost its way and had to push through a growth of high cane. The men hacked at it with their machetes, but could cut only a narrow tunnel through the dense reed. The stench of stagnant mud and rotting grass sickened my stomach. An eerie gray light filtering through the grass above our heads increased my sudden claustrophobia. I stiffled a rising desire to rush at the cane, push it back, trample it down, and fight my way out. After hours of grueling torture, we finally emerged from the cane into a glade.

Ten minutes or so out of the torturous cane jungles, we met some warriors who had run off at the entrance of the cane, and now formed up in front of a platform. The warriors' platoon called to our porters' line to halt. Thinking that their intent was evil, our men refused to stop and pushed on toward the river below. Hundreds of armed and decorated warriors ran beside us, excitedly pushing and jostling the nerve-racked porters, including me. Nearing the river the warriors formed an attacking square and rushed ahead to its banks, shouting and yelling wildly. Dancing up and down on their respective shores, brandishing bows, hurling insults and threats at each other, the contending groups warmed up for a foray, taking no further notice of our party.

My porters and medical orderlies shouted gleefully when I told them of my decision to erect camp here, a fair distance from the battleground. In no time my party built makeshift huts of branches, bamboos, leaves, and ferns to protect themselves from threatening rain. They put up my tent, in which they stored the medical supplies and provisions—mainly of salt, sugar, tea, and canned corned beef. A bush stretcher with mosquito netting on top was also constructed for me.

The party was now relaxed and soon made themselves at home. It was time to eat. They put stones in the fire on which they baked sweet potatoes, some taro, and vegetables, consuming heaped plates of food roasted over hot stones. This vegetarian diet is adequate for nutrition if taken in large quantities.

For myself, the long walk through the jungle-cane was a bit too much. I was dead tired, and my legs and body were scratched and bruised; but, to my amazement, after this ordeal I enjoyed the Stone Age meal.

When night fell, following the sudden sunset that is characteristic of the tropics, I went to my tent. I slid under the mosquito net, which was already occupied by a horde of buzzing fellow-travelers. They made sleep impossible. I crawled out from underneath the mosquito netting and tried to light a fire in the hope that the smoke would chase away the "uninvited guests." But my matches were damp, so the advantages of civilization were no good to me; my little magic sticks could conjure up fire only when they were dry. I called one of the medical orderlies for help. For a while he watched silently as I tried to get my matches to light. Then he picked up a branch and made a little heap with twigs and leaves. His movement grew more and more rapid, and the rattan thread moved up and down faster and faster through the tinder until it suddenly broke. The friction set up by the rubbing had burned it through, but in the meantime had set light to the tinder. Thus I witnessed the age-old "fire-saw" at work. To me it was another discovery.

At last the fire was lit and generating plenty of smoke to discourage some of the menacing insects. I lay down, crouched in my blanket, not so much warm as numb, feeling disembodied, rigid, and unrelaxed. I was convinced I would be awake all night, but fell into a deep, dreamless oblivion within five minutes.

I awoke, I thought, immediately, but discovered to my astonishment that it was daylight. The others were already up, and a new fire had been lit. I was chilled to the marrow and itched in a thousand places; my arms and ankles, which had escaped from the blanket's protection during the night, were speckled with insect bites. My nose was blocked, my head ached, and my eyes were puffed. But after I had forced myself to wash in the cold river, had swallowed some smoky, scalding tea, and was on my first cigaret, I felt much better. And, later, when the sun began to filter through the trees and I sat on a boulder turned, like a lizard, to the emerging warmth, I felt unfamiliarly vital.

The warriors approached our camp in full military dress: feathers, pig-tusk nose decorations, and soot-blackened faces with the resulting sinister expressions. Each man carried an assortment of arms—bow and arrows, stone axes, and bone daggers. They entered our camp ground with nods and smiles, the universal silent language, assuring our group that all was well. Nevertheless, my party was astir and wide-eyed with a sense of anxiety. Then the warriors placed in front of me an extremely well-built man of medium height, broad of shoulder, slim of waist, and muscular of limb. The warriors looked at me with a glint as if to say, "You must make him fighting fit— use your magic."

I scanned the dignified body of the warrior. He had to be some kind of chief, resplendent in the white and sulfa cockatoo and the gold and red bird-of-paradise feathers of his office, smeared with pig fat and smelling like a smoked ham.

The wooden handle of an arrow, about three feet in length, was protruding from his body. I ordered, through the interpreter, him carried into my tent and laid on my bush stretcher. Here I tried to pull out the long wooden shaft with its home-made barb, but it was immovable. He was in grave condition, breathing through a hole in his side. The first thing I did was cut off the protruding handle of the arrow. After that I made him as comfortable as possible and gave him as much resuscitation as I could.

I puzzled over what to do next. Should we carry the wounded warrior to the hospital, over four days' walking distance through his enemy's territory, knowing beforehand that he would not make it? The only way out of my quandry was to proceed with an operation on the spot. I also saw how it must be done; the arrow would have to be treated like a fish-hook. This solution would sound obvious to any surgeon if it were to be performed in a large hospital by a thoraic surgeon and trained team of helpers. But our conditions were not so amenable.

I had no idea where the point of the barb of the arrow was, for it was completely hidden inside the chest. My invaluable assistant, Sinoko, administered an open anesthetic of ether. I then resected the bowman's ribs above and below and opened the wound so that I could see along the shaft. The arrow had opened the pleura, lacerated the lung, and gone through the mediastinum (the space between the right and left lungs). But I still could not see the point of the weapon. It was a terrible risk to proceed with the operation; for all I knew, the point may be resting against the heart. I summoned up all my courage and pushed hard at the arrow. When I felt the point jutting against the chest wall, I angled it through the skin. I cut off the point behind the barb, then sterilized the shaft as well as I could and withdrew it. Finally I packed the track left by the arrow with sulfanilamide powder, and stitched up the external wound, leaving the usual drainage tube. Recovery was good, but slow.

By now our camp was milling with wide-eyed natives. They handled everything, leaving greasy black finger marks and a strong odor of smoked pig fat. Suppurating ulcers and festering sores of yaws were candidates for the hypodermic syringe and penicillin. Unprotesting, they presented their buttocks to the jab of the needle and its promised healing.

Later I learned that my former patient, the wounded warrior, not yet 30 years old, had accounted for more than a dozen men slain on the battlefield. Tribesmen spoke his name with respect and the enemy marked him as a prize target. He was already a "Bigman"—a term anthropologists use to describe a leadership status that is not hereditary—by the name of Koldom, and had four wives.

One evening when cool shadows lingered in the valley and the women came down from the gardens with their string bags filled for the evening cooking, Koldom entered my tent with one of the interpreters. He looked at me resolutely and announced that he was going to use our campsite as a place for the proposed armistice. When asked how long the proposed peace treaty would last, he just shrugged, which I took as a token "who knows?" And then he spoke, deliberately, taking his time as if to give the interpreter a chance not to miss the facts.

Here I relay the account of his talk translated by my interpreter:

Koldom's people lived in compact villages along several valleys on this side of the river. They were well off;

they had many pigs, dogs, women, and food gardens. Each village group had hundreds of units identified by their local and clan names. Interclan fighting, involving small bands from the men's house and the kinsmen of victims whose death could not be avenged on the battlefield, was practiced. A successful clandestine expedition into 'enemy territory' might result in the party bringing back a pig or two. A revenge action of this kind seldom precipitated open warfare on a large scale.

Clans were centered around a paternal leader and lived in small hamlets. Each hamlet had one large men's house where brothers, sons, and nephews of the headman slept and ate.

The current warfare between his people and the neighboring tribe, separated by a major topographic boundary, the river, and the mountain ridge, had started when a year-long truce had come to an end. Five days of fierce fighting ensued, during which the neighboring tribe had killed three of Koldom's warriors and severely wounded him. If not for my 'white magic,' he, Koldom, would also be dead. Furthermore, the enemy had raided a small settlement and driven its inhabitants into exile with friends and relatives in other villages of the region.

In the not long distant past, this particular enemy had frequently raided his territory, and eaten some of his warriors. He and his people would not forget this act of tragic perversion. Cannibalism was not tolerated by Koldom's people. If an enemy were killed during a foray into hostile territory, the raiders of Koldom's tribe would make every effort to bring the body home. If tactical exigencies demanded that the revenge party retreat without the victim, an attempt would be made to retrieve at least a limb.

Only once, he admitted frankly, had he had to consume the flesh of his enemy. It was not long ago that his warriors had beaten the enemy thoroughly, and now this enemy was again making war. Koldom had made many peace treaties, only to see them broken by this enemy. Finally, his tribe was forced to capture one of the enemy's men, whom they then roasted and ate, not for food, as one would think, but as an extreme form of punishment. He assured me earnestly, conviction in his eyes, that it was no pleasure to eat the man—he found him extremely tough.

Koldom needed the present armistice badly for he was still too weak from his arrow wound to go to battle. He wanted to recuperate completely and then, at the right time and place, lead his bowmen to revenge. For this he needed time.

His cajolery entered deeply into my mind. That night I scribbled it down in my field notes' scattered leaflets.

The early colonial administration had succeeded in putting down the intertribal fighting of some tribes. Previously, young men in those tribes had proceeded from tribal initiation to full manhood via this war-like activity. Now there was a vacuum. To fill this, as well as to provide labor for the plantations, the government introduced a system of indentured labor. Each man was examined by a medical officer and accepted only if healthy.

I examined hundreds of these young men, and the contrast between the malnourished and often diseased condition frequently seen among the incoming laborers and the fit and well-nourished fellows concluding their two-year terms was striking. Two years of enforced celibacy, however, brought many complications. But many of these young men, having once obtained a taste of civilization, were reluctant to return to the old village life.

War to them was the foundation of their religious system; souvenirs taken from enemy dead in battle became fetishes of importance in their animistic ceremonies. Although personally owned, they held communal significance in group ritualism. Consecration of fetishes gave a battle strength. Observation of food taboos protected life in battle. Sacred objects consecrated to give individual clans protection against sickness were directed against the enemy to his detriment and to their own success in battle.

The most important ceremonies were religious victory dances. To abolish this ceremony would be to shake the foundation of the tribe's religious system. It would mean a total collapse and demoralization of the community, unless it was replaced by something of equal value.

Koldom's affirmation of cannibalism was germinating in my brain. Is anthropophagic (man-eating) behavior "religious," or is it simply of a gastronomic nature? Is the cannibalism in this contemporary society an overlapping act of dietary value and symbolic expression? In Koldom's case, eating the captured enemy certainly indicated a symbolic expression of spite incorporated into an act of supreme vengeance.

Our cultural heritage has for thousands of years conducted experiments in the eating of human flesh, and it has not been uncommon. Today, however, the eating of human meat is viewed with extreme horror. It is therefore no wonder that the literature on the subject is permeated with grossly erroneous and prejudicial ideas about the practice. Few anthropologists have been able to study cannibalism because missions and governments have generally succeeded in eradicating the custom, which is thought to epitomize, more than any other, the alleged mental primitiveness and diabolical inspiration of people with simple technologies.

It is obvious that the enigmatic nature of cannibalism has invited many writers to speculate about its origin and its biopsychic basis. Yet no specific hypothesis can fully elucidate the cannibalism that these people have incorporated into their vengeance ceremonies. And certainly no understanding can be achieved by applying the precepts of Western thought.

In a missionary's travelog I read many years ago, the author, speaking of an African tribe, recounted:

"Once, when told by a European that the practice of eating human flesh was a most degrading habit, the cannibal answered, 'Why degrading? You people eat sheep and cows and fowls, which are all animals of far lower order,and we eat man, who is great and above all; it is you who are degraded!'"

A feast is the natural mode of expression of the Highlander. Death and burial, harvest, the completion of a men's house, the initiation of adolescent boys into manhood, marriages, and the termination of conflicts are all occasions to be marked with the ritual slaughter and consumption of pigs, with a few exceptions in which a human victim is found to be more stimulating. So it is natural that a feast should be made to mark the beginning of this new era of peace in the tribal history.

On the third day of Koldom's visit a whole day was devoted to the arrangement of the "peace treaty" ceremony, which absorbed the energy of the whole village. Some men erected temporary grass shelters for the forthcoming guests, making the camp site look like a grass-thatched town. Some dug pits and heated flat river stones in long shallow drains until they cracked and spat off chips of flint. When the pits were dug and lined with grass and leaves, each man and boy contributing his armful, the men picked up the heated stones with long wooden tongs and lined the pits with them. The women retired to the gardens. This sudden ebb of humanity left a peaceful lull, welcome after the constant flow of voices and shouts in the newly erected, overcrowded huts. During the late afternoon the tide of humanity arrived again, reaching a high crest of chatter and bustle, together with the squeals of pigs. The pigs were slaughtered and the carcasses thrown on the fire to singe off the bristles. The bodies swelled and stiffened as the air reeked. Then the animals were gutted and the flesh thrown into the hot pits together with potatoes, taro, corn, and beans wrapped separately in banana leaves. The pits were sealed with thick layers of banana and breadfruit leaves, more heated stones were piled on top, and the food was left to steam to perfection in the moisture from the foliage. Jets of escaping steam were quickly plugged.

While the pits steamed like volcanoes, somebody stood up to harangue the guests about the pig exchange that had not yet been made. Men grabbed bows and arrows and women scattered. Koldom, the spokesman of his group, and the spokesman of the opposite group strode to the center. They punctured their impassioned speeches with threatening rattling of arrows.

When both sides returned to their places still shouting, a group of warriors from each faction was signaled to drag a dozen squealing fat pigs into the camp for ceremonial exchange.

I asked the shrewd Koldom for two fat pigs in exchange for three axes and six hatchets. He accepted my offer with gleaming eyes.

Thinking to impress them with the killing force of the shotgun, I aimed it directly at the head of one of the two pigs, almost touching it. As the shotgun discharged and the pig's blood spurted, men sprang to their feet prancing, yelling, and pulling their bow strings. Raised voices proclaimed their intense disapproval.

I looked at them in dismay, trying to pacify their hysterical behavior. I then asked Sinoko to tell the men to kill the second pig their way.

One man rushed forward and grabbed the squealing pig by the forelegs, while another took hold of the hind legs. A third man, standing a few yards away, fitted an arrow to his bow and let it fly, piercing the pig's heart. It was praised by all with raving exclamations.

Finally the meat was done, the pit was opened, and the food piled onto carpets of leaves, with steam rising and reddish juices flowing. The savory essence of cooking meat teased appetites sharpened by long anticipation, and the din of voices became intense with women running hither and thither and men giving orders all at once with tones of authority. The portions of pork were distributed to attending guests and relatives of the person whose death was avenged. It was also distributed to the kin groups of a person maimed or killed in the war. Eligible people from other villages who would not participate in the festival were later sent pieces reserved for them.

My companion Sinoko and I were seated with great care, in order of priority and importance. By my estimation, about six hundred people partook of the feast; a good crowd for these dispersed mountaineers. Many of them were visitors for the occasion.

Toward the end of the repast, spokesmen for the two tribal groups harangued the crowd, extolling the new day of friendship. The two chiefs, who a few days ago had been enemies, each publicly broke one of their arrows, the sign of peacemaking. The war was at an end, but for how long, I wondered?

The "peace feast" was now in full swing. The natives danced in a circle, stamping in rhythm to the rattle and patter of drums. Sinoko gave me a breathless commentary on the dance as well as translations of their many songs, describing the significance of each movement and the meaning of each song. One dance was intended to make the gardens fertile, another to give the men more virility and power to procreate, and another to make their bow and arrow shots powerful against all prey. It also appeared that all ceremonial feastings were periods of licensed promiscuity, or better, a part of courtship.

As mentioned earlier, the men were traditionally segregated in houses of their own, separated from the women, girls, and small boys. When a girl reached the age of fourteen or so, she began to take part in courting, which mostly occurred during the feasts.

In this particular tribe, according to Sinoko, courting began with songs and "turn-head." A male partner sits crosslegged beside a girl and begins swaying his head gently toward her in a stylish fashion, while his friends strike up a particular song. The girl turns her face toward his, their noses and brows meet, they pivot twice on the nose, turning to make contact on each cheek, and then ducking their heads down together to the ground at least twice before moving upward again. In time with the song they repeat these movements many times. If the girl is moved by all this, she will then go with the man.

I felt drowsy toward the early hours of the morning but had no intention of returning to my tent. I was enamored by the "turn-head" of the group of girls and men nearby. Men changed places frequently, partnering different girls. As I observed now, "turn-head" required enthusiasm, skill, and endurance, for it continued marathon-like for hours.

Now both dancers and courting partners started to sing again in vigorous nasal tones. Many of their songs made use of natural imagery to convey a sense of emotion and atmosphere and give structure to the song. Mountains, rain, rivers, and mist, which predominated here and must be negotiated when one is going on courting trips, appeared in the songs as symbols of the difficulty of achieving one's desires, or the discomfort and sorrow that accompanies separation from one's loved one. However, the feeling of romantic loss and doubt in their songs is replaced by incitement or challenge, or a downright statement of sexual intent.

A few of those songs are recorded in my field notes. One song, for example, sung in the early hours of the morning to wake people up:

> *Walk up the slope*
> *Walk down the slope*
> *The place is bad, you'll say, and yet*
> *Its smell is sweet, like marsupial fur*
> *Girl, I like the way*
> *That you turn head*
> *Come closer, shift over here and*
> *Turn the head up, turn the head up*

The singer's place is mountainous with steep sloping pathways, and so it is "bad." Yet it is attractive, like the musk-laden smell of marsupial fur. They invite the girls to court with them, not to sleep.

The following song was used when a man made a rather bold challenge to a girl. In it, he compares his penis to the aerial roots of pandanus, saying it is slack and hanging down, but if she puts it close to her, it will feel her scent and rise. If not, well, they can always separate and forget about it.

> *Oh! The wild pandanus*
> *Roots fall down*
> *Fall down, oh!*
> *Girl, take it close,*

Make it feel your scent.
If it's no good,
We'll put it back, oh!

Another song, performed by a girl, complains that when she was small her parents gave her a lot of work to do, and they are still making her work for them. She protests that she is getting old now, her breasts have fallen down, and she is fully mature sexually—why don't they send her to a man?

When I was a child they made me their servant.
Now I'm grown up, but I'm still working for them.
My two fruits have fallen down.
Below, in the place, my head hair is growing.

Another song is sung by both men and girls. The references here are all sexual.

Men: *Beside the garden's edge*
         He eats sweet potato flowers.
         Since you were young you've had it in,
         Pull it out and place it in well!
Girls: *Beside the garden's edge*
         A rain mat lies unfolded there.
         You, boy, who say you've come to see it,
         Wear it as cape and go!

While Sinoko was telling me the meaning of the songs, a young girl, well-favored with pear-shaped, firm breasts tipped with two blackberries, approached Sinoko and said something to him. He said something equally unintelligible in reply. They began to laugh, and I asked Sinoko nervously what was happening. He replied with a broad grin, "She wants to 'turn-head' with you in your tent." Naturally the offer would have been accepted, except for one consideration: I did not want to lose face with the natives, and thought it inappropriate to show the white man's lack of will power. I was extremely green, the only white man among thousands of natives, and I did not want to do anything that would damage my reputation. At the same time, I did not want to fall foul of them.

So I asked Sinoko to tell the "belle" that I was too tired —the pusillanimous old excuse. As the explanation was passed around the group of girls, they shook and sobbed with laughter at the most melancholy and peculiar of all white man's sexual aberrations, timid continence.

I presumed that they had never before met a man who was too tired for sex, and I was told later that my modesty inspired a new verse for sing-song about the great white magician, Dokta, who was too tired for "turnhead" with a "beau ideal" whose body could launch a war. So I spent a solitary day while the rest, including members of my party, unhampered by the need to keep their status inviolate, were more sociable.

The "peace-feast" with its sing-song continued for the next five days. The young men and women were still grinning broadly at me, and I hoped I had escaped from the awkward situation with my reputation intact.

The message about my unusual indifference to sex spread around to the other clans, and I was never again offered a woman so directly.

The routine doctor's duties soon began again. I practiced from a small, crude surgery unit and visited nearby hamlets where an outbreak of whooping cough was occurring—four toddlers had died of it already. Whooping cough or pertussis is generally a childhood disease caused by a filtrable virus; it had been introduced by the white man. There is no specific cure for this deadly ailment, especially among youngsters: the only measures are protection from complications such as bronchopneumonia by antibiotics, strict quarantine, and immunization. The mass vaccination of toddlers was given priority on my list of future undertakings.

Apart from doctoring, my interest in the history and culture of the Highlanders was steadily increasing, and thus curiosity prompted me to pepper them with questions about their customs and past.

During my questionings I cross-examined one patient, a young man with hideous yaws and jungle sores, about matrimonial customs, cross-cousin marriage, and the other unique elements of Highland life that have always excited anthropologists and interested me.

The patient at last volunteered the information that many years before another white man had come to the village and had gone around like me, persistently asking personal questions.

Had he met this inquisitive man? The man said, "No Dokta, but there is a man in my village who did meet him and talked with him." "Could I see this man?" "Yes," he replied, "but you will have to go to see him. He cannot come to you because he is very old and can no longer walk."

He led me the short distance to his village and then through the usual domestic confusion of children, hens, pigs, and dogs to a hut on the periphery. In the dim recess of the hut lay a very old man, so withered and wild in his attire that he looked like a rag doll. But he stirred under his cloth when I came in and looked up with eyes as bright and frightened as a bird's. We tried to talk to him, but the old man was so senile and alarmed that all he could say was "yes" in a shrill, piping voice.

After this inconclusive dialog had gone on for some time, I gave up and went out into the sunlight. The old man's son told me later that his father had told him stories about the white man who had come long ago to live in the village and had shown him where he had pitched his hut. He led me into the bush on the edge of the village and pointed to a patch of tangled undergrowth of banana trees and vines.

"What did the white man do while he was in the village?" I enquired. "My father said that he asked questions; all the time he asked questions, and he gave 'tabaka' sticks to those who would tell him the answers." He looked expectantly at me. "What sort of questions?" "He wanted to know how we live, how we marry, how we make love, how we garden, how we fight, how we hunt, and about our spirits. All the time he asked questions and he gave 'tabaka' for the answers."

I ignored the hint and went on asking questions.

"Did your father like this white man?" The young man seemed embarrassed and muttered morosely about tobacco and I repeated my question. "No, he did not like him; this man was not liked by the village." "Why not? Did he do you any harm?" "No, he did no harm; but this man did not make love to women—he liked small boys."

I did not know whether he was telling the truth or simply trying to satisfy my overeager curiosity in the hope of being rewarded with tobacco. There was no clue to the identity of the mysterious white man, but the villagers said that their fathers had lied to him about their customs because they were harassed by his persistent questions and anxious to earn more tobacco.

So I discovered that one of the most important items of equipment in any exploration happens to be patience; it does no good to go up to a native and ask a question; one must first observe their behavioral traits and the ceremonies and lead up to important questions by a devious path. To simply approach a man and ask him about his lovemaking would naturally have embarrassed him.

Thereafter I tried to win their confidence first, and when they realized that I was not there to do them harm or to impose on their privacy, they came to me. I felt there were many secrets to discover; further adventures and a further slice of the unknown Stone Age with its unusual phenomena. Everything the analytic medico, anthropologist, philologist, social reformer, and crank had ever dreamed of could be satisfied here.

I found the natives to be as indirect and ambiguous in their dealings with each other as they were with me. If a boy wanted a girl, he never went to her directly and said that he wanted to sleep with her. Instead, he used a go-between to make the necessary arrangements with the girl or her family.

I did not find them straightforward in their ways. Even when they had something to tell me they never said, "I saw this" or "I know this." They always introduced an imaginary third person and said, "A boy told me this, and I know this boy speaks the truth."

The natives made up a lot of stories to placate the white questioners and to put an end to tiresome inquisitions. I found them to be simple people, but at the same time very cunning. I never expected to hit upon the truth in five minutes; sometimes it would take all day as layers of lies, invented to please or hoodwink the white master, were scraped away.

I was gradually getting closer to these strange people and their peculiarities; at the same time I was learning something of their language, feelings, and character.

Savages? Are they really cruel or barbarous? They are really not savages at all. Their society simply has different standards, and it is quite certain they would be as unhappy with our laws as we would be with their dirt. It is also quite certain that it would be utterly wrong to impose our way of life on these people within a short space of time.

* * *

My medical supplies diminished steadily, although the food stores were comfortably up to the mark. There was some tea, sugar, salt; and there were hens of a sort in the villages. For the staff I bought eggs and hens and tubular food from natives by a process of delicate barter and economics. Natives would bring me a present of fruit, eggs, or fowl. I would naturally accept and then, as an afterthought, would ceremonialy give a stick of tobacco and a sheet of newspaper to make cigarets. In this way everybody's face was saved from the accusation of having acted from base or mercenary motives, and I was put under no obligation to the natives.

Finally,I had used my last ampule of penicillin and my meager supply of nylon and catgut sutures was exhausted. It was time to curtail my "expedition" and return to the base at Goroka.

As it was everywhere on the island, it was difficult here too to find porters. Most of my previous carriers had absconded in fear of resumed fighting, for they belonged to another hostile clan. Sinoko and Muigi, the newly recruited cook, spent all day doing their best to engage local men. We finally recruited eleven, many fewer than needed.

Youths who were to accompany us, knowing they had to pass hostile hamlets, had stripped away their clan identifications; they even changed their names to Peter, John, and other characters and then, to their confusion, forgot who was who. They spoke in whispers so that their speech would not betray them to their enemies.

Sinoko and his assistants decided to change our original course and take a short cut that would supposedly save us considerable time. We had first to get to know the trackless, slippery, moss-carpeted forest and its tricks. We ascended about two thousand feet from our camp below. Then we descended about a thousand feet into the valley as far as the tumultuous river, which we crossed with the aid of a suspension bridge constructed from jungle vines, sweeping steeply upward across the roaring and tumbling river about fifty feet below. And again, like a yo-yo, we made our way up a slope on the other side of the river and went into the rainforest jungle.

Walking was made difficult by gnarled roots and fallen tree trunks, each lying in a different direction, and sometimes one atop the other. I went forward like a monkey, gripping first one branch and then another, dragging myself along, pulling myself up, and balancing my way along the tree trunks. Finally we reached a narrow gully-like path through the thick jungle. Here it went up steeply over liana-covered patches of chalk.

Meanwhile the carriers and the rest were laughing and shouting, moving with heavy loads over the maze of gnarled roots, branches, and trunks with the ease and elegance of wild cats. Unlike me, with my studded boots that gave no proper hold on the slippery trunks, they were barefooted, tripping along tree trunks with no difficulty at all. All of them were of an outstanding muscular physique, with biceps that stuck out like ropes.

Now I knew why it was that, after about six hours of tramping through jungles, I felt like death and had to rest, while my party could still do gymnastics amid the tree trunks like monkeys.

By now I was wet from sweat and when we finally came to a clearing I called a halt; my whole body was aching and bleeding from leeches, a terrible plague. For years I had waged an endless struggle against the bloody treacherous creatures. Often they let themselves fall from a tree or shrub when one passes beneath, and fix themselves to the neck, hands, and feet. It was, and still is, a mystery to me how they manage to live when they cannot suck blood. And how do they manage to find their unfortunate victims, humans, with such extraordinary celerity? Do they hear us, smell us, or sense our vibrations? It would be most useful for biologists and physiologists— not so much medicos, since leeches have no medical importance—to make a systematic attempt at answering such questions. I had heard that leeches increase in numbers only when they can find blood, like female mosquitoes, which need blood for laying eggs. But until our party passed through, these leeches—and there is no shortage of them—had lived in this jungle solitude without ever knowing humans. There are few mammals here, so how does the leech survive without blood? We don't even know how their loathsome species reproduces. In any event, it was a losing battle with leeches— there were just too many of them in the rainforest jungles.

The next day we crossed the rolling country, pushed through knee-deep grass, trampled down high reeds, and often floundered waist deep through hidden pits of old village sites. The track criss-crossed, seeming to lead nowhere. We wandered some time in a maze before finding a well-worn path, which indicated the presence of people, and took us through a dense forest ending at an enormous clearing. In the middle was a large vegetable patch with sweet potatoes, corn, beans, peas, pumpkins, and cucumbers surrounded by a fence made of palings.

We found many women industriously digging potatoes, and went down the hill toward them. Suddenly they saw us, and with a startled cry grabbed their bags, scrambled over the far fence, and fled through another garden and over another fence into the village. In a few minutes about twenty armed men streamed out of the huts.

Gathering together, they crept along the fences within a few yards of us. Both the warriors and our group, frightened and unarmed, stood facing each other, neither knowing what to do.

After a few pidgin English words and much sign language, we impressed upon the warriors that we only wanted some food in return for tobacco sticks or cowrie shells. At last they let us enter their fortified stockaded village, built on a high narrow ridge for security against raids. Soon women with heavy loads of sweet potatoes, other tubers, and water-filled bamboo cylinders approached the village. Just as everywhere in the Highlands, here too a woman who weighs only eighty pounds may carry a load over forty pounds in a string bag suspended from her forehead. In addition to the dead load, she often also carries a toddler riding on her neck. Steep descents and ascents of over three thousand feet must be made to the garden site, up and down the mountainside several times a day.

Fierce, sullen warriors armed with bows and arrows and some with stone axes slung over their shoulders, and naked children with their faces buried in their mothers' grass skirts, some standing, some squatting on their haunches, watched every movement I made. I suddenly realized they were behaving in a strange pattern already familiar from similar early contact moments elsewhere in New Guinea.

It consists of tense and anxious people acting in a way that at first seems like a self-conscious, stylized effort to be friendly, but that was, I slowly realized, an almost unconscious ritualistic copying of any facial expression, gesture, or utterance that I made. Thus, if I stroked their shoulders or reached for a handshake, they reciprocated in kind; if I nodded, they nodded; when I smiled or laughed, they too did the same; if I greeted them with a word not of their language, they at times repeated my utterance. I had observed a mimicking of my every stance and gesture, such as crossing their legs when I crossed mine, grasping their hands behind their backs, or rubbing them through their hair whenever I did.

I have now seen the phenomenon several times, with totally different groups, in first or early contact situations. This mimicking behavior appears to be carefully balanced between tension and anxiety, fight or flight reactions, and playful smiling and laughter.

After a rather prolonged scrutiny—on the one side mimicry of my facial expressions and gestures by chestnut-skinned observers and, on the other, a close study by me of their facial expressions—I felt that we had reached a mutual understanding.

The village site was extremely foul. There were all sorts of sores on the people; yaws and tropical ulcers by the hundreds.

A tropical ulcer is a vicious thing. It starts from a wound in the skin. Infection follows and bores in toward the bone. Later, a patch about the size of a pocketwatch swells around the infection and in due course falls out, leaving a round, open wound. This now spreads and grows from the edges and in a short time may be the size of a saucer or dinner plate. It is covered by foul-smelling slough that causes discomfort to olfactory organs, even at a distance of ten feet against the wind.

Yaws is no less unpleasant. It usually manifests itself first around the mouth and other orifices, where it erupts

in the form of a large scabby-looking running sore. Later
it breaks out all over the body, tiny little volcanoes that
erupt and grow. A large one on the face could at first lead
you to believe that the head had been broken and the
brain was protruding.

They were a pitiable group; they made me feel so
weaponless, being disarmed of my treasure, penicillin, as
I was.

We were offered an overnight shelter in a large hut
on the far end of the village. On our way to the refuge for
the night, Sinoko pointed to an old man sitting on a tree
stump. One of his legs hung from the stump, dripping a
glutinous stream of blood onto the ground, which was
licked off by several skinny dogs. Some of the villagers
stood or sat around him, watching and enjoying the unusual piquancy. I poked my finger gingerly at the ghastly
coagulation of blood, dirt, and flies, and asked one of the
boys to fetch water. He brought a piece of bamboo, twice
his size, filled with mountain spring water. I washed the
wound and uncovered a deep lacerated gash on the old
man's leg. He sat as phlegmatic as a giant snail. Carefully
I cleaned the torn flesh and tied torn edges of the wound
together as neatly as I could with the coarse thread of
pandanus fiber used for making string. Then I patted the
old man on his sound leg as if to say, "In no time the
wounded leg will be as sound as this one." The old patri-
arch grinned and held out his right hand. At first I
thought he wanted to shake my hand in appreciation, and
then I noticed it was covered with a piece of dirty string
bag. Under it was a bloody hamburger of a hand, on
which the thumb was crushed completely from the top
joint, two fingers were in shreads, and another was severely torn. I searched my brain for inspiration, then
asked Sinoko and his assistant to make as many threads

as possible from pandanus, but thin and fine. I washed the shattered hand while the villagers clustered around, leaning over the victim and chattering knowingly, like nurses at the operating table.

There was a flap of the skin left at the end of his stump of thumb, so I tucked it over and sewed it together. Of course I had no anesthetic, but the man did not move or make a sound. I became absorbed in the work and made quite a neat job of the thumb and fingers. I then wrapped the hand in my last bandage and strapped it across his body with a length of creeper. When the "plastic surgery" was completed, we retreated to the haven appointed to us. It was quite comfortable, though a bit cramped and infested with rats and all sorts of lice and vermin. I slept in my clothes as protection against cold and things that crawled along the floor. But I had no protection against the rats; I managed to cover my feet, but had no boots for my ears.

Many things went wrong the next day after we set off at dawn for the return journey. We were three days' walking distance from Goroka, according to Sinoko's estimate.

The party moved through the narrow passage and struck a midday bivouac by a small creek. We constructed a temporary lean-to with branches and leaves, and lit a fire. I felt marginally less tired than I had been before. In the direction of the creek the sky, which had been growing as sullen as my face, unnoticed, was now black and heavy. A few isolated drops of warm rain fell upon us—big, fat, drops. The drops increased in number, and the blackness beyond them swept overhead, creating a momentary rainbow before it obscured the sun and turned the day to twilight. A gust of cold wind blew down the creek, making me shiver. Then the rain came down solidly, churning the surface of the water and dousing our fire.

I looked around and noticed the nature of the banks for the first time. I knew we had to get out of there as quickly as possible before they filled. Sinoko and the rest had already started downstream, carrying the boxes and haversacks. It was now impossible to climb the banks. They were steep, almost vertical in places, or completely overgrown with dense foliage; and rivulets of brown water cascaded down them to swell the creek. This was rising rapidly and, even onshore, where we stumbled along clinging to overhanging branches, was almost up to our waists.

The natives, as I had noticed before, had an uncanny ability to walk in fast-flowing water, their bare feet seeking and finding footholds on the invisible bed nonexistent to insensitive boots, and their bodies leaning instinctively in the right direction to counteract the pull of the current. But I made very slow progress and at last, with water swirling around my chest, I stopped, clutching whatever twig or root that came to hand. And then it happened....I was swept instantly downstream, striking helplessly out for the shore, doing a totally ineffective crawl. I twirled around in the eddies and rolled sickeningly over a pile of submerged rocks.

Sinoko and Muigi did not fail to see me as I swept downstream. They saw me float by and both reached for me; Muigi missed and fell headlong into the flow. Sinoko grasped my shirt and was dragged after me, but did not release his grip. A few yards downstream was a rock bar and a steepening gradient. Boulders cut the surface and formed islands around which the waters curled and seethed. Between two of these was suspended a tree trunk and in front of this was an area of relatively calm water. As we swept in an arc around the trunk, Sinoko literally threw himself out of the current into the calmer water, wrapped himself around the timber, and dragged me to safety. The sudden cessation of violent motion was sufficient to bring me to my senses, gasping and spluttering, and I clung to the tree trunk on my own behalf.

When we had regained our breath we realized that we must get ashore promptly, for the creek was still rising and would soon free our tree trunk. We edged toward the nearest bank and, with Sinoko clinging to a branch with one hand and to me with the other, I cast myself into the water upstream and allowed the current to swing me around in a smooth curve, arms outstretched, until I could reach a protruding root. I let go of Sinoko's hand, clutched an armful of vegetation, and pulled myself up. After that it was only a matter of seconds before I had torn out a sapling with which to tow Sinoko ashore. We squatted in safety above the water level.

We made our way down the creek as fast as we could, searching for Muigi, but it was still raining and almost dark so we did not get far or look very thoroughly. We climbed the bank, found a relatively dry spot beneath a tree, and settled down to wait for morning.

The rain ceased in the middle of the night and by dawn the water level had dropped to no more than a few inches higher than it had been before the flash-flood. By now one could walk in the bed, so before noon the rest of our party responded to Sinoko's sonorous "yo-ho" and were strolling in from different directions. Soon the team assembled on our site. Muigi was still missing and most of our cargo was lost. We had only two haversacks now, which contained three damp blankets, seven tins of meat, some sticks of tobacco, and a plastic bag containing salt.

Sinoko, with some of the carriers, commenced the search for the missing Muigi, walking slowly downstream. They eventually found another haversack caught on a branch, and an iron box with some drugs. But there was no sign of Muigi.

We proceeded down the creek that grew wider and deeper, and I made relatively good progress, considering my swollen knee from the fall into the river. But after an hour or so of walking, the swelling enlarged my knee to almost twice its normal size, and any slight movement was painful. It was obvious I wouldn't be able to walk far. I continued to crawl, and Sinoko helped me as best he could. The carriers, who now had no load on their shoulders, eagerly removed everything possible from my path, but every foot of the way was sheer torture. One of the carriers offered to carry me, but what could a little, though muscular, man like that do with nearly one hundred and ninety pounds of live weight on his shoulders? He probably didn't realize how heavy I was. Therefore, I preferred to drag myself along as best I could despite the pain. When I came to a tree trunk I couldn't climb, I had to drag myself underneath it.

In no time they finally made a stretcher from bush material; on it they put two blankets, and then me, covering me with the third blanket. One carrier then got into position at the head and the other at the foot, and on their shoulders the others placed a thick pole they had quickly cut out of the jungle. Thus the pole ran in the direction of my body and right above me. Six men now took up their positions on either side and carefully lifted up the rope ends, raising me slowly and gently until my nose at one end and my feet at the other touched the pole. Next they tied the rope ends around the pole so that I was wrapped up like a mummy.

I felt rather comfortable through the following long hours. This native method of transporting the injured or dead seemed to work well. The pole, the rope ends, and

my body formed one piece, thus protecting me from sliding out. The fact is that our own form of stretcher is not
designed either for jungle conditions or steep mountainous paths. The greatest advantage of the native stretcher
was that when moving steeply, either up or down, I did
not slide backward or forward.

After several hours of tracking we passed the body of
the missing Muigi, now lying on the stones of the creek
bed, hideous and humming with flies. The smell met us
long before we reached the spot; I retched secretly for half
an hour on my stretcher while the halted group gave him
a "decent" burial on the hillside.

It began to grow dark, and now the bearers acceler-
ated their pace to such a tempo that they covered as much
ground as they would have in a full day of walking; they
obviously wanted to get to the nearest village before it got
very dark and, I guessed, were anxious to show me a thing
or two of their strength and agility.

And they succeeded; they stuck it out, those brave
"savages." The village we arrived at happened to be Sinoko's birthplace. I simply couldn't understand why he
didn't tell me beforehand. My question was answered by
his gleaming smile. Was it a surprise for me?

His people now carried me into a newly erected hut,
untied all the ropes of the stretcher, and brought me a
banana, cucumber, and sugar cane. Soon all was silent
and I slept with the help of tablets that Sinoko found in the
recovered box of drugs.

At daybreak I was feeling pretty wretched, but I told
myself that it would not be long before we were back in
Goroka, and this kept my courage up. The carriers were
paid off with tobacco and salt, which were rarities for
them. Sinoko also distributed the rest of the tinned meat,
and with loud shouts they happily departed.

Once again Sinoko's most hospitable folk made a "mummy" of me and lifted the stretcher as if it were a cradle with a six foot baby in it. In their enthusiasm they were trotting—there was no question of walking. A large number of young men insisted on accompanying the rest of our team.

On the last day of our journey we had to cross a very swollen river, the name of which is still in my memory— the BenaBena River. The bearers and the rest seemed doubtful about the advisability of attempting a crossing, so Sinoko organized a living chain of the toughest men he could find, and with linked arms they stood across the river in a chain to break the force of the current while the bearers carried me across. I have to admit that I was more than scared, because now I was not only in danger but absolutely helpless. Their faces were hard and set, and they even marched quite a good way downstream in the center of the now much broader river bed.

Finally, early in the morning, our eyes caught the most welcome sight of Goroka laying beneath us in bright sunshine.

Denizens of the
High Valleys

After several weeks of tracking passless mountainous jungles, I returned to the "civilian nook" at Goroka valley.

My knee—with its fractured knee cap and torn cartilage—was nicely mended by the erudite and skillful surgical hands of Lajos Roth, the newly appointed surgeon to the Highland region. I learned that he had been a noted surgeon in his former country of Hungary. He was soft-spoken, just past his prime, with hair graying at the temple, and an extremely well-kept figure. He gave the impression of being a zealous Esculapius, of the sort who draws strength and power from people's diseases and physical disabilities; himself, however, he could neither help nor cure.

He put me on three weeks' sick leave, and I was determined to follow the instructions he issued conscientiously, because only by doing so could I possibly hope to keep my next field trip's deadline. And this I felt I had to do to impede the stranglehold of widespread yaws, respiratory tract infections, and other fatal diseases.

While I was convalescing and hopping about on my crutches, I heard through the grapevine the most welcome news that another batch of the "bloody wog" doctors had been successfully recruited in Australia. They were already in Port Moresby awaiting their assignments. In addition to this splendid news, a policy giving top priority to the control and prevention of communicable diseases had been interposed.

Thus, through these "bloody wogs," who were not allowed to practice medicine in Australia, John Gunther, who more than anyone else deserves recognition for the introduction to New Guinea of rebuffed foreign doctors, was able at last to establish a modern health service in one of the least developed areas of the world.

There is no doubt that he was a noncomformist with streaks of eccentricity. His face would be a sculptor's delight, seeming to have been hewn of rough granite, with two front teeth missing, and the expression of a bald eagle. He was known as the "Laughing One," since he never laughed; but this I was to learn was both untrue and defamatory. By many he was regarded as "The Father of New Guinea Medicine."

He did a great deal for me and others. He showed himself to be a master of administrative leadership. He fought and won many seemingly impossible battles with high-powered politicians who were fanatically opposed to the employment of Australian doctors in New Guinea. Gunther also fought against "commercialist" doctors of Australia, those who manipulate the lives of their patients in order to line their own pockets; he categorically rejected the opinions of those policymakers of the Australian Medical Board, most of whom were inoculated with the belief that European medicine was little better than witchcraft.

He wanted to foster the development of a medical jack-of-all-trades who had the ability to cope single-handedly with all types of medical problems, and with a capacity to assume leadership in sundry affairs. Whatever he wanted was done quickly and efficiently; and as far as the Public Health Department was concerned, he wanted a lot.

One of many stories illustrates the difficulties with which he was confronted when he single-handedly carried out an extensive recruiting task in Australia. In one of the immigration centers, he wanted to interview newly arrived doctors with the intention of signing them for service in New Guinea. The senior Australian camp doctor happened to be somewhat antagonistic toward European doctors, and when John Gunther introduced his list of potential candidates to be interviewed to the camp doctor, the latter offered his "generous" assistance in the form of noting after each name his opinion of the person to be interviewed. Since Gunther could see no harm in this, he accepted the offer.

The next day, while going through the list of selected names, he noticed a new Australian doctor's name, accompanied by a remark stating that that particular doctor was a chronic alcoholic, though he was a fairly good medico.

Being, as he was, a man of his own judgment who tried never to perpetrate an unjust decision, he privately interviewed the alleged dipsomaniac. He asked, "By the way, Doctor, do you smoke much?" and received in reply, "Oh, ya, sixty cigarets a day or something like that." Then Gunther posed another question, "Do you drink, Doctor?" "Oh, ya, depends on how much I can get." "Suppose it was unlimited," pressed Gunther. "Oh, I could drink anything, and I have always been able to get something," he proudly told of his drinking prowess.

Naturally his name was deleted from Gunther's "shopping list." Lo and behold! Back in New Guinea, John Gunther received a letter from the Catholic Bishop of one of the Australian States where the rejected doctor

worked as an orderly in a mental institution. The Bishop
in his letter said that the "boozer" was a teetotaler. So
John Gunther interviewed him again. He asked him why
he had stated, during the previous interview, that he was
a chronic alcoholic and heavy smoker when he in fact was
not. The misguided medico said that the camp doctor had
told him to make sure that he tell Gunther that he was a
heavy drinker and compulsive smoker because, "Gunther is a blotto and a chain smoker, and he will not select
anybody who does not drink and smoke." The credulous
doctor was contracted for work in New Guinea and
proved to be a good medical officer.

John Gunther was subsequently appointed Assistant
Administrator of the Territory of Papua and New Guinea,
and before his retirement became the vice-chancellor of
the University of Papua and New Guinea, which was
created through his unbounded verve. In the later years
of his life he was justifiably knighted.

* * *

The fear that I would be marooned with boredom in
Goroka at first seemed to be realized. Although it was the
end of the rainy season, heavy downpours high in the
mountains had caused a torrent lower down, even as the
Goroka valley was basking in sunshine. Small streams
turned into rivers, and the rivers into moving muddy
lakes. Everybody stayed indoors. Inches of water eddied
and flowed through the town, carrying along all sorts of
flotsam. The town dogs took shelter under the houses,
scratching their mangy heads with each leg in turn.

I had nothing else to do but read books from the local
public library. Most were written in those pseudoscien-
tific terms acceptable to the majority of white residents
because they were written in the ponderous, apologetic

jargon of science; those perennially popular books that the West produces as an index of our ignorance about ourselves—Happy Marriage; Science and Sex; The Technique of Marriage; Recipes for Human Success; Achievement in Sex, in Business, in Making Money. Do this, do that; think this, think that; eat this, eat that; copulate in this or that manner, and you cannot fail to be rich, to be happy, to achieve an orgasm, or to get into heaven. All emphasis is on performance and ritual gestures and not on service or philanthropy.

Judging from the books' atrophied appearance, with their underlined sentences, paragraphs, and remarks on the back pages, it appeared to me they were in demand and well read. In one of the library books entitled *Joy in Sex*, I noticed a rather lengthy scribbled remark by a reader, "Our white men take native women, they take women regardless of color. Some white women like black men. I happen to be one of those, yet when a white wretch makes love to a black man it becomes an international incident. I have a white husband who is seldom at home. I enjoy being married to him, but at this moment I would prefer to be a black man's strumpet rather than his spouse. Any comments?" There were none, at least from me, since I felt sorry for the frustrated wife.

After three days of reading I became satiated with sex, doings and undoings, and recipes, so I gave it up.

For months I hadn't written a mature word. Should I begin again or at least try? But how should I begin to write again? My mind was like a tincture of many substances—bitter and sweet, fetid and fragrant. My discovery of so many alien things the last few months overwhelmed me, blotting out words. It made me intellectually excited, mentally constipated, stuffed with many notions that I was incapable of delivering. Within this

complicated self of mine there resided a small demanding demon, a vanity, a demiurge that was supposed to
turn everything into words, yet in my present state the
spirit was mercilessly reduced to perpetuating symbols,
mummies of my thoughts and emotions.

So, for a full week I joined the Bacchanalian ranks at
the Goroka Hotel and Goroka Sports Club, both of which
were for white folk only; and both of which were most
generous advocates, hastily marinating my meningeal
membrane with amber colored liquor for which I had to
pay dearly, not so much monetarily, but in the form of
"morning sickness."

And then I managed to divorce myself from this
addiction. I began to look more closely at the other people
around me, people of my race—that is, at my fellow
Caucasians.

I felt that I was beginning to measure them with my
deepest instincts, those that tell me exactly what people
are like beneath the bright chattering masks of intellect
they put on for show—their naked artless features, the
embryos within the armor—their delights, contentments,
obscenities, and fears.

At last I took down my shelved diary and thought, "I
will write everything that goes through my mind." And
I wrote, dating the page the month of April, Nineteen
hundred and fifty-five, making colonists my first subject.

* * *

It is not fair to say that the first white settlers left the
consequences of their crimes and fled to New Guinea;
they left the gray and placid contours of uninteresting
lives to seek these horizons peaked with mountains un-
imaginably steep and fringed with palms; they left
unwanted wives and pregnant lovers in the miasma of

the problems they had created and chased forgetfulness into a tropic idyll. Nor is it fair to say that New Guinea was the last land in the world where there was no law, where the individual stood as high as he cared to lift himself, where he held all law at the mercy of the weapon in his hand.

It is fair to say that the bulk of white settlers were, with few exceptions, composed of men who sought seclusion, a new kind of beauty, or the chance of rebuilding the sorry scheme a little closer to their heart's desire. This terra incognita with its encircling islands was a fertile hunting ground for the anthropologist, the philologist, the social reformer, and the crank and, on some occasions, was a political plaything.

It is also fair to say that the law came with the first ships and stood for social responsibility. When the men of God landed at or near their various destinations, their reports and temporal prayers were directed to those authorities that they recognized in an urgent desire to bring about the installation of government. Because of their convictions and courage, their reports carried a great deal of weight. They also brought the white women to the country. No one, apart from missionaries, acknowledged these as desirable imports; in fact, there was opposition to their coming and to their presence, for the first newcomers had native women in plenty who would keep house and cook meals and come when summoned to bed.

The missionary women were swiftly followed by others. After the first long skirt, their pale faces shaded from the sun by hats and sunshades, white women had come to stay. Soon New Guinea's world looked a little different—more stout, statuesque, and mature, the mini-culture was quickly saddled with a soft white civilization, but still full of hope andaflower with its special blossom.

Alas, I feel there are some disruptive effects of the
white culture's intrusion. The steel axe, chisel, and saw
were not only miracles of efficiency compared to imple-
ments of stone, wood, and bone, but also changed the
nature of the society itself, altering forever the ancient,
delicate balance of traditional forces and creating new,
previously unimaginable demands. The axe, making its
way into remote areas, often well before whites reached
them, took only a quarter of the time and exertion needed
to cut down trees and undergrowth with a stone axe.
Paradoxically, there was suddenly more time for warfare
and feasting than there had been, but there was less time
for looking after the gardens and husbanding the pigs.

But even if some went hungrier than before, the taste
for new things was firmly implanted, and as time went
by, more of the white man's possessions became desirable. Calico was preferable to plaited grass, and tinned
foods to sweet potato. Desire for the white man's matches
and candles, kerosene lamps and packaged salt, beads
and trinkets spread rapidly among people who knew
neither how they were made nor how they could be obtained. In the beginning the Highland native could barter
his sweet potato and some vegetables, the only "cash" he
owned. Later, with the establishment of the coffee plantations, he sought to offer the only thing of monetary
value he possessed—his labor.

When the first white explorers penetrated Goroka
Valley over three decades ago, the valley floor was a
vacant wasteland having no native settlement, no gardens, no trees, no houses, and no birds. The existing
native population had climbed higher, for security and
more easily defensible positions against intruders.

The initial embarkation into the high valleys of this
vast region was by the Catholic and Lutheran missions

and a small team of Australian gold prospectors in the early nineteen thirties. It was followed by the first Kiap (pidgin English for District Officer or Commissioner, believed to be derived from the German "Kapitaen").

I would argue against some New Guinea philosophers who say, "Most of the Kiaps displayed a particularly Australian style—anti-intellectualism, superficial egalitarianism of manner, and a quite remarkable lack of educated interest in the outside world. They, with few exceptions, have no tertiary education; their intellectual horizon is extremely limited and the effect of this on the governed is discouraging."

To most of them I would pay my respect for their spirit of real service, intelligence, pragmatism, courage, and great physical endurance. Many of them were exceedingly well-qualified in their departments, having spent many years acquiring experience, though with no degrees apart from a brief course at the Australian School of Pacific Administration (ASOPA) on the main subjects of law, anthropology, geography, and colonial administration.

It is true, however, that some of them, mostly prewar officials, exhibited a trace of the "master race" attitude, together with a paternalistic approach to the native. I regard this attitude as nonsense. In my view the only result of paternal giving can be an ultimate resentment on the part of the recipient, and the sole means of lessening such resentment must be repayment for the paternal gift. No matter how nominal the charge for service may be, that small charge will always maintain a retention of pride and personal self-respect.

It is apparent that this tiny group of Kiaps were tired men, feeling out of place in the new world in which they lived, and now counting the days until their retirement.

The majority of postwar recruits, I observed, carried out their duties with inspiring enthusiasm and responsibility, in spite of being handsomely handicapped by working under the vigilance of the Department of External Affairs in Australia. It is extremely difficult to avoid becoming cynical after years of life under constant surveillance, and being the tool of power-greedy, balderdashing politicians.

It is a complex task for the Kiaps, pressured by the United Nations Organization for a speedy introduction of civilization, peace, prosperity, and Christianity, to bring an illiterate Highland folk from age-old ways and ancient customs into line with contemporary civilization, particularly when this civilization is a highly technological one. The Kiaps do their best in endeavoring to stamp out feuding by persuading the natives under their control to abandon "payback" and leave it to white man's justice to deal with the offender. The natives can't grasp the benefit of these procedures, however, for the Highlanders find the shame of an unavenged wrong too great to leave to the white man's law to settle. The village elders shake their fuzzy heads and say, "The eye of the people is too dark for the white man."

It can be fairly claimed that the Highlanders owe much to the dedication, drive, and devotion of certain individuals, within both the mission and the administration, and in particular to the anthropologists who have shown that the traditional New Guinea Highland society is in no way contemptible, even if utterly different from our own.

* * *

I've reached my second week of renouncing Bacchus and begin to feel my old self again—sound in body and as certain in mind as the sunlit sensuality of the Valley, unobstructed from the reality of what ought to be, should be, but is not.

I have the feeling of someone who has been in the dark for too long, and on emergence into the light, everything leaps out sober, real, solid, into sight, into being. I am quite certain that I shall explode, but what a delicious explosion. And what certainty I have now that I am resurrected, when only a week ago I felt I was quite dead.

At the moment I feel I must sketch the characteristic features of the pale physiognomies whose names may be regarded a household words in the "High Valleys" of the mountains today.

The first name I immediately conjure for my sketchpad is that of Father William Ross, a diminutive (five feet, two inches) American who established the first mission in the Highlands over two decades ago. He appears to me noble and unselfish, unlike certain men of God that we see puffed with self-satisfied spiritual pride from doing something for lesser mortals.

He relayed to me his long and earnest struggle with the problems of paganism, which eventually modified his early views. When he first arrived, he had thought of Highlanders as heathen, totally devoid of religion and morals, but as he moved about among them, and especially as he began to know their language and could discuss ideas and abstract concepts, he gradually changed his attitude. He saw their spirit worship as the rudimentary manifestation of religion and began to develop the thought that the right approach toward Christianity for them would be to build on the foundation they already had, instead of first trying to tear it down.

Once he said to me, "The Highland heathens are very far from being irreligious. It is to our great advantage that

we recognize the religious faith of these people. Paganism is infinitely more cultivable than atheism. We gain
nothing by weakening or trying to destroy their veneration for diety. Don't look at them as hermits, savages, or
atheists. It doesn't matter how superior we may feel
ourselves to be, let us always see what is valuable in them
and utilize it in our labor for them."

Another person who comes to my mind is Jim Taylor,
a prewar Kiap and former Australian policeman. He was
the first official to settle in Goroka valley. I felt a leaping
attraction for this man with his inherent romanticism,
something of an Elizabethan temperament. He was a
keen reader, warm and outgoing, seemingly tireless, with
friendly grace.

After World War Two he quit the Administration
and became a successful trader and coffee grower, the
husband of a devoted woman of the Highlands, and the
father of enchanting, tender, tan-skinned daughters.

His descriptive accounts of the early explorations of
New Guinea wrought my low tide moods. After his long
march to the Goroka valley, he said, "Initial contact with
the Highland people was usually peaceful, but after the
wonder had worn off a second contact was sometimes
hazardous." Or thereafter, "At first we were people come
back from Paradise looking for our homes, later on we
were regarded as rejects who had been thrown out of
Paradise." Taylor was master of the bowman's sign language. Once, he recalls asking about a lake in the western
part of the Central Highlands. He encountered a native
whose language was utterly alien to him, yet it didn't
hinder his enquiry. As he puts it, "I asked a pleasant
looking young fellow with red, black, and yellow para-
keet feathers in his hair if he knew of the lake Kopiagu,
and he indicated perfectly by sign that it lay to the west.

I signed that I could not see it and he picked up a lump of earth to represent the mountain, and placed it in front of his eyes to signify that this was the reason I could not see it. He then pointed to a pool on the ground, suggesting that if I went to the top of the mountain I could then see the lake. While making these signs he did not speak a word, realizing that I did not understand his language. He hummed the negative and the affirmative."

It is time to renew friendship with this pure beauty of the spirit that is Jim Taylor. Tomorrow I will take him up on his offer to "drop in any time" and pay him a visit.

* * *

I feel a similar respectful affection for a postwar recruit, Mick Foley, a dominant figure in the Kiap group because of his size, if nothing else. He was tall, heavily built, and broad-shouldered, powerful in frame, with great vigor. His movements were not those of an athlete, but he walked with an easy gait. He was an effigy in stature, but the antithesis of the inner-self of his superior, the District Commissioner—a sycophant with an executive smile and a doctor's paternal smirk. A rather forbidding official in his stiff office. With the steely glint of his eyes, a look intolerant of dissent, he reminded me of a consummate politician. Since I have no love for politicians, he was a "misfit" for my sketchpad.

I respect Mick with a slightly mixed complicity, regarding him as a "boong lover," which means that he takes his responsibilities as trustee for indigene welfare seriously, perhaps too seriously; and that this responsibility is his obsession. I see him more espoused to his job than to his family of four.

Our fondness for each other is unrestricted despite our frequent disagreements. It is Mick's opinion that since the Highlanders pay nothing for their medical and

other services, they have no right to any say in how services should be administered. The only policy is to tell
them, "This is what you need, we happen to know, and
this is what you are going to have given to you."

This philosophy with its disparagement of native
understanding does not surprise me. For many years the
people had been deprived of responsibility over their
own affairs, and in the process their reticence and timid-
ity had been interpreted as ignorance and stupidity.

It was my view that we should not break new
ground, but merely revert to the ancient tradition in
which the people had a voice in all things. But Mick says,
"This has been done in the past and has never worked."

One day we had our customary session, in the company of dark rum for him and ruby wine for me. It was
a lengthy one, lit by my comment that many officials were
as much in need of health education as the natives if we
were to improve the general health of the people.

"Now wait!" Mick responded cooly. "I've seen as
many as you, and who can deny they are a hefty looking
bunch of natives for anybody's money, plenty of food to
eat, plenty of energy for their squabbles and dancing too."

"Oh yes!" I shot back, "They sing and dance, but did
you notice the way some of them walk? On the outsides
of their feet, because the soles are so cracked open with
neglected yaws they can't bear to put them to the ground.
We all know that many Highlanders walk like crabs and
make fun of it. So would you walk like a crab if your foot
was open and bleeding. Poor devils are ill. And they are
hefty looking, aren't they?"

He had an answer for that too. "Ill, you call them?
Show me one place in the tropics that doesn't have yaws,
malaria, hookworm. Just show me! Everyone knows
there is nothing to be done about that."

"I can't show you one, that I'll admit, but I can show you the reports on research, the medical surveys, and the totals of money being spent every day of the year by people who think that something can be done. And I am one of those people. It won't be long before we are made aware of their poor health, and won't be able to conceal our knowledge and ignore them forever."

"I have no doubt that you'll play your part in bringing the day of reckoning nearer," said he, without a trace of sarcasm.

"No, Mick, that won't be so, but when the day comes I am going to listen, and if it is humanly possible, I am going to help make things better, whether helping purely as a medical man or as just an interested person."

With his Irish eyes of loving kindness and engaging deep husky voice, he retorted, "Our administration has given the best we have to offer. If the natives have not prospered it's because they couldn't understand our motives, and that's hardly our fault."

I felt disarmed and only able to say, "Another man answered that kind of statement better than I can. 'The fault, dear Brutus, lies not in our stars, but in ourselves.'"

He patted my shoulder kindly as he led me to the door. "God bless you and the Highlanders. Sleep well." He meant it. I looked forward to our next duel of "entente cordiale."

* * *

The next sitter for my sketchpad is not the Kiap, but one of my counterparts, another "bloody wog," medical officer like myself. I discovered him much later during a visit to the western part of the Central Highlands.

He was, with the strange Lithuanian name of Vladas Ivinskis, I must admit, in some ways an odd man, but among all death fighters certainly the most profoundly original. He was past his fifties, almost bald, a big fat man, not handsome, but beautiful, for his was a genius of the heart, maskless. He was a real Lithuanian, like his predecessor Leo Petrauskas, as happy as they know how to be happy in Lithuania. In the milling crowd, with its compulsive gaiety and agitation, he looked to me the only sane human being. Apart from air travel, there was nothing that he disliked. His respective enjoyments were focused on gastronomy, tippling, and, as he called it, "roasted coffee beans"—the fawn-colored maiden's bosom on the topless brown supple body with long, firm nipples. He and he alone, the "papa bilong al," as the local dark folk addressed him, was privileged to fondle any of the smooth and shiny pear-shaped twins he chose.

During his Saturday promenade in the local market there would be a number of pubescent girls, either in the company of elders or alone in groups, showering him with demonstrative affection and solicitously proffering their young virgin breasts at the first cast of his glance. The natives were convinced that his "magic touch" would enrich the supply of milk after marriage, for women here were proud of their supply of milk, often demonstrating their capacity for his benefit by squeezing the breasts to show the generous stream they produced.

His fondness for caressing the firm young breast was more for the pleasure of being "privileged" rather than from any carnal intent. His every "magic touch" was accompanied by a soft chant in a language alien to the native, which they regarded as a beneficial spell.

He loved everyone. A two-or-four-legged creature, naked, furred, or feathered, people of all tempers, tastes, creeds, and beliefs, evil or good, ugly or beautiful, rich or poor, all were on a par with his gentle breeding. Only pious frauds were kept in the background.

Unlike me, who chose my friends as I chose books—few, but choice—to Vladas all were friends; there was no place in his vocabulary for the word aquaintance; he was friend to all, a friend who accepted your "aye" or your "nay."

Half jokingly, half seriously, Vladas loved to say, "A foe should be despised only as far as one who may one day be a friend."

His abode was like a haven of rest and enjoyment; the hungry were fed with a rich variety of Lithuanian cuisine, mostly made and cooked by him; those thirsty were refreshed by assorted beverages. His abode provided secure lodging for countless stray dogs and cats.

Vladas Ivinskis was not a wizard. Nor would I class him as a "crown specialist." He was a humble man with an essential understanding of the nature of illness—more important to a good doctor than being trained in the natural sciences from childhood. He says:

"Many of us assume that the primary aim of education is the collection of a number of facts whereby the mind can be furnished. But a house must be a home, and lived in as well as furnished. It is possible to store the mind with a million facts and still be entirely uneducated; the fact must be used as a basis for thought and criticism. The purpose, therefore, of education is to produce the all-round person, one who can put his or her specialty in its proper place. We are in grave danger of regarding our specialty of medicine as the be-all and end-all of our lives. It is a learning so absorbed that we may be forgiven if, in our early years, we feel that it is a subject worthy of our total devotion."

"It is clear that our 'scientific' surgeon can be, and usually is, a master of the technique of appendectomy and other operations, but is he able to make the diagnosis of organic appendicitis as clearly as one who has been trained in a knowledge of humankind as a thinking and sentient individual? We have only to remember the number of appendices that are found to be normal after an operation to remove them to realize that diagnosis has failed because of the inability to appreciate the emotional antecedents that may be the cause of pain, vomiting, and many other symptoms. Examples can be given repeatedly. The humanities teach us that each human is a personality distinct from most other humans, and therefore in diagnosis and in treatment a patient must always be treated as an individual."

"We, as doctors, must deal with people who are vehicles of various diseases, mostly functional, and not with disease as an obstruction lifted out of the individual. As soon as our work brings us into close association with people, we need more than technical knowledge, and that is something that can only be derived from a wider culture of the mind, rather than from the study of a pure technology. It is therefore more than ever necessary to guard ourselves from the mental sclerosis that awaits us should we fail to employ the mind in all its capacities."

As to health, in which respect our progress with natives is indisputable, Vladas comments befittingly:

"Is it worth living longer if our lives are not correspondingly richer and happier? Is it worth being preserved by medical science as a human vegetable, or in order to be thrown into an old people's home by children who cannot be bothered to care for us? Or to die of old age in material poverty such as is never found in any traditional New Guinea society where there is always enough because there is never too much? Medical science, moreover, is to a large extent responsible for the disastrous population crisis, destroying the balance between the human population and the rest of the natural world, in a sense making man unnatural and threatening his future existence. These mountain folk seem to find more purpose to life than to live in an excess of wealth and comfort, and they find security in the natural world, including other human beings, rather than in technology."

His prescription: "Let us look at specific cultures and peoples and see in what ways they are different from each other, and in what ways they are alike."

There is space left on my sketchpad for Rhys Healey, the loyal adjutant who bore a great similarity to Vladas. Rhys loved to play the wild Irishman, but his elaborately casual manner could not conceal the dour and able fighter that he was; like Vladas, he was deeply conscientious, a tremendously keen student of all things connected with the Territory, and a fascinating raconteur.

Before the introduction of Australian doctors, most medical services on the Island were efficiently carried out by former military medical attendants, called here European Medical Assistants. Of these, in my opinion, the one most gifted in administrative and medical ability was Rhys. He laid a firm foundation for the management of medical services that, though it might totter in political earthquakes, would not fall. He was a qualified accountant; every item of expense, no matter how minute, was skillfully and carefully scrutinized; he would lop off here and whittle there, waging a successful war against the common failing of the padded expense account.

Together, Rhys and Vladas were ideal superiors and a great team. They, like most department heads, were forced to battle the ghosts of past abuses and bureaucratic machinery.

Such was the power of their personalities that it pervaded all health workers under their guidance. The "esprit de corps" was raised to such a pitch that everyone worked without regard for their own interests; even local Aid Post Orderlies—lowest on the rung—were heart and soul a part of the movement and firmly convinced that if Rhys and Vladas were not there, the wheels of life would stop.

Argus-eyes that snapped in your face, a lively temperament, a veritable passion for music, photography, and numerous topics dominated Rhys' life. He possessed an unusual ability for quick learning; after a few years' assisting in the operating theater, he became a competent "self-taught" surgeon in emergencies; treating complicated fractures, appendectomies, hernioplasties, and the like was to him "just like shooting fish in a barrel," according to Vladas.

Like Vladas, he is a remarkable character, although he would be the last to recognize this, for he has a very low estimate of his own attainments. I have known only a few men or women as humble-minded as Rhys and his wife Dorrie, a crown to her husband; a mother of five, pretty, unblown urchins; a woman whom Providence has provided with beauty of spirit; a faithful companion who is ever at his side, sharing his every thought, rapture, and victory!

* * *

In the Highlands it is said that you make acquaintances, but not friends. This is true, I am afraid to say. Apart from Mick Casey, I was estranged from the local private enterprise sector and the "social whirl."

Mick, a former Major of the Australian Army, is the manager of a large, partially cultivated, and remote coffee plantation. He, with his closely knit family—wife Margaret and two gilded youngsters—lives in almost total isolation, and to live on one's mental resources is a cruel test of character. Unlike many who destroyed themselves by nursing their fierce resentment against their lonely surroundings, Mick created an inimitable life by giving himself up to new experience, reaching out for new ideas and interests. He did not talk about solitude—and he, of all people, knew what this implies, for his plantation was a three day tramp from Goroka, over high ridges and deep canyons. He accepted such conditions as a matter of course.

Mick is something else too, however: gifted, unsentimental, sympathetic, and superbly original. Mick and Margaret are a divine unity of two souls, and I consider myself privileged to have met them and become their friend.

* * *

There is no definite place either in my "sketchpad" or in my sublime mind for the local, shabby gentility. To me they were beings of another strata. Most of their lives here have been passed semiconsciously; I mean, not keenly alive, alert, noticing, questioning, comparing, thinking, probing deeper. I find most of this human fauna to consist of misfits—setting one's life deliberately against one's environment, making adjustment very difficult, if not impossible. They live in self-imposed seclusion, succumbing to frustration, neurosis, and the inability to enjoy living, unable to remove the veil of prejudice from their eyes, not wanting to see the truth of life for all humanity and live in tolerance of all humanity.

Liquor and profit, profit and liquor—a vicious circle —comprise a large part of their lives. Parties of various celebration—birth or death, arrival or departure, separation or reunion, the natal day, the Saint's day, you name it—are incessant.

At first these social gatherings were to me a kind of satisfaction, a triumph over myself, for, being a narcissistic type, I guess, I found the admiration of women and the attention of men more than agreeable, and even desirable. But gradually this faded and all *fête champêtre* became to me humdrum.

A christening party, for example, that I was obliged to attend as the chief of baby delivery, was a replica of other parties. It was an evening garden party. Ice tinkled in the glasses, beer foamed, champagne spouted, and the liquid sound of laughter and the murmur of separate groups of conversation swirled, bubbled, and eddied like the meeting of two currents. The erotic puppetry that I had idly imagined was in abundant evidence. Casual illicit liaisons between sexually active swains and members of the fair sex in the form of a "promiscuous stroll" were evident. Adjacent casuarine and dense coffee trees provided avenues of gratification for these hasty, furtive encounters (commonly called quickies), concealing them from heedful eyes.

To reach the bar to refill a glass, one could hardly weave through the strings of the puppeteers jerking and manipulating the figures that seemed to sit, stand, or talk quite lustily. I sat on the garden bench beside the inviting figure of my former inamorata. Our carnal relationship hadn't lasted long; I had been viewing her through the veil of desire, and thus had seen nothing but the shape of her body, not the shape of her inner substance. She is still my friend.

She was sipping her Bloody Mary and I my beer, slowly and silently trying to divert my libidinous mind from the rapture beneath her braless cashmere jersey. Looking across at the hills, away from the lighted garden, all I could see were the dark hills silhouetted indistinctly against the night sky. I tried to visualize the familiar movements going on in that unseen vegetation; tried to focus my mind's eye upon it so that, like a smooth sheet of paper through a microscope, it would reveal itself amorous yet chaste, unkept yet silken. For a moment I succeeded. I could see the branches and leaves and vines entwined and chaotic, I could smell the damp earth and feel the green canopy of grass as vividly as I had not long ago, as I lay with my face on the yielding marble of snowy breasts, looking at the paps, the center of delight, viewing them as they must look and feel to an infant.

All of a sudden the scene was erased by a blatant voice saying to the host, the father of the baptized baby, "Now, Jim, that you have proven your manhood, women will adore you all the more. It's like those dear savages Margaret Mead writes about. They despise virgins. The way to be alluring is to bring forth a bastard. It proves that he is virile. Do you reckon it is true, John? You should know better, being Kiap with your fundamental anthropology learning from ASOPA."

I noticed a young man with a boyish face a little off to one side of the bar, holding a full glass of rum, and half listening to the conversation.

"No, those dear savages you refer to have no bastards; all their children are legitimate, though from different wives, and, what's more, they don't brag about their f...... potency, they just do it, effectively," said John *sotto voce*.

"But surely these women were bringing forth bastards," my companion added.

"I know that, love, I am going beyond her, actually," the tall talker replied.

The talk went on. By now more liquor was going in and more wit coming out, and my blood was boiling.

Thanks to my charming "chaperon," it was simmered down by generously served drinks.

The discussion turned to an argument—not a spat or a quarrel, but a long, simmering argument in which the prattle lost its formal politeness.

"Well, Steve, what do you reckon. Think you'll like the Highlands?" "I don't really know yet, I..." Steve couldn't finish his sentence before he was interrupted by another voice.

"It grows on you. You might go South after a term stuffed with dough saying you've had enough of the bloody place, but you will be back, I tell you. They all do. Best place on earth!"

"Yes, it is nice, but it's a bit isolated," said Steve.

"Wherein its beauty lies," John murmured oddly.

"You said it, John," agreed another coffee planter enthusiastically. "Gee, when I think of that rat race, Sydney, it gives me the creeps. Every bastard in a hurry; knock you down as soon as look at you. You go to work, leave at the same time every morning with a million other blokes; get on the train and there are no seats, can't even unfold your bloody newspaper. You...."

"What he means," interposed one of the well-off planters, "is that you have to earn your living down South. No black kanaka to do the dirty work."

And another muddled voice thrust in, "That is all they are fit for, the dirty work. They don't really want a job, they don't want to work, any of them, lazy bastards; no loyalty, no responsibility."

"For two dollars & fifty cents a month you would be lazy too," John grunted, by now hitting his fifth stiff rum with no obvious sign of inebriation.

"They're not worth two fifty a year," the first talker snapped. The others nodded shrewdly in agreement, as if it were a matter all had devoted considerable thought to, and had agreed that the first speaker expressed it well.

It was already after midnight. I felt rather dozy, whereas my woman friend in need, at this time of night and after many Bloody Marys, was full of life force. I asked her if she knew John well. "Surely, and pretty well too," she sang out. "Naturally, not in the sense that these impotent boozers think."

And here she gave me a concise account of John. His surname was MacArthur. He came to the Highlands as a Cadet Patrol officer a few years ago. Now a fully fledged Patrol Officer, he was assigned to a very remote region, as yet uncontrolled by the administration, to establish a government station and to initiate the road that would link Goroka. He took a profound interest in the region and its people, so much so that he refused to take a long overdue recreation leave. So, the battle between him and the administration was joined: they trying to push him out and he stubbornly kicking back. According to her, he was a very quiet and shy young man, and having no desire for either grass skirts or hot panties, grog was his only mate.

She summed up by stating that the "local nobility" regarded him as an incredible blotto and dumb kanaka lover. During his rare trips to town, accompanied by native porters to collect rations and building materials, he was invited to the parties through pretended pity of his being a loner and an unfortunate blotto.

"Judge for yourself, lousy lover," she chuckled and beckoned to John.

He had a nice voice, unaffected by the booze and singularly refreshing to me; the cadences, a certain mellowness, not harsh and without the edge of nasal inflections. He looked young for his age, which he told me later was twenty-five.

I learned that the region assigned to him had a mountainous terrain and lay southeast of Mt. Michael in the Central Highlands.

John's area was regarded by the colonial administration as "restricted" or "uncontrolled." The government stuck that label on those places that were still little known and therefore considered dangerous for white man and resistant to progress and pacification. It was his assignment to establish a permanent Patrol Post at Okasa (Okapa) and to thus pacify the "Stone Age warriors." The next step would be the road to Goroka, which would gradually introduce the progress of civilization, or so at least it was hoped.

John told me also that he had ignored the order of his superior, and instead of a Patrol Post in Okasa valley, he had started to erect it at Moke on Pentagori village site, miles away. John felt that Moke would be healthier, and more central to the people, for Okasa valley was heavily infested with mosquitoes transmitting malaria. The Administration was not aware of this modification, and thus official maps showed the post at Okasa, not Moke.

I returned to the subject of health, and was told that there were many health problems such as those that existed elsewhere in the Highlands. Yaws, dysentry, pneumonia, and bronchopneumonia among children were the main causes of morbidity and mortality among the population. He asked me if I had received the extract from his patrol report to the Headquarters where, in the health section, he mentioned briefly a small girl he had observed during a recent patrol. She was sitting beside a fire and shivering violently, with her head jerking from side to side. He was told by the villagers that she was a victim of local sorcery, called Kuru, and that she would be dead within a few weeks.

Upon my negative reply, John, talking now in jerky spasms with distorted and ravaged features, poured out a frenzy of Anglo-Saxon profane swearing. This was uninterrupted vitriol with the common Australian adjective of "bloody" and the four-lettered word beginning with 'f' addressed to his direct superiors. It flowed as freely as the beer at this party.

All of a sudden, he spoke calmly and pleasantly again. He began telling me that on return to his "domain" he would send one of the knowledgeable and reliable chieftains to accompany me as adviser and guide to Moke, where he was now building a permanent house.

As I write this I wonder, which is the real John? Is he the simple, likeable schoolboy who would never grow up—a dreamer, the man who found a satisfying life among "primitive savages" and unrestricted intercourse with men of his own outlook; or is he the dual personality of a mind in an untidy state—in layers like geographical strata—and without conscious psychosis produced by prolonged isolation, being torn out of his normal environment and replanted? I wonder....

Here I must halt, for a swarm of gnats, moths, and flying ants, fatally attracted by the minisun of my desk lamp, now fly to their death. I try to chase them away; shade the lamp, but they persist in their suicidal urge toward the light. My desk with its scattered typed papers is covered with a thick layer of still wriggling bodies.

So be it—the last line of today with my thoughts of tomorrow.

The Mountains Fretted with Evil Spell

A man apt to promise is apt to forget. So I thought at first about young John's assurance of sending me one of his trustworthy guides to lead me into "the mountains fretted with evil spell," as they were called by him.

Two months had elapsed since I first met John at the party, and there was no sign of him. Was his unconstrained offer to me just a semiconscious alcoholic garrulity? My ego refused to take it so. How could he be so fuddled with drink when he talked so pleasantly and soberly about his "territory" and its people, and with such frankness—even allowing that he had shirked some things rather than face up to them; it had been a most courageous confession that surely no drunkard was capable of making.

Another month went by with no word from John. I nursed my patience fondly, for I had discovered from my experience that one of the most important items of equipment in any expedition is patience. And if one thinks he can hurry up government officials, or even native carriers, one had better stay home. In this stiffling jungle country, a philosophy of "take it easy" is absolutely essential. It is the only way to adapt to a new and strange rhythm of life, and it is a joy to do the adapting. After all, I wanted something from the natives; they didn't want anything from me. I needed John's unexplored fascinating mountain region, for I felt there were many secrets to discover, a further slice of the unknown Stone Age with more unusual phenomena than an analytic medico had ever dreamed of; but, again, did it need me?

This was made very clear on a minor excursion into the mountains and valleys. Natives naturally led the way, not I. They knew the tracks, or found them, they did the hunting, they carried the loads, and they decided where I was to camp, not I.

So, at ease, I awaited word from John, remembering my school motto, *vincit qui patitur* (patience conquers).

That day in September, in the year of Grace nineteen hundred and fifty-five, still remains a vivid impression, although it happened well over a quarter of a century ago:

A large yellow moon rose over the mountains, shining dimly through the scattered pine trees of my garden, spilling silver across the fronds of the solitary palm tree. I sat on the porch with no want of thought, sipping wine and listening to the cicadas' constant chirping and the croaking of frogs, watching a lime tree studded with fireflies flicker near the house. There were thousands of them around it, all flashing their green lights together, like fairy-lights going on and off. I counted their flashes, like the heartbeats of the tree—seventy to the minute; later it might be eighty. No matter, they would always beat and flash in unison.

Was it not Cicero who said, "I am never so alone as when I am not alone?" The loneliness of the mountains and the jungle has something magnificent about it; their peace and quiet induce a mood of solemnity. I often prefer to experience it without company and words.

While I was enjoying the tranquil surroundings, the moon rose higher, reflecting silver on the trees along the narrow path leading to my lodging. I saw four dark shapes slowly ascending the moon-beamed path. One of them, lean and long limbed, I recognized as being that of Sinoko, my invaluable assistant. The other three were stocky fellows and complete strangers to me.

Sinoko, with his broad grin, handed me a small bundle of breadfruit leaves tightly wrapped with jungle vine, saying in Melanesian pidgin: "Masta Dson (John) Kukukuku no lusim tink long yu, em salim pas long yupela." (Mr. John Kukukuku, pronounced Cookucooku, didn't forget you, he sends you a message). While unwrapping with scrupulous care the "dispatch pouch," I was puzzled by John's *nom de guerre* of Kukukuku. Did the natives label him by this name, like John Bull for the typical Englishman, because of his heedfulness of the Kukukuku tribe, which he called "manhunters in bark cloak?" I could only guess.

The communique was a neatly pleated note of few words, like a telegram: "Follow Apekono. Stop. Be my bunkie, no tucker needed. Stop. Grog and penicillin appreciated. (signed) John-Blotto."

Which of the three strangers was Apekono? I picked one who appeared of different stock from the other two. In the full light of the moon, against the dark background of the spinney, his face was tense and luminous with intelligence. He was darker than his companions, and his features were more finely shaped. His nose had a bridge, his high forehead was aggressive, his eyes were large and brilliant. His body was lithe and extremely muscular and well proportioned. He carried himself with an ostentatious pride, and when he addressed me he used his hands to make supple expressive gestures that seemed to give life and wings to what he said.

He planned my journey to his parish like a travel agent, but went one better by accompanying me on it and was my guide and adviser. Just a few hops ahead, he was slashing down a projecting branch here, warning me of a hidden stump or pothole there, lending a hand on the greasy surfaces of the tree trunks, and testing the different jungle vine-suspended bridges before I crossed a river. And if our day brought us, as it often did, to an old deserted hamlet, Apekono would hustle his men and in an hour have a tolerable shelter made of brushwood and leaves for me for the night. In a word, Apekono did for me what Longfellow's Hiawatha did for Minnehaha:

> Cleared the tangled pathway for her,
> Bent aside the swaying branches,
> Made at night a lodge of branches,
> And a bed with boughs and hemlock,
> And a fire before the doorway
> With the dry cones of the pine-tree.

I had told Apekono of my intention to visit as many villages as possible, since he knew all the tribal land and miles beyond it. This he agreed to do.

We discussed arrangements at some length. Apekono assured me that it was best to leave the final arrangement till we reached Hogoteru village because it was from there we would strike out over the mountains and get a fresh supply of carriers. On our way to Hegeteru village, a two-day walk of six to eight hours each, we came across a small village, a mere handful of huts. We turned onto a faint track leading to a small dilapidated hut that I had thought uninhabited. Apekono nudged me and pointed through the doorway of the hut. I stepped warily to look inside. On the ground in the far corner sat a woman of about thirty. She looked odd, not ill, rather emaciated, looking up with blank eyes with a mask-like expression. There was an occasional fine tremor of her head and trunk, as if she were shivering from cold, though the day was very warm.

I asked Apekono and Sinoko to carry the woman out from the hut. She lay outside in the sun with chill-like generalized tremors of her whole body.

I told Apekono to inquire whether the woman felt any pain. She could not speak, only utter some sounds with a negative head shake. Through Apekono I asked her husband and his other wife what was the matter. The answer was that she was very sick and "klos dai pinis." Then the husband and his second wife retreated to their private world again, withdrawing from the conversation.

I realized now that the woman was chronically ill, perhaps with consumption, more probably with a neurological disorder and the knowledge that a malignant spell had been put on her so that she was bound to die.

I decided I might as well try my own variety of magic. I asked for my tattered kit bag. I fumbled in it and pulled out a tube of jelly I had carried for rubbing on my legs and feet when they were tired from walking. It was an embrocation of the family of Sloane's liniment. If applied unwisely to a sensitive part of the body, it stung like an angry millipede. If rubbed gently over the lower legs, it was supposed to warm the skin and loosen the muscles. It was the best available counter-magic that I could lay my hands on. Holding it up, I turned and faced my small audience, putting on my most dramatic voice and announcing: "The sorcerer has put a bad spirit inside the woman. I am going to burn this spirit so that it comes out of her and leaves her. You will not see the fire, but she will feel it. The bad spirit will leave her and she will not die." This was translated by Apekono with impressive gestures.

I squeezed a gobbet of liniment onto the woman's stomach, rubbed vigorously, and asked through the in-

terpreter if she felt the "fire." I squeezed more jelly onto
the woman's belly, adding some to her inner thighs, and
rubbed even harder. "Do you feel a big fire now?" Apekono translated. The woman could only nod. Perspiration was running off her. For that matter, perspiration
was running off my forehead and dripping on the
woman's face. I turned and said, more boldly than I felt:
"There is a big fire burning in this woman. Your evil spirit
has left her. She is going to live." I waved my liniment
tube, then turned to the woman and said in a patriarchal
Old Testament voice: "Get up! Walk!"

She looked at me appealingly, but made no effort to
rise. I took her by the arms and lifted her; she sank limply
back to the ground. In even sterner tone I let out: "Stand
up!" The woman struggled feebly as if to rise, then, exhausted, started to tremble more violently, making a
sound of foolish laughter, akin to a titter. I lifted her
again; again she sank back. Only now I realized her
helplessness. I realized also that during my effort I had
erred on the side of medicine.

The audience looked at me triumphantly and cack-
led, and I suddenly felt as naked as a conjurer whose
white rabbit had burrowed too far up his sleeve and fallen
down his trouser leg.

There was a long pause. People bowed their heads in
deference, almost as if they did not dare look me in the
face. The woman's husband stood with his eyes tightly
shut against the white barbarian intruder.

That day we camped near a small mountain stream.
Apekono put his men to the job of building me a shelter
while he went off to the bush to try his luck at hunting.
Without Apekono's attention they worked very slowly,
but when he returned a few hours later covered with mud
and perspiration, carrying in one hand his inseparable

bow and arrows and in the other a small wallaby, he spurred them on considerably with tones and gestures that were good sound abuse in any language.

Less than three days from attaining its full circumference, the moon rose over the mountain tops into the grapeskin sky that was already lighted by a huge concourse of stars and dimmed the brightness of the camp fire. The evening breeze was still blowing; the whole sky was cloudless. When we—Apekono, Sinoko, and I—had drunk our coffee from enamel mugs and eaten our frugal meal of baked sweet potatoes with a delicious chunk of tinned corned beef, I asked Apekono how the arrangements were for tomorrow's trip. He looked at me in silence as if to say, "It's a long story so pull up a chair." "I am sorry," he said, "it's going to be a long walk, and if all the bridges are alright we will reach Hegeteru village before dark." Then, after a few sniffles, he added, "Dokta, don't use your magic medicine any more. It will not win our strong sorcery. In my place you will see plenty people dying from this." Then he nudged Sinoko and they left me alone with fervent thoughts of sorcery. Even with intelligent fellows like Apekono and Sinoko, I did not attempt to discuss this subject. I did not ask for so much as his tribal name because I knew that even his name is taboo. And of course I didn't ask the name of their sorcery, although I knew it from John—Kuru.

The Australian administration had discouraged sorcery, as it discouraged polygamy. But underneath this thin crust of inexplicable alien law, the old Highland beliefs persisted; the belief in taboos and the awful penalty for breaking a taboo—the self-inflicted penalty of death, he or she would probably be told to die, and would die because the sorcerer had said so. At the decreed time on the decreed date, he or she would sit down and die.

What a wonderful administration of justice I thought—
no prisons, no courts. Which of us would sit down and
die because we had broken the law? Is it merely autosuggestion carried to lengths we cannot grasp?

I have witnessed many cases of autosuggestion. One
of these occurred when a native thought he was bewitched by the sorcerer, fell down in a fit, and lived only
three days. He was moving, muttering, twitching, but
unconscious. Was it some kind of visitation paralyzing
all his faculties until he died? That dominance over their
own vitality was extraordinary to me. It is the power that
the sorcerer wields, which must have the victim's cooperation. At least, this is what I learned—not here, but elsewhere.

There was little sleep that night. I rose at five and jot-
ted down a few notes by light of the hurricane lamp. Apekono and the carriers were anxious to move and so was I.
All we needed was the first grey light of dawn to make the
track discernible. By a quarter to six sufficient light had
penetrated the overhead canopy of leaves to serve our
purpose. We moved like ghosts through the fog that still
clung to the mountain tops.

We had now crossed the mountains some forty miles
west of Goroka and consequently Hegeteru village was
well to the east. The terrain became more inviting, hilly
but not mountainous, with a good open track.

Mt. Michael rose as straight as a wall behind us with
wooly clouds sleeping on its emerald top. We were not
heading in the right direction, however, and I learned
from Sinoko that the carriers were not on speaking terms
with the neighboring people living in scattered hamlets
on the hillsides. Thus we had to make a three-hour de-
tour, walking uphill through muck and slush and slimy
fetid rain jungle, before we reached Hegeteru.

We found the whole village in a "saturnalian" spirit. This was an unpleasant surprise, at least to me, since I felt it would delay our journey to John's parish.

A dance was in its beginning phase. Men stood opposite each other in ranks of ten or twenty—there was no regular or ordered planning in their dancing, it obeyed only the changing time and fervor of the drums—and when the drummers beat more urgently, the women came in behind the men, dancing more widely than they and changing above the voice of the drums their brutal endearments or enticements to battle. Each rank of men then turned about, and men and women danced to a tumultuous rhythm in an obscene and violent parody of the sexual act, to which the moon gave inhuman dimensions by throwing on the pallid ground enormous, elongated shadows of leaping breasts and arms beseeching, legs demanding, and heads nodding in agonies of desire.

Gradually the pace and fervor of the drums diminished, and the women, with a casual and slouching gait, retired from the dancing ground. For a little while the men turned and pranced in solitary frenzy and then grew tired of their play. The men were given the best hot chunks of half-roasted pig, which they gnawed and swallowed with almost declamatory greed. Women wandered here and there between the fires, taking now a stringy rib and then, by favor, a piece of sizzling hot kidney or heart, or clumsy pieces of viscera.

At last our group was noticed by the busy host and some of his guests. He recognized Apekono and was now moving toward us with a small body of men. After shaking hands with Apekono and talking to him in an alien prattle, he addressed Sinoko in fluent Pidgin. Pidgin, or Melanesian Pidgin, was becoming a common language of communication and is the one chiefly used at present.

The influence of Pidgin has been tremendous, for it has
allowed the European to get in touch with the natives and
the members of different tribes to communicate with one
another. The words of this *lingua franca* are mainly English in origin, but the idiom is Melanesian. However, the
English words are not faithfully reproduced for two reasons: the average English speaker is slovenly and careless
of diction and is a victim of his hometown pronunciation;
and also the native is unable to reproduce many sounds
common to the English language; for instance they will
say P for F, S for Sh, D for J and Z, and P, B, or V for W.

Our host seemed to me to be much better fed than his
fellows, so I asked him if he had worked on a European
plantation. He answered negatively, but told me he had
just spent six months in the Goroka jail for killing one of
his wives. He felt that he had been wronged: six months
in jail! Six months for killing an old wife "a lapun meri,"
who was "no gut" and was already "klos i dai pinis."

I felt that the conversation between Apekono and the
village leader was not overly cordial. A few sticks of twist
tobacco, however, put him in a happier mood and he
agreed to let me use his shelter for the night.

I did not sleep at all that night, for the drums began
again and beat more loudly, more urgently. Wiping their
greasy hands on naked thighs, the dancers went forward
to revive their ritual frenzy. Above the hilltop where they
danced, the stench was a mixture of wood smoke and
gross humanity, the moon exaggerated their postures in
a caricature of leaping shadows; but within their parochial minds there beats a faith, responsive to the drums,
that blessed their dark broad shoulders, their trumpery
ornaments and greasy flesh with a rapt and fearful joy.
The clamor of the drums was now accompanied by a
hoarse and rhythmic vociferation.

To my eyes it was the germ of poetry and ballet; their minds were in a turmoil of creation. It was a dance of Walpurgis night, in monochrome, and the to-and-fro movement of the larger crowd had raised a thin powder of dust. There were no clouds over the mountains, and the promise of the sky was a clear morning for our final stride into the land of puissant voodoo.

On our arrival at Moke, now officially named Okapa, the air grew cool and sharp with excitement, and the gray sky came down to meet the crests of the mountains.

Apekono's parish, called Fore, appeared at first like a dream. But after a little while it wasn't like a dream; it was like being more awake than I had ever been before.

It had to do with coming here. This feeling of being awake meant more than a widening and gladdening of the eye at seeing the mountain peaks thrusting out from closely woven treetops, giving a curious effect from a certain distance, as if I were looking at a two-dimensional movie. This happens especially if the distance is steep, as is so often the case, for then you see the ceiling of the forest suddenly uplifted from the horizontal plane of tree crests, giving a perspective so different that the mountain seems much nearer than its surroundings.

Okapa is no great distance from Goroka as the crow flies. But the crow's flight has not the same meaning in this mountainous region, where we reckon a distance by so many days' trek. Measured on the map with a ruler, Okapa was only about fifty miles away, but to march there over the mountain tracks takes four solid days in the dry season; no one attempted it in the wet months. The only communication with Goroka was by radiotelephone, when it worked, which was a rarity.

The armed force at John's disposal consisted of a native corporal and six constables. He also employed an interpreter who spoke three of the hill languages, a couple off houseboys and a carpenter. His only white companion within two days' march was a German missionary.

John MacArthur had spent two and a half years in the district, and thought his life had been peaceful. He lived a busy, strenuous life, but in these years he himself had never been in grave danger. A half-wit had tried to shoot him with a broad-bladed arrow, but he had never had to order his constables to open fire or draw his own revolver. In the Highlands, as in all Australian territory of Papua New Guinea, there had been for nearly eighty years a fastidious disapproval of manslaughter as an aid to pacification, and every officer in the service had been taught that a calm display of confidence was not only preferable in moral judgment to gunfire, but was more effective and much more economical. Those who, like John, were untroubled by nervousness, quickly accepted the teaching; the others did not survive their period of probation.

But now the simplicity and relative peace of John's life were threatened by an emotional, visionary belief that had already spread like smallpox through a score of villages—belief in the parochial sorcery called Kuru, associated with the ritual vengeful killing of the alleged sorcerer, here called Tukabu.

The last hour of the day was richly colored and the mountains, now imminent and sharply focused, were enormous but seemed benign. The sky above was a pellucid veil, the hue of pomegranates, and the distant grove of trees was as dark as cucumbers.

I sat with John on the veranda of his bungalow, which, like the other buildings in Okapa, stood on stilts above the ground. John had built it with pride in his labor, and he was pleased with his ingenious achievement. He and I were living in it, though it was far from finished.

The doors were unpainted, there were no louvres in the windows, and at night the lamp attracted a thin drift, then a cloud, of soft and clumsy moths that dimmed the pale kerosene pressure lamp with their fluttering curtain of wings. But in spite of its deficiencies, the new bungalow was vastly preferable to the old one 20 yards away, which John had abandoned because of its grass thatched roof, too long a breeding ground for small snakes, spiders, and rats. It had begun to sag in the middle and threatened to bury him beneath a mattress of rotten timber, dead palm leaves, and the nests of its uncountable population.

I told John of the events of interest that had occurred during my "marathon race" over the mountains, not omitting the episode of "magic with liniment jelly." I then proceeded, brimming over with subjects of new interest: Kuru and Tukabu.

John confirmed my previous observations that information must be collected piecemeal from natives. Subsequently one fits the pieces together like a jigsaw puzzle. It is rare that a native realizes the white man's curiosity and hunger for knowledge, for neither is a factor of the native mind. Facts have to be dragged out. Thus, during one of his numerous patrols, the native showed John only one case of Kuru when he happened to pass the victim's hamlet. Likewise he would not have mentioned Tukabu.

John MacArthur believed in the necessity of patience and forebearance in all his dealings with dissident tribes—a belief often justified, but always exasperating. He was convinced that any disorder of people's mind would be cured, in time, by mere exhaustion. To interfere with them would, however, deepen their credulity. He was uninterested, or only superficially interested, in the nature of the infatuation with Kuru sorcery, which he thought was a kind of mass hysteria. As far as he knew,

Kuru meant "chill" in the Fore language, or trembling, or shivering, from cold, fear, fever, agitation, or exultation; all of these were expressed by the word Kuru.

It is an offense under the law of the Australian colonial administration to profess to practice sorcery, but it is extremely seldom that the Highlander will lay an official complaint against a sorcerer. With no exception, the natives feel that where sorcery is concerned, the white man, who cannot understand such matters, can be of no help. "The only course to them," John asserted, "is to take the law into their own hands, then accept the consequences as far as the law is concerned. To natives, there is no such thing as what we rather comfortably call death from natural causes. If a relation or friend dies from a sickness, they immediately look for a sorcerer as the culprit. If there is a practicing sorcerer in the area, he will probably be the suspect. If not, suspicion will fall on some perfectly innocent person, perhaps a personal enemy, perhaps merely a person of unusual appearance or habits, or perhaps somebody seen behaving in an unusual manner. Many innocent people have been killed because of entirely unfounded suspicions that they are sorcerers. There is a particular problem here in Fore of ritual killing because of suspected sorcery, which is locally called Tukabu."

He went on. "Take for instance the girl I mentioned in my report. She died a month after I last saw her, as was predicted by the natives. About three months ago I had the opportunity to observe yet another case of alleged Kuru sorcery. It was a young woman shivering and trembling, unable to talk and sit up, just lying on the ground of the hut. She died within a week. Natives were saying that she was the victim of Kuru sorcery."

In spite of John's excellent rapport with the natives, particularly with the Fore tribe, he could not discover the *modus operandi* of Kuru sorcery. It was under the seal of strict taboo against the white man's prying eyes and ears. About the ritual vendetta murder, Tukabu, he could tell me that it was accompanied by physical violence and carried out by the "willing party," accompanied by at least one other person of the victim's kinsmen. The alleged sorcerer is attacked from ambush and then violently beaten by pounding of the jumeri and femurs and of the anterior neck with stones or wooden clubs, biting of the trachea until it is fractured, and crushing of the external genitalia with stones. The victim is then left alone at death's door.

Once he had witnessed a dead Tukabu's prey with a sharp, slender bamboo probe inserted into his penis through the urethra protruding on the lower abdominal wall. This "operation" was labeled by John as "excruciating surgical death." And he concluded: "I take my stand against sorcerers! As I said before, there is a law against sorcery, black magic, but law is only convention and sorcery is a social problem. How can I prosecute a sorcerer when there are so many? According to natives, any male can perform Kuru sorcery. You see, Doc, where the black cat is hidden; jail all men and the problem is solved, eh? So, let me concentrate on road building and schools. You erect your hospitals and initiate Kuru studies and find out the remedy for it. Thus, perhaps, we will be able to convince them that it is not sorcery, but that the person is sick."

That day we missed our supper. Was it after midnight or just before dawn? I couldn't tell after my share of one and a half bottles of rum. I could hear John's healthy snore carrying his moot points away. Crashing onto a stretcher, I was still conscious of the music of bamboo flutes, with their spectacular exhibitions, which

I was hearing for the first time. The music was a real, and delightful, experience; it has no rhythm, inflexions, syllables, cadences, or any form that can be used to describe it to those who have never had the privilege of hearing it. There seems to be an undercurrent of deep sounds that suggest organ notes. One can only speak of it as "celestial" music, beyond our language or song.

My time was already running out for I had to replace Bill Symes, an Australian doctor who was going away for a nine-month postgraduate course. I had to get what I could from this place in a hurry, to see as many cases of Kuru as possible, to ascertain whether it was just a fixed idea of the Fore—a fantasy or reality.

I found here, as everywhere else, that the youngsters were the best companions and invaluable informants. I built mutual trust by learning the native names for everything in sight. This invariably broke the ice. I would point to some object and a youngster would supply the name and then try to correct my pronunciation. This would cause bubbles of laughter, for I found the modified vowels extremely difficult to hear and reproduce. To my amusement they were soon one group, all talking at once, then turning to make me repeat a word as though I were another child. By the end of the day the youngsters were delightful company. Through them the formidable barrier of prejudice and mistrust was broken down; through them, as it happened, I had the opportunity to witness nine cases of different stages of the Kuru malady—nine cases in less than two weeks.

Returning home one day by the main track of the hamlet, one of the youngsters drew my attention to a battered hut. A small woman was sitting on the ground in the doorway. She was holding on her lap a limp figure, grossly emaciated to little more than skin and protruding bone, the shivering skeleton of a boy, looking up at me with blank crossed eyes. On both his hips were large bed-sores, and when I tried to apply a dressing to protect them against blowflies his tremor became more pronounced and from his cracked lips came a moan-like sound. He could not utter a single word. Conversation with the woman was necessarily by sign, for she knew no Pidgin English, and her language was completely foreign to me. When I asked about the child, the woman held up one finger to signify that he was her only one, and when I pointed to myself, pretending shivering, and then back to the boy, she muttered the word "Kuru." It was useless to attempt to probe further and I decided to return in a day or two with the interpreter. Alas on my revisit two days later, the mother of the boy told the interpreter that he had died the day before and she had buried him alone. I discovered that her clan was some distance away; the ground she was living on belonged to her husband who had died from Tukabu.

Another case of Kuru registered that may be of no interest to anybody but myself.

Apekono invited me to see "Masta Dson Kukukuku" in action blasting rocks on the road under construction. On the way to the road building site with Apekono and a bunch of chattering youngsters, we had to pass several hamlets with nearby gardens situated on ridges and hill-sides. Every hamlet was surrounded by a fence made of palings—reminding me of my home in the Baltic. Apart from fat pigs and scraggy dogs, most of the hamlets were deserted. Just before the last descent to the road construc-tion site, I was attracted by a small figure of a boy dressed in dirty, weather-battered shorts, obtained from a neigh-boring mission, I guessed. Over his narrow shoulder he was carrying a long thick bamboo tube filled with water.

It appeared to me that he was staggering with his bamboo pipe as he tried to cross the narrow passage of the fence. This, to me, was rather unusual. As a rule all Melanesian children exhibited extraordinary coordination and equilibrium associated with balance.

My anxious question "What is wrong with the boy?" was met with Apekono's shrug of the shoulder and a reply in Pidgin, "Skru bilong em i lus, Kuru i kamap," meaning his knees were weak; he had Kuru. The tiny water carrier's success in stumbling through the passage was accompanied by hearty laughter from the group of youngsters and, to my amazement, was joined by the little fellow with the bamboo tube. Was I confused that the laughter of the waterboy sounded debilitated, a foolish laughter? At that time and place it appeared as such.

"Yep, you call this road building, eh?" was John's response to my acclaim. "Pick and shovel, a few crowbars and a bloody miserable supply of dynamite. And the rest ... just these miserable creatures with their hands. No bulldozers, no graders, no chain saws to cut these giant trees down. Everything by hand. As you see, it is strenuous and sometimes outright dangerous work." Wiping the sweat from his weary, unshaven, and muddy face and producing from his side pocket a bottle of aspirin, he took four tablets and, crushing them between his teeth without water, gulped them down, remarking, "These bloody fumes from 'blasting thunder' leech my brain. Have to medicate it with bolus, it relieves my headache for at least a few hours." Sadly looking at him as a potential candidate for gastric ulcers or some kidney malady, I had nothing to say, for I knew it would be of no avail.

Goshawks speckled the air, swinging in and out of the valleys. And crowds of little sunbirds came and went, and there were scores of cockatoos startling the echoes.

We walked on the newly built road, six miles or so in length, now going over the wide, squashy loop of a recent landslide, which a large group of natives was laboring to clear in order to lay the roadbed and parapets. As we went ahead, the road began to hypnotize me, the everlasting winding and looping and turning and twisting, ascending all the time. At last we arrived at the foothills where the new road ended.

In a few minutes, there were only hills around us, soft and crumbly, flecked with mica, swinging, rising, and falling. At first all the slopes were fields, lentil shaped, descending like giant stairs to the narrow gully-like valleys below, still filled with brush and trees that became thicker. It reminded me of a broody and violent sea, a sort of psychiatric playground that must somehow be spared the irrevocability of modernization. Here we were encumbered with rows of laborers. Here and there woodcutters, chiefly men and adolescent boys, were enlarging the passage of the pegged track. Women and girls with string bags strapped across their foreheads carried chips of blasted rocks, and sitting workers were breaking stones. The pegged track swung ever upward, cut sheer in the cliff, and the raw face of the cut showed its layers, grey and flecked with mica, somehow porous. In one corner was what appeared to be a slip of grey stones like granite, but when the natives clobbered it with their digging stick, it yielded like mud. It was obvious that cutting a road through this land was not easy; the rock was dust in the dry season, and sleezy mud in the monsoon. It could begin to fall around them in fine ash, in grain, in pebbles, and then in larger rocks or boulders, boulders heavy and hard, yet still washable into mud. And later, after rain, a whole hill might pour itself down, sliding upon the road and covering it with a red-brown

ooze. And behind this fluid earth another hill, and another, and another.

We stopped at the gully that was John's base of
operation. It was an assembly of grass huts on the bank
of a stony stream that would be a torrent in the monsoon.
I picked up what looked like a piece of granite and crum-
bled it easily in my hand.

"Gigantic mudpies, aren't they?" said John pointing
to where about fifty feet of good stone leaned against the
hewn bare fence of the rock, a wide, large wall, holding
up the hill.

"That stone had to be quarried two miles away and
brought here by Apekono's people," announced John
proudly, pointing at Apekono. "He will tell you that the
secret of a good road is drainage. Drain, drain, and drain.
Don't let water accumulate anywhere. Put culverts
everywhere you can, for after rain these hills swell and explode very suddenly. Now, let's have some coffee."

It was four o'clock. The drizzle had ceased and the
sun shone from a washed forget-me-not blue sky. Steam
rose from the thatched roofs of the huts; it rose from the
pathways and the floor of the jungle, swelling up in white,
loose, billowy clouds and padding each mountain range
with a layer of white cotton wool.

This was the idle hour of the day for the men, the hour
to lay off from work; the hour before the big meal and
verbal intercourse. In a short time quite a gathering of
men was formed. John introduced me to the senior members of his "task force," sitting around the "garamut," a
drum-shaped, hollowed out log a few feet long that is
used for tapping out messages to neighboring villages.
The men were smoking and yarning. To satisfy everybody's curiosity, I did some tapping on the garamut. I did
not think it was quite so funny, but they seemed to derive

extraordinary pleasure from it, slapping their thighs and rocking to and fro with delight. They proudly showed me a pig's skull and other trophies of a chase. I pretended to believe this to be a human skull and, holding it on an unusually long piece of bark, I questioned "Kukukuku?" I thought the cheering would never stop. My popularity abounded because I had disparaged a fearful neighboring tribe.

This was all quite silly, but what other common topic could we find for a few passing moments of conversation? Had I carried out an enquiry on Kuru, it would have been met with a blank stare—the strange white man on display, like the elephant of the circus.

The round grass huts looked dramatic in the last light of the day; slanted low across the gully, it set them in a lambent frieze against the evening sky. To me it was a noisome place, dark and redolent of unwashed bodies anointed with pig fat and wretched, mangy-haired dogs. My distaste was intensified by the weird howling of the dogs, alternately shrill and deep, reverberating in the confined space until I felt myself dissolving into it as though my mind had become a sounding board for the massed yowl.

The oratorical refrain of the Highlander, "Pigs are our hearts!" may also be applied to the dogs. Descending unchanged from the Quaternary age, they cannot bark, but they certainly do howl. Although the muzzle is pointed like a ferret's, they look like terriers, but stand higher. The long, thin tail does not wag, but is kept in cowardly fashion tucked between the hind legs. The beast is always being scolded. Just skin and bone, it is constantly on the lookout for food, not being fed by the owners. Since it is used in hunting, the natives prefer to starve the canine to keep it keen on chasing game. A good precaution is to hang one's boots as high as one can lest the dogs, drawn by their smell, devour them during the night.

While we ate our evening meal—baked sweet potatoes, corn, sliced bully beef, tomatoes, shallots, and a pot of tea sweetened with condensed milk for Apekono, Sinoko, and the two boys, plus a large enamel mug of Nescafe with a solid dash of rum (known here as "coffee royal") for John and me, John was telling me about dog's meat. "For some reason," he was saying, "natives consider dog's meat so choice a dish as to be good enough for crowned heads. I well remember the first time I tasted dog meat. This occurred during my visit to Amusi village. While sitting on the front porch of the men's house with one of the "big men" and talking about the proposed road, he shouted out some orders. Two boys seated behind me, one of whom is here in the camp, immediately stood up, each with a stone in his hand; they pounced on a skinny old dog that was crouched by the house trembling either from fever or hunger, similar to the quivering girl. The dog was mercilessly butchered before my eyes, with blood and froth flowing from its half-broken mouth. There it was left for some time since we had to wait till the women came back from the gardens. Big green flies soon infested the pitiful carcass. As an aperitif, I must say, it was pretty unsuccessful."

Here John halted and, looking at me sheepishly, as if to apologize for spoiling my apetite, poured rum into our mugs (this time diluted with water), and continued the story.

"The women eventually filed past us, laden with their vegetable nets. The Big Man, Epaia by name, property owner of large gardens, three wives, a dozen pigs, and dogs with their offspring, slowly got up. He moved toward the slain dog, which he then began to skin and dismember. Women removed some "joints" that were covered with hair and dust and began cooking them with the sweet potatoes in the ashes of their open air hearths. Half an hour later, they solemnly placed two wooden plates in front of Epaia and me."

"The portion of dog meat lay in shapeless black patches against the dirty yellow of the kaukau (sweet potato) that the wives of Epaia had peeled with their long nails. But I was hungry. Besides, I had to give due honor to my host by doing justice to the food that I had heard was only for the VIP. So I forced myself to pick up the skinny leg that lay within my reach. I summoned all my courage...and then bit boldly into it. I managed to detach a few thready pieces and chew them for a moment, when I suddenly felt one of my grinders gone. I could not go on....I retched, then discreetly put the hideous mouthful in the palm of my hand and managed to force it between one of the gaps in the floor. All this was accompanied by tooth sucking sounds intended to show my keen appreciation for so succulent a morsel."

"Honestly Doc, there was no hypocrisy on my part; only elementary politeness, the other side of etiquette."

I was flabbergasted, not so much by the gist of the story as by its presentation. It was a tribute to John's narrative gift that he made the story so hugely amusing. He was a splendid raconteur, indeed. I almost choked on a piece of kaukau laughing. Although not having the slightest idea of the reason for my "outburst," Apekono and Sinoko joined in with their Melanesian laughter, high pitched and glottal.

John turned the stud on the pressure lamp and the light went out with a hiss and a smell of kerosene, taking with it all evidence of the white man's intrusion into this lonely jungle notch. The night now differed in no way from anynight for a 1000 years; the moonlight, the mountains, and the river; the frogs and the cicadas, the dying fires, and the scourge of evil spirits—they were as ever.

A rinse of my mouth, a splash of icy cold water on my face, and a hot mug of coffee put me in high gear for my return to Okapa the next morning.

John was engaged in deep conversation with Apekono and a small assembly of local chieftains. Hearing only bits and pieces, I guessed the important points of their discussion were the road and Kuru. Coming closer to camp, I could hear John persuading, "Tokim olgeta man na meri ol i kam wokim long rot (Tell all men and women to come and work on the road). Sopos yu helpim mi bai mi helpim yu (If you help me, I'll help you)."

After several orations from the chieftains, Apekono summed up: "Masta Dson em i tok stret, em i no gaiman (Master John is telling the truth, he is no liar). Mekim dai kros yumi (Let's settle our quarrels). Na brukim bus bai wokim rot (Cut the road through the bush). Rot bilong mipela, mipela yet mas wokim (We must build our own road). Yupela no lusim tok (Don't forget what we say)."

Then with an impressive gesture Apekono declared, "Tok i dai! (The matter is settled)." And turning to me with a voice attuned to brief authority, he said, "I moa beta yu go nau long Goroka, na bai yu kisim em i kam strong pela medisin bilong yu pitim poison long Kuru (It would be better for you to go now to Goroka and bring your potent medicine against Kuru sorcery)."

His sharp and troubled gaze over my shoulder caught my attention and, turning around, I spotted the figure of a youth staggering along the narrow path toward us. His scissor-gaited motion, rigid and frozen-faced expression, tremulous frame, was quite mesmerizing. Was he yet another prey of Kuru?

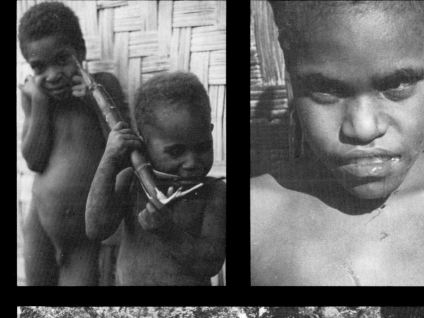

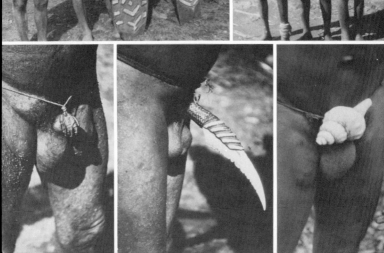

I learned from John that the youth was from Amusi village, one of the two boys who had stoned the dog and whom John had brought with him to the camp. According to John he was an exceptionally bright lad, learned Pidgin in no time, and was a most effective worker, active—perhaps too active—cheerful and trustworthy. He was a little brother or nephew of Kasinto. A month or so ago it had come to John's notice that the boy's behavior was changing somewhat; he became rather sullen, timid, and very much reserved, his speech appeared slowed down and he developed a kind of "drunkard's" gait. He was convinced that he was poisoned by Kuru.

Now observing him within reaching distance, I was struck by his expression, resembling the melodramatic face of Pagliacci in charcoal, minus tears. Here he stood, erect on a wide base, holding his hands together in an attempt to control the involuntary tremors and maintain his equilibrium. When asked by me about "Masta Dson" eating the dog's meat in his village, he excitedly uttered, "thu, thu" instead of "tru" and then, making an arduous effort, slurringly said, "M-m-m i k-k-hat k-k-k-uru."

So far he had stood on the same spot with his feet wide apart, and was now trying to touch the end of a cigaret. His hands wavered and, aside from singeing his short-clipped fuzzy hair, he had no success. One of the youngsters put the lit cigaret between his lips, but after a single puff it dropped from his mouth.

As if he sensed, in a very slow motion, some threat from behind, he gradually turned his head to one side. With his outstretched arms, he uttered a single rasping inarticulated shriek of laughter. He couldn't keep his balance any longer—I caught him before he fell.

And suddenly everybody, including the duped, began to laugh and laugh and laugh. It was the kind of

squeaky and curt laugh that one chiefly hears in an asy-
lum. It put me momentarily into a "rough-and-tumble"
state of mind. Was it just an extraordinary fatalistic attitude with which the victims of an alleged lethal Kuru
sorcery and their kin accept witchery? Are they so callous
that they lack the reaction of grief, I wondered?

The young "Kuru prey" was now sitting in an awkward fashion, bracing himself with one arm to avoid
dropping to a lying posture, while with the other trembling arm he continued trying to puff the cigaret. His
head was shaking slightly. The face tried to smile at me.
He had an inexpressible neoplastic aura—silky, smudge
skin, and haunted eyes with a moderate strabismus. The
cigaret dropped from his mouth again and he tried to
speak, brushing his lips with unsteady hand as if to pull
the words out of his mouth. He became so aphasic that I
silently attempted to reassure him , kneading and strok-
ing his shoulders. Finally he lay back, exhausted—the
lethargy of increased intracranial pressure, so I thought.
At that time I was a greenhorn in neurological diagnosis
and its prognosis. Neurology to me was merely a superb
diagnostic specialty that rarely offeredd any therapeutic
help, and usually could provide only fruitless diagnoses.

I encountered four other cases of alleged Kuru sorcery in one remote small village called Yasubi, a few
hours walk from Okapa. Here again I had to give my
thanks to the little fellows who, like cocker spaniels,
sniffed out and guided my direction.

It happened to be in the "women's territory," a cluster containing half a dozen women's huts, fenced in, near
a cultivated plot of land with pigs loitering in the hamlet
yard. Judging from the number of pigs, their corpulence,
and their dedicated women caretakers, it appeared, as
elsewhere in the Highlands, that pigs were highly regard-

ed. Some pigs were gathered closely to glean handouts and scraps, and two were suckling at a woman's breast. One, fat as a porpoise, was prostrate in a puddle and was being deloused by two pairs of unsteady hands. The arms of the two females were quivering so badly that every effort to cast a crushed parasite into their mouths failed by several inches. This was most unusual among High-land women; normally, when delousing each other's luxuriant scalps, every single vermin skillfully, without a miss, popped directly into their mouths.

Both females, one of an advanced age and the other in her pubescence, foolishly giggled after every failed attempt. Spotting me, they stopped giggling andtried to rise from the ground. The elder woman, pushing herself up with her arms, arduously tried to get up, but in a second dropped back, her entire body trembling intense-ly. The girl, however, got up, though very awkwardly, and bracing herself with a stick, studied me. With the corner of her little mouth lifted, a slight tremor of her slender body, and with the shadow of a timid smile, she looked forlorn. She could not yet be eleven. It gave me a queer sensation, which was detracted from by a small group of women sitting around the fire. One of them was stuffing kumu (a spinach-like leaf vegetable) just picked from the nearby garden into a bamboo tube to be cooked in the coals. Another was preoccupied with beetles and larvae of the Longicorn beetle, which in the Highlands was considered a culinary delicacy. The third one, sitting cross-legged beside the fire, was peeling sweet potatoes with a bamboo knife. The jerky movements of her arms whetted my curiosity. And when I did cast a glance at her, her tremor became more violent, assuming the char-acter of shaking palsy. Now she had to interrupt her task, and when one of her companions spoke to her, she muttered some reply so slurred that it was unintelligible. Her appearance was most pathetic.

My "undercover force" of youngsters was jestingly shouting; "Kuru, Kuru, Kuru!" Bedazzled by their indifference to the tragic plague-like malady, I was hustled by my guides to another place.

Walking on a steep, rough, and muddy footpath that connected the hamlets, we came to a single garden house, a rather large shack, as windproof as a five-bar gate, for the blue canopy of heaven could be seen through the roof. There, on a stack of dry grass, a middle-aged woman was sitting beside the naked figure of a small boy, lying on his side. With one hand she was wiping off brown porridge-like feces from the boy's puny buttocks with a handful of grass. Each soiled grassy wad was tossed to the pig waiting eagerly for the flings. Her other hand was fondling the boy's penis and she was talking to him. There was no response from the still figure.

I moved closer and put a hesitant finger on his cheek. Then I knew that there was no need to check his pulse or his pupils, for his cheek was as chill as metal. The little Fore boy had been dead for hours. Saddened, I imagined the mother's fondling of a few hours before, under different circumstances. Then the gesture had probably been pleasurable; at present, alas, the boy was under eternal anesthesia, inanimate.

Interrupting her action, she busily tried to chase two wretched dogs away from the boy's stiff body. One beast had managed to lap up quite a bit of the gray-yellow maggot-filled slough from a huge bedsore on the boy's hip. The other beast was obstinately trying to follow suit, but was driven away by a kick from one of the boys.

Turning away from the small chilled body, I was surprised at my fuzzy-haired scouts, solemnly observing the lifeless figure of their doomed playmate. The woman uttered something emphatic to the boys. The word "Kuru" was in it. With a cursory look at me they were running toward the village, leaving me alone.

Humbled, I took off to John's house—a chill passing through me; bringing sorrow—not so much for the dead boy, as for those Fore people who were still living and who any day, any hour, any minute, might become the prey of Kuru's frantic spell and cruel vengeance of Tukabu.

Now, walking alone on a footpath trodden down by abominable Snowman-like soles, I started thinking of all the Kuru cases I had seen, scissor-gaited, frozen-faced, rigid, tremulous, mobile, an almost total helplessness. I felt an almost masochistic curiosity about new cases. Perhaps they would be more challenging, calling for acumen and finesse. I suppose I shared, deep down, the egotism of most medicos—the feeling that my diagnosis and handling of unusual diseases was new and unique. The intellectual victory was certainly pyrrhic....

Probing deeper, I asked myself: Is my curiosity merely the product of vanity? Is my motivation for research born without any humanitarian instinct? Without a deep identification of the value of research? Is my present involvement with Kuru sorcery a particular manifestation of my curiosity, rather than the ability to experience the joys of discovery along with the responsibilities of a humble and honest researcher?

My questions were not simple and, as far as I could tell, no guidelines to them existed. "Something must be found that will reverse the awful curse of Kuru malady, and let moral philosophy go to the native dogs."

In this sweet mood, with decisions made, I stepped into Okapa station.

A pair of natives were carrying a small, shriveled old woman on a primitive litter consisting only of two fallen branches, roughly trimmed. The men were in a jocular humor, and when they saw Sinoko and me, they carried her onto the veranda. One of them began at once to talk with tumbling speed in his own language, which apart from the word "Kuru" we did not understand.

She was a pitiable yet ludicrous figure. Her small body still decorated with the remnants of her tattered finery, her malevolent, mask-like face with inward-turned eyes like chocolate drops in discolored whites, her parched mouth and fluttering gestures, made her look farcical indeed. She drank tea that Sinoko gave her with a nodding head while a thin straw-colored stream ran down her chin. Sinoko, leaning against the rail, studied her intently, while I gave her a physical examination.

After examining her for over half an hour, it was difficult for me to pick the important facts and summarize them in a few sentences. She was all too easy. She was approximately forty-five years of age, which is old by Highland standards, a woman having trouble speaking, getting up, and feeding herself, owing to severe ataxia (incoordination of muscles) of her arms. She did not complain of pains, headache, or fever. There was no evidence of muscular weakness and all reflexes were normal. The important findings were lethargy, dysarthria (impairment of articulation), and intermittent tremor. The whole story suggested the stark simplicity of a psychogenic disease. "So where is the trouble?" I posed the question.

My deduction at that time that Kuru might be an hysterical disorder was based on past and present anthropological data and personal observations.

Hysteria is a neurotic mechanism that an individual unconciously uses in order to avoid psychological distress associated with emotional conflict. It is frequently accompanied by physical concomitants such as paralysis, deafness, blindness, impairment or loss of speech, and the like. These secondary physical conditions provide the individual with an effective means of escaping problems that would otherwise cause psychological uneasiness.

Hysteria implies a heightened suggestibility, which is the most effective psychological mechanism employed in bridging reality and unreality. A consideration of the native's behavior, beliefs, and attitudes, and of his nervous disorders, would be quite uncomprehensive unless viewed in the framework of a continuous state of suggestibility.

The native lives in a world in which there is normally very little difference between reality and unreality. He is so entrenched in his environment that he believes himself a part of it. Trees, animals, and stones are part of the dynamism of which he and his ancestors are an integral part. He has no difficulty in incorporating illogical beliefs into unified thinking. It is this function that allows the native to handle his environment and its accompanying tensions without too much trauma.

The native's belief in magic and the supernatural provides ideal soil for the growth of acute suggestibility. He is thus well equipped to make ready use of hysteric mechanisms to relieve anxiety. When this does occur, the concomitant disabilities produced are colorful and dramatic, and can be related casually to sorcery and magic.

Furthermore, an individual of acute suggestibility is often a good subject for hypnosis, which had been used successfully by me to carry out minor surgical procedures and to cure minor hysterical reactions. It is of some interest that hypnosis can be induced by using a translator as means of communication.

The loss of function, localized or generalized, usually prevents the individual from following a normal mode of living, and so excuses him from facing his problems. Thus, it is an avoidance technique. Its form is similar in both Europeans and natives, but rationalization of the conditions differ. Europeans usually say that the loss of function "just came on" and offer no explanation for its occurrence. In contrast, the native expresses the firm conviction that the occurrence is the work of spirits or the result of sorcery.

The following case histories exemplify states seen by me in the Highlands:

A male of about twenty years had held his left arm in a tightly flexed position for two years. At times his speech was infantile, and at other times he was dumb. He said that immediately prior to the onset of his paralysis he had gone out to cut trees and inadvertently cut a tree that was the property of a spirit (massalai). When asked to demonstrate how he used an axe, it was obvious that he was accustomed to using his left hand to swing it. He stated that his disability was cured by taking a native medicine (the bark of a tree), but that shortly afterward he suffered an attack of fever and the disability returned. He does not know why he was attacked by the massalai, but stated that if he were able to make a large payment (to someone not specified), he would recover the power in his arm. As in the case with most hysterics, the hysterical paralysis was an unconscious form of punishment for his action or determined deterrent against repetition of the act.

A young woman was brought to the hospital with an almost complete paralysis of both legs. There was no involvement of her bladder, and no abnormal neurological signs were elicited. She was depressed and stated she wanted to die. She said "puri-puri" (sorcery) was done to her. She said that prior to the onset of this illness she was engaged in an adulterous affair and feared her husband had learned about it. Her father was a man of high social status in the village, the owner of many pigs and three wives, so she felt she could not go home and face her husband, although she knew she had to.

There are many other examples of minor hysterical reaction. A married female of about thirty years had been ill for about a week. When seen in the hospital, she was whispering and trembling continually. At times she was almost ecstatic and at others giggled in a senseless way. She appeared to be aware of the examiner's presence and reacted relevantly, but in an exaggerated manner. She was heavily sedated and the next day was quite well-behaved and professed no memory of her illness.

In general, hysterical "overlay" occurs rarely in association with severe physical illness. However, I am able to demonstrate one case of hysterical "overlay" occurring in a native patient with severe neurological disorder.

A female of around twenty years had an attack of encephalitis resulting in severe paraparesis (partial paralysis of the lower limbs). There was clear evidence of a neurological lesion and the patient had been unable to move any muscle of her lower limbs. There was apparently complete absence of joint sense at both ankle joints. There was no wasting of muscles. After induced hypnosis, the patient was able to move her ankles and was later able to stand and walk when supported.

With regard to Kuru, which is universally ascribed by the natives to a specific form of sorcery, this factor, in my opinion, was of considerable importance in assessing the psychological consequences of the disease. However, there were certain features of the illness that favored rejection of the psychogenic view.

These included the incidence of a fatal Kuru in young
children, for example, and the remarkable uniformity of
both the disease pattern and its march to a fatal conclusion, with certain clinical features indicating clear neuropathological patterns that are highly unlikely to be produced as hysterical features.

   In brief, the physical features in Kuru include the
early appearance of disorders in gait and balance, spreading later to the upper limbs and trunk. Although this
instability proceeds to a completely disabling degree,
there is the concomitant appearance of shock-like tremors affecting most of the muscles of the limbs, trunk, and
neck, diminishing during rest and sleep. This tremor
shows a steady progression. Associated features include
strabismus and emotional lability. Complete incapacity
proceeds to decubitus (bed sores), coma, and death. It
appears that "intelligence" and "memory" remain intact
throughout the disease and thus contraindicates cortical
involvement.

The all-too-brief review of Kuru did illustrate a pattern I faced in my struggle against the ravages of the
degenerative disease that did not come in outbreak
waves. My tired mind was sliding into philosophy,
where there were no answers—just endless questions
criss-crossing the void.

The night before my return journey to Goroka, while
awaiting sleep, I was still searching my mind for an answer that did not seem to exist; an answer to a disease
syndrome that was new to Western medicine.

Cheerful Optimism

The months flew rapidly by, and every month was the same. Like a pendulum, the BenaBena river swam its ominous, beautiful arc between two ranges of hills a few miles apart. Crows and cockatoos filled the air with strident alarms, voracious and quarrelsome. Their tearing voices in no way ruffled the peaceful existence of the Goroka valley. Kestrels poised like small black pins in the sky. Parakeets, swirling like trails of wind-blown leaves, called in great excitement across the gardens. And nowhere was there anxiety among the birds, only boldness in song and presence.

Not so with my inner self. My head was spinning with numerous questions. What causes "Kuru syndrome?" Is it infectious? How many people fall victim to it? Could it be contained or eliminated? What was the treatment? Was the disorder really fatal, and how long had it been among the Fore people?

In my university days I had been a rather easy going student. Never had I studied with such urgent need, never had I exercised my cerebral capacities as sequentially and in the well-organized way I did now. I read all the material on diseases of the central nervous system that could be obtained from the Public Health Department Library at Port Moresby. This was another of John Gunther's conquests. He believed the library to be an essential tool to medical advance. The library to him was medi-

cine for the mind. It was richly equipped and run by another "bloody wog" whose name was Clarissa de Derka,
a Hungarian Doctor of Philosophy and competent librar-
ian. She was queenly in appearance; tall and erect, she
had the figure of a showgirl. She moved deliberately and
slowly like a yacht. She had blond hair and bright blue
eyes and the whitest teeth I have ever seen. Later I learned
that she had aristocratic blood: I thought it was visible.

Clarissa confided in me and I in her because, I guess,
we saw early that each of us was moving toward the other
with no thought of sex. I felt an intense dedication to her
because of her inner quality. She liked conversation and
had many friends. "Friendship is heaven without God,"
was her saying, and she was consulted as a woman of
wisdom by many others. She worked all day, every day,
reading or writing, thinking or entertaining. The library
she claimed as her own, her literary home. "Reading provides the gymnastics of the mind, and gymnastics are the
reading of the ailing body and soul," I have heard her say.
She was married once and was afraid of getting married
again; afraid, like me, of losing something.

Our rendezvous took place partly at her small but
gemütlich government apartment, which she shared with
her mother, a superb culinary artist. We saw each other
twice or thrice a year during my official trips to Port
Moresby, but mostly our communication was a long epistolary intercourse—hers handwritten and mine typed.

And so, the more I read, the more I felt tight, angry,
frustrated, felt myself sinking into apathy and disorienta-
tion. And the more I racked my brain, the more the notion
that Kuru was a psychosomatic entity faded. There was
no doubt that this unusual phenomenon, this plague, was
a rare syndrome of which my medicine had no knowledge. Clinically the disease was closely akin to several

categories of genetic neurological degeneration, including the cerebellar ataxias. However, none of the many descriptions of those neurological illnesses fit the pattern of disease seen in Kuru. The tremorogenic, congenital, hereditary degenerative diseases exhibited more regular symptom patterns than Kuru, and were not associated with the profound disturbances of posture and balance, or the impaired articulation and emotionalism found in Kuru. Furthermore, they lacked the rapidly progressive degenerative character and fatal course of Kuru.

Eleven months had passed since my first visit to Okapa and things had taken a new shape.

John MacArthur had completed his task of road building. But instead of linking Okapa with Goroka, he had conjoined it with Kainantu, approximately sixty miles by road east of Goroka and just over a hundred miles from the coast. Kainantu was regarded as the "Gateway to the Highland," and was rapidly becoming populated by the white settlers. John reluctantly left for Australia without seeing Land Rovers ride the thirty mile road over which he had sweated and cursed for so long.

Another John, John Colman, my old fellow boon, was now in charge of Fore territory. He was, in many respects, a carbon copy of John MacArthur—a proud young man, but not vain, who also spoke with a conservative voice.

In the course of eleven months the Goroka Valley had received many overseas visitors, most of whom were crafty officeholders, trustees of the Government paid in honors and gold, from Australia's capital, Canberra. During the winter season in Australia, they swarmed into our high valleys of neverending broiling sun to harass and eat away the spirits of the field personnel. Naturally, they were of no use to me. I was desperately seeking practical medical scientists with a knowledge of neuro-

logical disorders, or at least with a keen interest in unusual phenomena. I met several colleagues to whose
attention I brought Kuru, but who, disappointingly,
showed very little, if any, interest in this extraordinary
malady. They knew even less than I of neurological and
virological fields.

There were a few "callers" whose visits still vividly
register in my mental notebook. The first was Professor
Maegraith, the Director of the School of Tropical Medicine in Liverpool, England, who was accompanied by Dr.
Peters, a malariologist, from the same quarters. Both of
them were here on official invitation by my superior, Dr.
John Gunther, himself an outstanding malariologist and
persuasive fighter against crippling and deadly diseases.
Priority was given to the control of malaria, followed by
tuberculosis and venereal diseases, and little attention
was normally paid such oddities as Kuru.

Malaria in this vast island, as a whole, was and still
is the greatest single public health problem and the most
important cause of illness and death. The transmission of
malaria in the lowland region was extensive, far greater
than elsewhere in the West Pacific region. To Gunther,
malaria was a disastrous phenomenon—one of the para-
mount factors limiting the development of the country—
and thus his prime concern.

He did not disparage the new strategic approach to
the eradication of malaria taken by the World Health
Organization. This involved spraying DDT in all local
dwellings twice a year, in some cases in combination with
mass antimalarial drug distribution. A man of uncommon wisdom, he merely raised the question whether the
goal of eradication set by international organizations was
not too ambitious and impractical. There were no reservations in his mind that this new strategic approach to

malaria eradication would produce an excellent reduction and, in some remote islands, would almost completely interrupt transmission. The eradication of malaria from a single huge tropical rain forest, such as the mainland of New Guinea, however, he looked on with considerable skepticism. Not only were great distances and areas involved, but the extraordinarily difficult and varied terrain, seasonal fluctuation and rainfall, and paucity of population hindered this kind of operation.

My impression of his thinking was that he regarded the World Health Organization's "Eradication Program" as a highly elaborate, exceedingly expensive project that confronted numerous obstacles and needed excessive resources: dedicated personnel, material, and money. Total eradication could prove to be a political and financial impossibility for the future independent Government of Papua New Guinea, even with international help.

While the World Health Organization's grand moguls were flaunting their banners with the watchword Eradication, based on the assumption that full eradication of malaria might be achieved in a few years, and swelling their ranks with "Eradicators," but far fewer malariologists, Gunther gave his *verbum sapienti*.

"Fight a war of containment, a war of control—control must be our watchword...control malaria and double the expectation of life; control malaria and halve the infant death rate...." John Gunther was looking for malariologists who were "bionomists," students of practices of the cultures served, and the mosquito vector's behavior pattern. The "Eradicators," to him, were just "house painters," like high-pressure salesmen trying to sell their whitewash to a consumers, *caveat emptor*.

I found my two guests, Maegraith and Peters, to be happy men bubbling over with *joie de vivre*. Far from

being bigwigs, both men were facile and unusually tal-
ented in tropical medicine. They were most attentive to
my searching talks about Kuru, which had become my
passion and anxiety. Although my graphic account ended with their dismissal of the subject as "fandango," they
introduced fresh views that had never occurred to me.

According to them, physical disorders may be responsible for the production and aggravation of mental
abnormalities and neurological disorders. Such disturbances may be transient or permanent. The following illnesses occurring in New Guinea may cause neurological
or psychiatric disorder: malaria, including cerebral malaria; infectious disease, including measles; pneumonia;
acute encephalitis; sequel to meningitis, chorea; birth injury with neurological signs and associated medical de-
fects; degenerative cerebral disease with associated trem-
or of the "Parkinson's" type; probable cerebral tumor and
cerebellar ataxia of unknown cause.

Both Maegraith and Peters thought well of John Gunther's measures to control malaria and tuberculosis in the
Highlands.

The danger of introducing malaria and tuberculosis,
which were prevalent on the coast, into the Highland districts by the returning laborers was Gunther's greatest
headache. Realistically enough, he acknowledged that
recruitment of Highlanders for employment on the coast
could not be stopped, nor could the Highland tribes forever remain locked away from the world in their moun-
tain-ringed valleys. Through him, medical teams began
a vigorous campaign for BCG inoculation against tuberculosis in the eastern part of the Central Highlands, the
area most exposed to the danger of contact.

Despite protest from the majority of the oldtimers
who had returned to New Guinea after the war, Gunther

successfully introduced an ordinance whereby planters were compelled to administer antimalarial drugs on a weekly basis to all Highland laborers. In addition, all infected laborers returning to their home districts after completion of their contracts had to be quarantined in a government hospital for one week, during which they received an antimalarial treatment.

These two welcome visitors, Maegraith and Peters, left Goroka after a three-day sojourn. Our valediction was unpretended and, with no more ado than a firm handshake with a touch of sympathy reflected in the Professor's eyes, eyes that could understand and speak as if saying, "Young man, I bemoan the medieval incubus of your fanatic obsession with Kuru," later paraphrased by him when we met again, 12 years later in Teheran, at an international congress on Tropical Medicine and Malaria.

Another visiting consultant to the Highlands happened to be a prominent nutritionist, a senior member of the South Pacific Commission. He, Doctor Oomen, arrived at Goroka Valley in the company of two assistants, one of whom was Lucy Hamilton, a dietitian from our Health Department who not much later became a valuable member of our Kuru research team.

To Gunther, a miniature edition of Oomen, there was no doubt that anemia, poor nutrition, malaria, and hookworm, or a combination of all four, were the chief reasons for the generally poor state of health among the indigenous population. He would say, "The expectation of life is half what it should be; the infant mortality twice to ten times what it should be...they sustain themselves with less than eighty percent of their food requirement." So he invited Oomen to assess the effects of dietary deficiency on the capacity and performance of otherwise healthy New Guineans.

Oomen was from the Netherlands and I found him, in character and status, a contrary portrayal of his "Vaderland," defined by someone as "the cockpit of Christendom and rendezvous of all adventurous spirits —naturally cold, moist, and unpleasant."

He was in his fifties, thick-girthed, a man as big as a church-door frame; a profound searcher and philosopher, whose spirit ran away from his body, leaving him alone with what he called "metabolic credo." Like nearly everything else about this man of deep warmth of feeling and human kindness, he was a rare, honest man of true good nature.

Being a master of persuasive argument and bull-necked energy, he swimmingly merchandized his cumulative evidence of the catholic role of nutrition in the maintenance of good health and in the prophylaxis and therapy of disease.

After a few days of efficacious verbal inoculation by the Dutch luminary, my previously dubious views about the significance of nutrition grew clearer. Gradually my interest in and understanding of the problems of tropical nutrition awakened.

The notion of yesteryears' medical school—that the fetus develops more or less independently of its mother— now appeared erroneous. According to my guest, in addition to interrelated anthropological factors and infections, malnutrition also effects the unborn child long before it takes its first breath. Thus, he said, "Like specters, the malnutrition factor haunts it virtually from conception through a toilsome, inglorious, and fast-withering life to the grave."

The infant born of a mother suffering from malnutrition is usually immature and underweight. It may also be that orthopsychiatric disorders resulting from malnutrition in early life contribute to their backwardness and seemingly low order of intelligence; and, he deduces, this apparent inferiority should not be considered dysgenic.

From Oomen's observations, the nutritional deficiencies in infancy and childhood usually become manifest at a time when the supply of breast milk is failing and supplementary feeding is begun. The most serious and widespread of these nutritional disorders is Kwashiorkor, or malignant malnutrition, the result of a reduction of both total calories and total protein, with animal protein absent or minimal, and which, he guessed, is widespread in the Highlands.

As I had foreseen, he was thoroughly roused and shared my excitement over the discovery of Kuru. To my enquiry whether nutritional factors, dietary deficiencies were the cause of Kuru, he shook his head, clearing his mind, and commented:

"There is solid evidence that the deficiency of pantothenic acid may produce a locomotor incoordination. Although the neurological changes are irreversible, the object will grow to maturity. In severe cases, however, complete posterior paralysis results, followed by death. Copper sulfate deficiency can also cause neurological disorders, such as gross ataxia of gait and stance, and other symptoms similar to Kuru."

His information put me in an expansive frame of mind; my eyes perceived the sheer potential of the causes of degenerative diseases. I agreed with most of his arguments. For example, the role of drugs in infections. According to his assertion, they are sometimes precious. They decrease excessive and disordered reactions. Drugs, serum, vaccines—all can be indispensable in an acute crisis, but should not be used until one has tried other methods. And, in using them, one must be aware that the problem is only suppressed, not cured. When the trouble is suppressed, it inevitably transfers its cleansing effort to some other organ with aggravated circumstances. Since the purification of the organism has been hindered, the drug or vaccine will have caused a supplementary chemical or microbial intoxication in a patient. In using a drug in urgent cases, one must also remember that this is an emergency; afterward the physician must treat the patient through a long course of detoxification and general revision of his whole nutrition and mode of life.

In his words, we all carry millions of microbes with us. They are harmless as long as we are well. Why do they suddenly become virulent? Because, he thinks, of the weakening of our "organic territory," as he termed it. Various microbes can cause precisely the same disease in a patient and, conversely, the same microbes can produce very different diseases, according to the temperament of the individual who harbors them; the same streptococcus will cause erysipelas, or an inflammation of the skin and subcutanous tissues, in one, angina in another, or septicemia in another. What counts is the trauma and weakness of the subject—the "nutritive territory."

On a rainy dawn, barely two days after commencing his survey of the nutritional status of the Highlanders, I received an urgent message from a Catholic priest in a remote mission that my scholarly visitor was acutely ill and required immediate medical attention. We landed safely in the old-fashion aircraft—the Dragon—on the small missionary's paddock and took off with the feverish and semicomatous doctor on board. My provisional diagnosis of acute appendicitis proved to be correct. He was operated on and after three days of hospitalization, took his leave home, giving me his hand and, with emotion hidden in banter, said in Dutch, "Tot ziens, boeken wurm, en dank U." Thank you for what? It was for me to say "dank U," since I felt deeply indebted to him for those swift and persuasive decisions, and especially for his genuine interest and his unasked-for assistance in my studies of Kuru.

The fourth and last visitor at that particular time happened to be the Director of one of Australia's leading medical research institutes, the Walter and Eliza Hall Institute of Melbourne. I had heard of this institute from my confidante Clarissa, who wrote to me about two doctors, Anderson and French, who successfully isolated an encephalitic virus (Murray valley encephalitis) transmitted by birds. It gave me an inkling that Kuru might be caused by the same virus group.

So here he was, the pope of Australian virology, already crowned with the title of Sir—Sir Macfarlane Burnet in the flesh—standing in the grounds of Goroka Hospital and eyeing me sharply as if expurgating a book. For obscure reasons I felt like a gnome stranded in a remote stagnating backwater. I had the peculiar sensation of being constipated, my guts filled with solid substance, but incapable of egesting it. To his leading questions on health problems in the Highlands I could only utter "yes" or "no," followed by "Sir Professor Burnet" instead of Sir Macfarlane.

Somehow I managed to give him a full medical account of Kuru. He pretended to look adequately interested, nodding and smiling whenever he guessed it to be appropriate. There was something distinctly impish about him. I felt he must look upon me as a freak, obviously unbalanced. Perhaps, I thought, my description of Kuru was delivered with too much gusto, giving an impression to this austere figure that my discovery was just a new obsession.

The days of his visit frittered away, leaving me in doubt about his promised cooperation in the investigation of Kuru.

There was a general saying among government officers that the only permanent appointments are temporary ones, meaning that if you were appointed to some district with full formality, something always occurred to change it, but if you were casually asked to lend a hand to some fellow officer for a weekend, you would most likely continue there for several years.

My "temporary" appointment came in October. This was to be at Kainantu and lasted for nearly eight delightful years. There was more than enough work for any one medical officer in the area. I had inherited nearly four thousand square miles of mountainous terrain, and an indigenous population of over one hundred thousand, composed of seventeen diverse linguistic groups.

My legacy also included ten coffee plantations with several hundred imported laborers, one gold mine, a government agricultural and livestock station, three missionaries of different denominations, and the Summer School of Linguistics, a Christian organization consisting of a dozen families. Its main purpose was to learn local languages in order to translate the Bible into tribal lingua. Catering to the somatic needs of these Highlanders left very little free time.

I found the local Kiap, Harry West, an amicable character, though perhaps too much imbued with *amour propre*, too thirsty after promotion. With his platoon of native policemen and five Australian Patrol Officers, he impressively introduced the Pax Australian policy, encouraging his young subordinates to go on frequent patrols.

The word "patrol" here has a different meaning from the dictionary definition of "small group of soldiers sent on a mission" or "to traverse a particular district, as a policeman." These patrols were a mixture of prevention, wisdom, resource, good humor, and fortitude, and basically followed the theme of an old Chinese poem on the principles of proper approach:

> *Go to the people, live among them,*
> *Learn from them, love them,*
> *Start with what they know, build on what they have.*

I was pleased to encounter here a young man named Glen Jonson. He happened to be a third year medical student dropout, recently married to a much older woman. His wife, Nancy, a qualified nurse and teetotaler, safeguarded him in a motherhen-like manner from backsliding to his past failing—the "luscious liquor." They were a great team, expediently managing the essential medical orderlies. To me they were a substantial asset; without this couple I would never have been able to familiarize myself with the physical aspect of my "temporary assignment."

I had envisaged the Kainantu subdistrict as a small parish, but it was in fact a district, and quite an extensive one at that. It was nearly as vast as the Papuan mountain region, which I had left five years ago, but lacked even the primitive Papuan amenities of beaten tracks. Here, the hinterland was nearly trackless, almost a primeval forest; it took me several years to learn what a primeval rain forest really was.

Ever since my last brief visit to Fore, I had had my mind set on the southwest of Kainantu. Besides a pioneering instinct, a physical fascination for high valleys, blue sky, blue mountains, white clouds, and, maybe, roaring rivers and thundering waterfalls that would exercise any healthy soul, there had been another motive to revisit that far mountainous spot. Up there, the enthralling phenomenon of Kuru was causing the population to dwindle, and this knowledge was to me like an unopened letter. I would do my best for the Fore people, I thought, even though my best might be very little.

Ultimately, I hoped that by going back I could document a more accurate picture of the alleged Kuru sorcery. Thus I would be able to plead with the Director for relief from some of my duties as medical officer, so that I could spend more time in Fore studying Kuru.

Finally, by juggling time, I was able to make a trip back to Okapa. It was at the end of October, nineteen fifty-six. Glen Jonson drove, I navigated, and Sinoko, who had by now become my shadow, and Liklik, a very shrewd native medical orderly seconded to me by Glen, served as back-seat drivers. We set out for Okapa in a British-manufactured Land Rover.

At first the road was not too bad—wet and rutted, but rideable. As we drove higher into the mountains, however, the twists and turns became sharper and narrower. The road swung ever upward, cut sheer into the cliff, and the raw face of the cut showed its layers, gray and somehow porous. At one corner was what appeared to be gray stones like granite, but when the Land Rover's wheels went over them, they yielded like mud.

The Land Rover was now driving over the wide, squashy loop of a recent landslide on which people were working; planing, smoothing, and pushing the mud and soft earth until it slithered in great lumps down the slope. On one section the road had looked impassable, but we winged over unmade portions rough with boulders and stones, potholes, and narrow places where small cracks had dented the road badly. Then the Land Rover tilted and I had an uncontrollable urge to throw myself inward and away from what I had not noticed until now—the precipice, a hundred feet down, which bordered this section of the road. I unclenched my teeth and started breathing again as Glen clamped the steering wheel sharply to the right and took his foot off the brake. Down went the car, completing the curve with no more than a few inches to spare on either side.

Sinoko and Liklik were sitting tightly on the patrol boxes, packed with essential food and medical supplies, with an air of intense happiness.

Liklik, as I said earlier, was a shrewd fellow. He was also a great actor, an innocent liar of the most magnificent proportions, and hence very good entertainment.

He was now in form for story telling. His mouth was full of the red juice of the betel nut and lime; his sluiced lower lip wriggled dexterously to collect a run of juice that was only too often trying to escape. Sometimes he could not quite manage it and two red streams would flow down from the corners of his mouth, hop off his chest, and splash his lap-lap or sarong with red blobs. And then, with a few "fleeeeps" and "prrrrts" out of the side of the Land Rover, he got rid of his betel nut, took a small homemade cigar butt from above his ear, looked deprecatingly at it, and replaced it saying loudly, too loudly perhaps: "Maski, never mind!" As a nonsmoker and abstainer, being indoctrinated by the Seventh Day Adventists, Sinoko ignored Liklik's "see through" intimation. Unlike him, accepting this broad hint, I gave Liklik the makings.

"This is only a story," Liklik said, "something I tell my children so they will not be bush kanakas (simple peasants) and to make them go to school."

"There were two men in my village," he began, "Makis and Takis. Makis was a true bush kanaka. Takis went to mission school when he was a boy. One day Takis went up to the bush to see a pandanus tree. When he arrived, however, he found that the pandanus wasn't bearing any nuts. So instead he climbed a pandanus tree that belonged to Makis and his wives, and began cutting the nuts. One of the nuts fell near Makis' hut."

Makis asked one of his wives, "What fell there near the door of the house?"

"A pandanus nut," she said. They asked the pandanus nut, "Where did you come from? Did a kokomo (hornbill) throw you down?" The pandanus shook its head. "Did someone climb you?" The pandanus nodded.

So Makis went out to see Takis sitting on top of the pandanus tree. He went back to get his two teeth to fight with and put them in. He returned saying, "Hey! Who said you could climb my pandanus? Do you think that's a wild pandanus?"

"It is not your pandanus," Takis answered.

"If you talk like that, how will you get down from there today and get away? If you come down, I'll eat you!"

"I will come down."

"You will come down, eh? Where will you hide?"

"I will hide in the bottom of the wild ginger." At this, Makis cut down all the bottoms of the wild ginger with his teeth.

"Now where will you hide?"

"I will come down. I will come down in your number one wife's hair." Makis cut his number one wife's hair.

"Now where will you go?"

"I will go hide under your number one and number two wives." Makis went and killed his two wives.

"And where will you go now?"

"I will hide under your balls." So Makis bent down and cut his balls with his teeth. Now he was no man. Then he died. He couldn't come back to his village as a spirit without his balls. So Takis ate his fill of pandanus nuts, and came down and left.

With Sinoko's exclamation of "Oh man, man oh man," so ended Liklik's tale, together with our hectic six-hour ride.

I felt immensely privileged to be back at Okapa. It might have been the effect of the rough ride, but the first thing I noticed on setting foot in this place was a sensation of stepping onto a weightless orbit. The ground seemed to lift to my feet and the distant mountain appeared to swing around my head.

This was not the same Okapa that I had known so well not long ago—just an earth's crust, wide open to the sun; there was nothing nearby except the tall russet grass, clumps of ancient bamboo, and the semifinished house of John MacArthur, surrounded by scattered grass huts.

One hut stood in the deep shadows of a casuarina grove, submerged, from above as well as below, by a hundred hues of plants and shrubs. It was completely absolved of its previous homelessness.

The soft wooded casuarina tree grows rapidly, and it did not take long before it topped the thatched roofs of the village houses, extending branches to cover the sky and shut out the surrounding landscape. The wooded air of the present settlement had a beguiling charm, a romantic remoteness, an integrity and completeness of its own.

When we stepped onto the small verandah of John Colman's house, now completed and painted in white with blue trim, I was confronted by the dark, tall, and dignified figure of Apekono. He spoke a few rapid words, then, with flair, stepped back and came to attention in the approved manner, his arm lifted in a smart salute. He was now Luluai, or Mayor. Without thinking,

I arranged my arms to receive and give the customary embrace, moving my hands down his back and thighs. Later, it came to me that Apekono had been surprised when I met him this way instead of shaking his hands. This had not been my plan, but I was glad that I had fallen automatically into the local greeting, for I am sure it disarmed him, paving the way for the closeness between us that would develop later.

This renewal of acquaintanceship, however, was rather strained for me. Apekono and I sat down together on the bench while John and Glen left to load the Land Rover with vegetables for the return trip to Kainantu. I did not know what to say to Apekono. His slightly languid manner, most uncharacteristic of him, did not help. We smoked for a while in silence and I became more discomfited. At last I managed to ask him about the nine Kuru cases I had seen during my last visit. I received a laconic answer, "Olgera in-dai pinis na planty moa Kuru i kamap," meaning that they had all died and plenty more Kuru was appearing.

Apekono showed no signs of distress, and when he rose to leave, embraced me naturally; the ease of his gesture went far to relieve the weight he had placed on my mind. All nine cases of Kuru dead within less than one year —this seared into my brain like a hot iron. Was Kuru then always a fatal disorder?

The first few days were among the most difficult I have ever faced. I had to find a way to obtain the necessary information from this human laboratory, information of vital importance for fruitful research on Kuru, which I feared might eventually affect the entire population of this particular community.

From John Colman I had obtained important ethnographic information on the region: It had a geographical

elevation of three to seven thousand feet, and its mountainous terrain was dissected by broad, deep valleys. The
total population of all the villages and hamlets was over
thirty thousand, spread over about a thousand square
miles. The entire region was inhabited by eight culturally
and linguistically different groups. The Fore ethnic
group was the largest, with approximately ten thousand
members, and extended into the neighboring groups of
Yagaria, Yate, Kanite, Usurufa, Keiagana, Auyana, and
Gimi peoples. Deep in the southeast there was a remote
settlement of Kukukuku people who had no contact with
the neighboring groups, and who were separated from
the rest by the formidable barrier of the Lamari river.

Here among the Fore and its neighboring groups, as
elsewhere in the Highlands, there was no chief in the
accepted sense of the word. Groups of villages had established a special bond, based mainly on their proximity to
one another, and each group, each village even, enjoyed
autonomy in its own affairs, guided by the general tradi-
tions of the tribe. The arrangement was similar to that of
the British Commonwealth. The different units of the
tribe were held together by virtue of the strong internal
cohesion of a common outlook, interest, or language.

The Fore people were polygamous. Wives were usually obtained from within the same group, but would, on
occasion, be sought from some friendly neighboring
group.

According to John, the cultural and social structure
was relatively uniform throughout the region, apart from
the practice of child marriage among the Gimi linguistic
group, revenge killing for Kuru sorcery, called Tukabu,
and ritual cannibalism among Fore society.

Although this information was valuable, I needed
more explicit knowledge. I needed broad ethnomedical

data on the region that John could not provide. I recognized that a government patrol officer can hardly be expected to give the same critical attention to a census record that an anthropologist, demographer, or epidemiologist might. Thus, it is certainly true that critical demographic or epidemiological work cannot be done with the usual census records and sketchy ethnographic information. Each linguistic group required its own approach.

The question of how to collect expedient ethnographic data perturbed me from the moment I arrived. The answer was vital for my forthcoming epidemiological studies of Kuru.

I remembered the advocacy of my friend and mentor Camilla Wedgwood, the anthropologist, that a basic requirement for biomedical research or any anthropological field study is an adequate medium of communication. Significant means of communication include language and the formation of trust and understanding with the selected community. This, in her view, would be a great aid in learning the traditional beliefs and practices of a particular group. In addition, establishing close contact with children also helps create a genial social intercourse with the community, and New Guineans are very fond of their youngsters.

All this was more easily projected than accomplished. In spite of my friendship with Apekono, the general attitude toward me was one of suspicion and even fear. I hoped that their suspicion was more of an observant, scrutinizing, and cautious character than complete distrust. I was keenly aware of their black eyes upon me during my rounds of the community. They seemed to be taking me apart, examining the depth of my smile and sincerity of each spoken word. They would cordially greet me and invite me to the men's house,

where I would be enthusiastically welcomed and show-
ered with a proud host's unstinting attentions. But once
out of this ritualized hospitality, I was again under the
cover of their suspicion and fear.

Only much later did I realize that this warm friendli-
ness that accompanies the ritual was genuine, deeply felt,
and extremely moving. In the men's house, these martial
men who will fight to the death for their own gardens, for
someone else's garden, for their pigs or women, or to
avenge any slight to their honor, were the epitome of
cordiality, gentle dignity, and brotherly affection.

Their metamorphosis was not altogether surprising.
In a society in which survival depends upon a man's
physical and psychological toughness, there is little
chance to express such emotions as affection and tender-
ness. The guest in the men's house fulfils in ritual fashion
the role of the idealized friend. This dream of the perfect
friend, always a man, was the fantasy of every male of
Fore and its neighboring groups. The friend, however,
had to be a stranger, for all Fore and the adjacent linguistic tribes were, by the very nature of their harsh and com-
petitive society, rivals and potential enemies. Naturally,
given these qualifications, friendship, trust, and understanding among these people were rare indeed. Yet the
dream persisted and was acted out in the rite of hospitality whenever the opportunity arose.

I do acknowledge Camilla's philosophy that a man is
worth as many men as he knows languages. In this mountainous countryside, however, there was no common language. Their were eight distinct languages, and which of
these I should learn was a vexing question, a barrier that
had to be overcome.

I found myself fingering the events of the recent past
like a rosary. Each occurrence, each learning experience,

each mistake was now a bead and its own space, creating
a string of beauty for remembering and enlightenment.

It is so easy to do the wrong thing, even when you
mean well. It is so easy to mistake the intention of the
natives or for them to misinterpret your meaning, even
when you are acquainted with their customs, beliefs, and
language.

For example, when you come to a village for the first
time, you may see a little child, and wishing to show like
a parliamentary candidate that you love children, and
also meaning to compliment the parents, you pat the child
on the head and say, "Atta boy, Tootsie-Wootsie," and
move along swollen with good-will toward all, thinking
that perhaps you have initiated a friendly relationship.

It will never be forgotten, however, that at such and
such a village on such and such a day you patted little Ero
on the head. And since a few days later Ero got a fever and
died, it is now known from one end of the tribe to the other
that you cast an evil spell on him. Didn't every one see
you do it? Wasn't that child all right until you did it? Your
next visit will not be a glorious success.

One must avoid trying to make a good impression,
and be satisfied and grateful simply not to make a bad
one. Should someone seem very friendly with you at first
sight, it is usually best to dismiss him after a polite inter-
val. You never know what reputation he enjoys among
his own; he might be just a "rabisman," a person of no
account or without honor. To Highlanders, a loss of hon-
or is worse than death, since it renders them unworthy of
the name of Chimbu, Goilala, and so on. Most often, your
first acquaintances are such pariahs; but the Highlander
produces the best wine last. Showing aloofness may well
be preferable to an exaggerated affability. These people
are not easily fooled; in fact they are not fooled at all.

Look again through the eyes of the tribesman. He has seen you visit his village and cure his sick. If there is a doctor-boy or native medical assistant, you will come more often and the villagers will never again be sick and will increase in number and make a powerful village. There are always old scores to be settled.

Even when you have established contact with a tribe and work is ready to begin, there are still problems that will frustrate and delay conversation for years.

For example, village A is assigned a doctor-boy. He is a good fellow, but cannot help being young and handsome. You can guess the rest. A mountain lass fastens her eye on him and says "Hai! Carry-leg with me!" She jilts her own boyfriend, which the villagers will not hear of. Trouble brews, and the only solution is to move the doctor-boy. So you replace him with a married one. That will fix things, you would think. A few months later, however, you get a message from the doctor-boy's wife. She wants to go home so off she goes with the doctor-boy-husband trailing behind.

A year has elapsed in village A and you are right back where you began. And if there are hundreds of villages, the difficulties will be proportionally increased.

Meanwhile, you ask the locals to let you send a few young boys to doctor-boy's school. If suitable, they will come back later. Well devised, you would think! They in turn offer you a boy who is hard of hearing and crippled— of no use to the village, so let's give him to the government. You are expected to teach a half deaf and crippled boy, and he is expected to look after all the villages of the clan. You then agree to take him if you also get four more of your own choice. The bargaining gets you two.

The villagers now want to know if the lads will return to their own clan when trained. The villagers are as cunning and as cute as pet foxes. No villagers are willing to supply boys to be trained as doctor-boys if they are later to be posted to another clan: Why should we supply boys to help advance others while we ourselves lag behind?

You may try to get out of that by pairing off the clans. Thus you say to the people of clan A, "When your boys are trained they will be posted to clan B and the boys from clan B will come here." "Oh no," they respond, "the people of clan B are always casting evil spells on our people."

Then you say, "But you will have clan B's boys here so their people will be afraid to try any tricks on your boys. Anyway, clan B's people say you are always casting spells on them!"

A witty reply awaits you, "Oh no! We don't do that. Those fellows are only a mob of liars at best. And if their boy happened to die—just die, you know—they'd say we had bewitched him and we'd have to pay compensation even though we didn't do a thing."

"And if your boy died in clan B, wouldn't they have to pay?"

"Ah, that's different! You see no one just dies in clan B. They are all bewitched."

"Isn't it true that some of your villagers bewitch one another?"

"Yes, it is! But we can undo those spells."

"All of them?"

"Some of them," they would demur.

So you post a doctor-boy only after long deliberation, and no matter where you would send him, you always realize later that it was the wrong place.

After a few days of mental labor, of searching for a way to obtain the medical and cultural facts on Kuru, and how to generate an atmosphere of trust, I arrived at a conclusion. I decided to be cool and cautious; observe and learn slowly, engage in a process of discovery rather than attempt instantly to absorb an endless mass of material, losing sight of this jungle disease's forest because of its impenetrable thickness of vegetation and trees.

John's proposal that we partake of his well-prepared patrol to Kukukuku countryside was eagerly accepted by Sinoko and, with some reservations, by me.

I considered that an exploratory patrol to a territory unknown to the white man, a territory of "manhunters in bark cloak," was unjustified. I had come here to study Kuru, not to search out a new image of God, though this was very tempting. Then I had second thoughts. Why not? To gain a brief glimpse into a truly neolithic world would not deflect me from my ultimate objective. Besides, I could check to see whether the Kuru scourge was also known there.

John's forthcoming patrol was intended to be a joint venture with the number one Kiap, Henry West, covering an unexplored terrain of the left bank of the river Lamari, which is the demarcation line between the Kukukuku and their neighbors to the northwest, the Fore.

Because of the long distance to be covered and the sparseness of the population, John expected to be away for at least twenty days. By long distance I do not mean hundreds of miles, but rather distances that take an unusually long time to traverse because of the rough terrain encountered or a complete lack of roads or even crude bridle paths. Distance in the Highlands is never referred to in miles, but in hours—four hour's walk, eight hard hours' walk, three days' walk, and so on. Mileage is deceptive. A mile-long walk along the beach may take only twenty minutes, whereas a mile in the pathless mountains may take as much two hours and be as fatiguing as ten.

When one decides to take on a twenty-day journey, as John did, he must prepare accordingly. Knowing the unforeseen delays that can occur, one should add fifty percent to his supplies and make provision for thirty days. After all, boxes of food and trading items may be lost to a flooding stream or river; or one may be marooned for three or four days; or one may encounter unfriendly villagers who refuse to sell any part of their local food supply. Or, again, one may find it necessary to stay longer in some villages than anticipated.

Just before I teamed up with John and Harry for their long march beyond that wall of serried ranges and turbulent unbridged rivers, John prepared me with a short account of Kukukuku tribal histories.

Probably the most refractory people in all of Australian New Guinea were the ill-reputed Kukukuku, who have been described as notorious killers, living in independent groups, isolated by valleys and ranges and mutual hostility.

Most of the Kukukuku tribes have been contacted repeatedly by government patrols during the last four decades—and a number of patrol officers and other trespassers have been wounded by these diminutive but ferocious mountaineers. Their territory extends from the southeast side of Kainantu and almost down to the coast.

In spite of the Australian Government's intense policy of pacification, the general attitude of the Kukukuku toward any invader had not become friendlier. Not even the establishment of a Patrol Post far southeast from Kainantu was able to pacify these "stubborn" stone age warriors. And a year or so ago an American ethnologist still found the Kukukuku country, except for a few small groups that were considered to be under "control," unsafe for anyone but a strongly armed party. One of the last groups of Kukukuku untraced in this zone were two Kukukuku linguistic families—one in the southwest and the other in the northwest section—whose domain was represented by steep grassy ridges and slopes high above the Lamari river.

In order to avoid tedious circumlocutions, I shall give a summary of my four-day unsentimental venture into the "uncontrolled" area beyond the Lamari. The following notes are based on both insider's information and personal observations. A few peculiar findings were supplemented by John Colman's studies concerning the population on the "other side" of the Kukukuku country.

Waiajeke, a bright young lad and one of the ugliest ducklings I have ever encountered, whom John brought to Okapa from his patrol, was an extremely helpful informant. He spent most of his life with the Fore, although he was a Kukukuku—a fact that facilitated and enriched our conversation in many respects.

I was satisfied with finding no evidence of Kuru among the Kukukuku, who categorically denied knowing anything about it. Medically, there was a fair amount of severe yaws and tropical ulceration of the legs, which certainly indicated extensive problems. Coughs and incipient bronchitis were fairly frequent. Differing from the Fore, these people did not use deep pit latrines or any other kind of sanitary arrangements. They relieved themselves anywhere, often in the bush immediately adjacent to their settlements. Their hygiene was therefore inadequate, as was the rubbish disposal, which was not confined to prescribed places.

Gardens were well fenced and decorated with borders of flowering plants. The houses were often encircled with floral borders and flower beds. The Kukukuku obviously had an eye for decoration, color, and esthetics.

Landscaping gardens and villages was a fine art among many Highland natives, but especially the Kukukuku.

All villages were stockaded and isolated on ridges and well-protected prominences. The settlements consisted of six to twelve thatched round houses, mostly on stilts. Except for a house of igloo-like shape without the raised floor and built from kunai grass, the residence for the young unmarried men, each house in the village was occupied by one family. The household consisted of a husband with up to four wives and their children, minus the boys after the second ritualistic initiation. Each village or hamlet had a headman, who had a certain amount of authority in everyday life and warfare. The chief's eldest wife was said to be the "boss" of the women.

Among the Kukukuku only the males had to undergo initiation rites. At the age of five to seven, the naked boys' noses were pierced and their names were changed. They were also then given a fan-shaped pubic covering made of grass. The next initiation ceremony took place when they were considered adolescent, at the age of at least 12. Piercing of the nasal septum was performed again, and the nose was fitted with a short piece of yellow bamboo, often thicker than an ordinary lead pencil, or wild pig tusks. Once more the youngsters' names were changed and now extra grass skirts with diagonal, yellow-braided chest bands and belly bands were supplied. This, then, was the clothing and adornment of an "initiated" youth and continued for the adult men. The fan-shaped grass skirts were fastened one atop the other and, together with girdles of human or cassowary bones, were never taken off. The under-layers were left on, even in sleep, until they rotted and new ones were added on top.

The Kukukuku's menu consisted of quite a variety of food. Some imported vegetables, such as sweet potatoes,

taro, yams, bananas, sugarcane, and the like, were cultivated in the gardens using digging-stick agriculture.
Others were collected in the bush as seeds, nuts, berries,
fruits, certain leaves, and roots.

It is noteworthy that some Kukukuku groups from
the upper Lamari had a marvelous engineering ability for
irrigation and manufacture of salt. They terraced the
sides of the mountain's deep slopes, delivering water to
the terraces by irrigation using bamboo pipes stretched in
different directions. The vegetable salt was produced by
burning and extracting water-soluble salt from the ash of
local pitpit or cane.

Meat was said to be difficult to come by. Wild animals, which were relatively scanty, were hunted with
bows and arrows. Slings or even spring-traps were used
for wild pigs, possums, and cassowaries, though the latter were sometimes captured as chicks and raised. They
were locked in the men's house during the night, thus
serving as a living alarm device, similar to the famous
geese of the Roman Capitol.

Religious thoughts and feelings of the Lamari Kukukuku concentrated on the spirits of their dead relatives.
Without hesitation, they admitted that they were afraid
of these spirits; even of the spirits of harmless little children who had died. These spirits were believed to bring
sickness and disaster, rather than good. Contrary to the
Fore people, sorcery, especially "poison magic," was not
practiced by the Lamari Kukukuku. The spirits of the
dead did enough mischief without being especially asked
to and they were considered to be quite independent in
their activities.

The funeral customs were not the same throughout
the Kukukuku tribes. Among some tribes smoking and
mummification had been practiced for battle victims and

VIPs. In other groups earth burial in the sitting position was the rule. Among the Lamari Kukukuku, when any member of the group died, the whole "family" (often more than one village) came together in order to mourn and lament for several days. Then the body was carried away to a remote place where all deceased people were "buried." A wooden platform would be made, then covered with a series of parallel pieces of sugarcane. The body was then placed on the sugar-bed without adornment or clothing, and the whole setup was placed in the branches of a tree. Months or years later, when only the skeleton was left, the rotten corpse was pulled down and the bones were thrown into the bush. Some of the bones, such as a mandible, clavicle, and tibia bone were put into a net bag that the women hung around their neck, and were used by the men as waist decorations.

The practice of cannibalism, ritual or otherwise, was strictly denied by these Kukukuku tribes.

I took an instinctive liking to these "bark-cloaked man-hunters." Their louse-infested grass kilts prudishly concealed their genitals, their vanity, their independence, and their arrogance, and their acquisitiveness made them an intriguing people to study. They were more fascinating than any other New Guinea natives I had yet encountered.

The Fore region, which seemed so large at first, appeared to shrink with time. The fact was that I was becoming accustomed to it. I had also made some mental adjustments. If I had to go to a village 20 miles away, I began to realize there was no need to set a speed record, or to return the same day or the same week for that matter.

I began to flirt with the Golden Rule: Never put off till tomorrow what you can do today; and came up with a version that seemed more suited to the local situation:

Never do today what can be done as well tomorrow... convinced that it would recompense my study of Kuru.

I approached cases of alleged Kuru sorcery with the greatest possible sympathy and tolerance, and encouraged people to speak openly to me about it. The results were slow to come at first, for I did not try to hurry them. Later there would be more Kuru cases than I could study.

Though I scored a pleasing result in "case detection," the *modus operandi* of Kuru sorcery was still concealed from me under the aegis of strict taboos. It would take a long time, possibly forever, to break this immutable distrust. My pessimism and expectation now rolled into one. The only hope of exposing this strongly guarded secret was Liklik.

Past experience showed that members of an indigenous population, though from different cultural groups, can converse much more intimately about their personal circumstances to those of a similar cultural background. Thus, Liklik was very useful in establishing contact and trust with the Fores because he knew a few of them already. The ancient tribal incisions on his forehead gave him prestige with the Fore; the older men would say, "Here is a man who can tell big stories, here is a man we can speak to, trust, and understand."

I had told Liklik of the Tukabu and Kuru in general and also of Apekono's story. He was now to work alone quietly and find out all he could about Kuru sorcery while I continued to study Kuru case histories.

By mid-December I was fortunate enough to be studying the clinical aspects of the twenty-seven cases of Kuru brought to Okapa and another eleven in surrounding villages. It appeared to me that most occurred south of Fore. The disorder affected principally females, but almost one quarter of the cases were in children of both sexes.

It was noted that Kuru was remarkably uniform in its symptoms and clinical course. In fact, so unvaried was the clinical picture that its stages were described by the natives in almost unvarying form, and both the disease and descriptions of its stages had become part of the traditional magic lore of the Fore people.

The sharp-witted Liklik, as I might have foreseen, proved himself to be a first-rate emissary. Typical of his nature, he commenced his story about Kuru sorcery with a rather long preamble. "Hear me, Number One," he said one rainy evening at John's place. "I am not afraid of Kuru sorcery. These Fores don't know a thing about real magic! Not like us, the Tairoras! They call it sorcery, ha! It is simple to make Kuru poison. Boys can do it; every man can if he has the right stuff. Very well! I am not afraid. OK. I am not afraid of even the biggest wild pig. Did I ever tell you how I killed a boar with no bow or arrows?"

Without waiting for my response he continued.

"Well, it was like this. I had one dog, but he was only a pup. I had a bow and arrows too. I saw a boar deep in the bush close to Aiyura village. The dog stopped him and I came up with my bow and arrows. OK! I shot at him, but it only scratched him. He attacked the pup, but he ran. He was only a pup. OK. Then the boar came for me. I dropped my bow and arrows. All right! I tried to pick up my bow and arrows when the big boar, big fella true, attacked me. Very well! Just as he was about to pierce me with his long tusks I jumped. I jumped on his back and sat and held on. Oh man, oh man, says I, I'll be here till sundown. No! I took off my laplap and twisted it around his long nose. Very well...then I pulled his head up and up, till I shut his breath. I killed him like that. That is true. Ask anyone. My little brother (cousin) Tarako, he is dead now, he saw me."

After puffing away at the fourth fag of my pernicious weed, he told me at last all he had found out about Kuru sorcery.

There were no specialized Kuru practioners of execution. It could be inflicted upon the intended prey by any male member in the community. Kuru was worked upon its victim by a variety of methods, but basically it involved the following:

The sorcerer requires a portion of the victim's excreta or a fragment of sweet potato thrown away by a potential victim. He places it in a "magic bundle" made up of special pieces of bark, twigs, and leaves, with fine grass, taro leaves, green croton, and sweet potato leaves. This is bound tightly together with a twig protruding. The bundle is named along with the burying, at which point the victim has his or her first sign of sorcery in the form of unsteady gait or "loose knees." The sorcerer returns to beat the bundle intermittently, and at each beating attacks are intensified until the victim spends most of his time in his own house, or hobbles around with a stick. As the magic bundle begins to disintegrate, a stench rises from the victim's body; tremors appear and the victim is unable to move at all. Finally maggots appear and death is imminent.

Another procedure is to obtain a piece of the female victim's grass skirt, and place it in a wild taro root; this serves as the base of the "magic bundle" (made up of special leaves, bark, and similar ingredients), which is placed in swampy ground, and left to disintegrate. The victim's skin becomes cold, she starts to shiver, with intermittent loss of muscular control: she can walk only with the help of a stick. The attacks become more severe, until finally she is confined to her hut, her body begins to stink, maggots appear, and she dies.

In some instances, a "magic bundle" may be placed in a native pit latrine, ground and left to disintegrate. The victim's skin becomes cold, she starts to shiver, with intermittent loss of muscular control: she can walk only with the help of a stick. The attacks become more severe, until finally she is confined to her hut, her body begins to stink, maggots appear, and she dies.

In some instances, a "magic bundle" may be placed in a native pit latrine, where constant defecation causes it to agitate and accordingly shake its intended victim.

There is yet another method to induce Kuru. The sorcerer collects a piece of sugarcane fiber discarded by the victim, warms it over a fire, and prepares a "magic bundle" by adding the poisonous leaf and binding it with prickly twine. He then places it in the nest of a special bird. The nest is constructed of twigs at the base of a small bush. All around its base are bird droppings, together with fragments of possum, pig, cassowary, and human excrement, and pieces of moss collected by this bird. The sorcerer makes a hole in the nest with a stick held at arm's length, throws in the bundle, and covers it up. The bird eventually returns and moves from twig to twig shaking both the nest and the bush. This causes the victim to "shake." The shaking increases as the bird flies to and from its nest carrying old fragments it has found. The victim becomes quite debilitated with even more severe trembling and finally dies.

Liklik's constructive account of Kuru sorcery, though of unverified authenticity that called for checking, cast aside some of my presumptions.

One point I could not determine to my own satisfaction was how much the Fores really believed in their Kuru sorcery. I sometimes had a feeling (it was only a feeling) that the individual might harbor a doubt, though he never wavered in the slightest manner in public. I tried to nourish that little doubt if it was there and create it if it were not. Alas, it seemed to me that belief in Kuru among the Fore was deep-rooted and unbending. It was a phenomenon that western medicine could not in any way influence or control. The Fore may say, "We understand how strong Kuru is—medical scientists do not."

On the whole, the attitude toward Kuru was one of resignation and despair. The only sound remedy for this attitude would be for a significant number of Kuru sufferers to be cured. Until that could be done, it was improbable that any amount of explanation or propaganda would achieve much in removing the main cause of suspicion and insecurity in an otherwise harmonious society.

Christmas drew nigh. I did not find the answers to the questions I asked about Kuru, yet I did discover that there were questions for which answers might be sought, and felt now better equipped to seek them.

Back in Kainantu, on Christmas Day, I wrote a report to John Gunther. In a few words, without technical gibberish, I postulated, "on October 22nd I left the station (Kainantu) for Moke area to investigate a form of encephalitis in this area called Kuru...."

With resolute confidence I awaited his usual prompt and inspiring response.

Opening the Pathway
to Kuru Research

Yuletide is always a time for great festivity and what
is known as sing-sing among New Guineans. The celebration continues nonstop for days, undeterred by cloud-
bursts of rain or darkness of night. This year's annual
sing-sing attracted thousands of natives of both sexes;
hundreds of maidens and warriors gorgeously plumed
and bedecked in dazzling colors assembled to dance and
celebrate, in keeping with a centuries-old tradition.

The arrangement of this event was a tremendously
important affair for all the people. For weeks the men
were busy making traps for wild pigs, wallabies, cassowaries, possums, and birds, and rounding up all domestic pigs of worthy size to be killed on the appointed day.
The boys chopped wood from the mountains and afar for
the fires. The women brought load after load from the
gardens: taro, yams, tapioca, bananas, sweet potatoes,
and other foodstuffs. And when the pyres of firewood
were laid across the mouths of the earth ovens to cook a
few hundred pigs, along with uncounted pyramids of
potatoes and other vegetables, and all was in readiness
for the ceremony, the people were called together.

Opinions vary on the significance of the sing-sing.
My impression seemed to confirm the belief that the rites
are performed to propitiate the tribal spirits and so ensure strength. Strength in this Highland society does not

refer to physical qualities only; its larger meaning signi-
fies a constellation of traits and skills that characterize the
ideal man—qualities and aptitudes that the society seeks
to encourage and instill in all its boys. For groups such as
the clan, strength is measured in wealth and number—
mainly the number of men and pigs. Indeed this was seen
clearly in the vast prideful volume of the men's voices, in
the massive slaughter of pigs, and in the spectacular and
gaudy decorations.

The "repertoire" of this year's sing-sing was exceptionally colorful. One particularly deliberate and impressive ceremonial display of "Mudmen" attracted my attention. This began with the dancers' appearance, one by
one, from among the bushes, their naked bodies smeared
with white clay. They wore gigantic clay heads, distorted
and framed with pig's tusks in the masks' mouths. Their
dress was eyecatching to say the least, and their bodies
were grayish rather than white, giving them the bizarre
aspect of supple and insubstantial ghosts.

The dancers advanced silently with slow, rhythmic
steps, shaking the leafed branches in their hands. Then
another group of dancers, identically dressed, made its
appearance, carrying bows and arrows. The two groups
approached each other cautiously, step by step. They
moved slowly at first, then suddenly with flaring tempo.
The mime became frantic, until the climax was reached.
Then, in utter stillness, the dancers, still brandishing their
bows and arrows and branches, vanished into the bushes.

The significance of this dance, Liklik assured me, is
to portray a great victory of the past over the enemies of
the tribe, which was won by the ruse of lying in ambush
in a swamp, covered by mud.

My interpretation, however, was that the gray-white
forms of the dancers symbolized the souls of the departed

brave ancestors. In fact, these two interpretations are not necessarily contradictory. Why shouldn't it be performed to simultaneously commemorate a victory and to represent the spirits of those who won the victory?

For the first few days of the festival, I was one with the crowd of admirers, fascinated by the showmanship and elaborate dress of the participants. Every one of these magnificent warriors seemed to stress the value of human decoration. Far from being actors' costumes, the feathers, headdresses, and paints were part of a well-defined rite. They symbolized and expressed a tradition. The plumes and feathers had a religious significance not unlike that of priestly vestments. The ceremonial dances, beplumed and garnished with dazzling color, were part of their culture for uncounted centuries. The bone and other objects worn in the nose were signs and symbols as well.

The decorated, dark-skinned maidens were particularly attractive, with heavy thick pigment applied to the face, neck, and arms in patterns of red, yellow, and black, and perhaps other colors. The painting was done in definite patterns of triangles, squares, and other symmetrical designs.

The belles were of sturdy build, well muscled and without a discernible "figure," in the Occidental meaning of that term. They wore the traditional dress of the Highlands, which consisted of a rather provocative skirt with a narrow panel of fiber cords that dangled from the waist to slightly below the knees. To my eyes it was more of an ornament than a covering, for it moved with every movement and concealed little or, in most cases, nothing. All were topless and carried themselves so as to exhibit to best advantage the large, well-formed, bouncing breasts that nature had so generously bestowed upon them. Their bodies were smeared with a glistening unguent that gave a tawny cast to their dark skin, catching and reflecting every ray of sunlight that filtered through the trees as though they were clothed in see-through satin.

The men's paints and plumes were even more spectacular than the women's. They were decorated in the full splendid panoply of war. Chests and faces were daubed with paint or pig grease mixed with charcoal, which gave an ebony cast to their muscular bodies, as though they were clothed in polished steel. This was punctuated dramatically by the silver mother-of-pearl crescent around the neck. The headdress of tossing array, made of plumes of cassowaries, parrots, and birds of paradise, was a towering structure that added several feet to the man's normal height. It waved in the slightest breeze and undulated when they moved. It was a gleaming brilliant mass, matching their intricate dancing steps. In their ceremonial decoration the men appeared like walking shrines.

The most lasting impression for me, however, was of the ritual display of the sing-sing itself. As the great festival progressed, the voice of the singer grew gradually from two or three syllables to long strings of vowels of "oo-ooo-yee-yaah-eee-yooo," slowly joining the deep-throated shouts of the men. The ululating notes of old women trailed away in lonely sobs of "oo-ee-oo," then rose again. These stylized cries told with genuine emotion that the spirits of their dead lovers were among the dancers. The cries of the flutes, the deep beats of the hour-glass-shaped drums, and, rising above all, the iridescent orchestration of a hundred plumes were accompaniment to the pounding sound of bare feet crashing on the dancing ground. They danced with increasing seriousness, completely absorbed by their rhythmic movements. Their faces were expressionless and their eyes fixed on some distant point only they could see.

My personal interest had faded during the first set of sing-sing. By the fourth day the feast, now whipped to an emotional frenzy, grew stale and detestable. The celebration continued, with the squeal of the pigs heard for days as they were bludgeoned to death. The warm carcasses were split open, spilling blood and entrails on the dusty sing-sing ground. The steaming smell attracted scraggy dogs who sneered distrustfully near the scene of the carnage. The pile of refuse grew and the air became heavy and nauseating, with the smells of raw flesh and singed bristle, of sour, rotten greens, and, from nearby bushes, of malodorous human waste. The noise and movements were overwhelming, as was the stench of sweating, unwashed bodies, pressed against each other. The flames from torches of pandanus roots threw leaping shadows over the faces of the dancers, making them no longer recognizable. Frenzy could be seen in all of the faces, glittering with perspiration, red paint trickling into their eyes.

I felt as if I had been plunged into an inferno. This sensation was reinforced by the wriggling bodies of the women. With their hands of mutilated fingers—cut off at the joint while mourning the death of husband or pig—they quivered nervously in front of the male dancers, their breasts vigorously swinging from side to side like the long ears of a playful spaniel. Their skin rippled between throat and navel while they contorted the upper parts of their bodies.

When it was all over, I settled in with thoughts of sorrow, my attention wandering, passing above the heads of the crowd. Slinging their net hold-alls over their backs, the natives began to trudge back over the muddy mountain tracks. The great festival had come to an end. Sounds had ceased, leaving only a momentary echo on the threshold of days to come.

When experiencing happiness, we are often unconscious of it. Only when time passes and we look back do we suddenly realize—sometimes with astonishment—how happy we had been. But on that day—the first month of the New Year, nineteen hundred and fifty-seven—I knew I was happy. I read two freshly arrived letters with fumbling excitement. And I was happy. The letters had been short and to the point, but the few lines of impersonal typescript contained all that I could wish to read.

Kuru, the dreaded, abundant scourge, was now on its way to the research laboratory....

One letter was from John Gunther, who gave the green light for Kuru research. In securing expert laboratory facilities, he never dreamed that one of the most exciting adventures in virology would soon be brewing in his own department.

And Gray Anderson, the distinguished Australian virologist from the Walter and Eliza Hall Institute of Medical Research in Melbourne, in his separate letter to me, expressed his sincere willingness to examine the specimens for Kuru investigation in his laboratory. At that time he had no idea that he would be testing the first serological and organic specimens of Kuru, tests that would much later prove a door ajar into the shadowy mansions of other cerebral disorders.

We—the newly appointed native driver, Liklik, who had now become my right hand, and I—were riding once again to Okapa, this time in a brand new Land Rover laden with a kerosene-operated refrigerator, a hand sewing machine for Sinoko's family, and a luxurious cargo of imported freezer goods, such as butter, steak, calf's liver, rabbit, and, my favorite, sheep's brain. Naturally there was a case of claret and some bottles of dark rum, known by Liklik as "kus marasin," or medicine against colds.

The road had improved noticeably since my last ride on it four months ago. The narrow paths had been widened and many new bridges erected. The bridges were not works of art in stone or steel, with graceful arches and sculptured balustrades and statues of nymphs and lions thrown in for good measure. They were primitive yet ingenious structures that spanned about forty feet of gorge cut by mountain streams. The bridge flooring was most uneven, since it consisted of small round tree trunks lashed with vines to large, hard wooden beams. Not a nail was used in these bridges, yet they were strong enough to carry the Land Rover without difficulty.

At Okapa we were met by Sinoko and Apekono in John's deserted house, where a hurried scribbled note of miscellaneous directives was pinned on the wall. The last words of the note, "I shall return," never transpired. To my bitter disappointment, John never did return to Okapa, for he resigned while on leave. When he returned to New Guinea, this time married, he settled as a private citizen in Mount Hagen, the western part of the Highlands. John's decision to resign, revealed to me by the bush telegraph, had been triggered by an unfortunate incident. There were great rewards and great problems during the period of John McArthur's and John Colman's road building. In this particular incident, Colman encountered a human problem concerning a native named Asisi, a "big man" in his tribe and a fine orator.

Bridges were absolutely essential for the success of the road-building project. They called for heavy hardwood timbers from trees that grew high in the mountains. Natives of the tribes were told how many trees and what size would be needed. They agreed to bring them to the bridge and the building sites, where they received a fair price for them. All went smoothly until Asisi began his campaign of defying white man's authority, the government. By doing so, he could hope to boost his stature in the tribe.

Asisi succeeded in pursuading enough of the men to stop delivery of the logs to end the building of the bridges. John took no action against Asisi at first, since he was convinced that such an ambitious blusterer was bound to trip himself up in time. So the bridges were held up for a while and Asisi, heady with temporary victory, spoke louder and louder.

John did not have to wait long. Understanding the native psychology well enough to guess that Asisi might gain greater prestige, and might wield even greater authority than before in convincing the natives not to sell him the hardwood logs, John decided to undercut Asisi's influence. To do this, in spite of its risk and danger, he had to make Asisi lose face in front of his followers.

So word was sent out to different tribes that the Kiap wanted to talk to the tribes that brought the logs from the mountains. He succeeded in assembling a thousand or more natives, including a large crowd of Asisi's followers. John addressed the great assemblage of natives, many of whom greeted him in unfriendly fashion. He saw Asisi among them, and although tempted to face him in this large gathering, did not even look in his direction. When they were all seated on the ground, he launched into a lengthy oration, knowing only too well that natives had no respect for short speeches. Moreover, he was dealing, in the case of Asisi, with a great orator. He repeated, in as flowery a language as possible, all the things his predecessor John had told them before about the many advantages the road would bring them. He spoke of the bridges and the logs, and the price he would offer in advance. He then gave an order to his men to open patrol boxes containing trade goods such as twist tobacco, bush knives, tomahawks, and precious mother-of-pearl shells. He also displayed a cash box filled with silver coins, and offered the native workers the shovels and axes when the road building was completed—a good work incentive.

Last he mentioned Asisi, still not looking in his direction, saying that he had been hearing a great deal about this man—how he had tried to stop villagers from delivering logs and how hehad said he would kill the pigs of any man who worked at bridge-building. Then John declared that this Asisi seemed to be a very "big man," a very important man indeed, to do and say all these things. He would be happy and proud to meet such a man and pay him in a way befitting so outstanding a personage.

Every eye turned to Asisi. John then looked at him for the first time. Asisi was naturally flattered at the attention given him by the Kiap in front of such a large crowd, but at the same time a little uncertain at this turn of events, which he had obviously not expected.

John asked Asisi to step forward to receive his special prize. Asisi, suspicious though he was, could not resist the temptation of a small pile of shells on the ground in front of John, and stepped forward. To exalt his authority, Asisi exclaimed, "I see no shells," meaning that he did not see enough of them. John counted more of them, but Asisi was still "blind," although the pile had grown considerably. Next, John asked Asisi to hold up both hands to receive the largest mother-of-pearl shell. Asisi did so eagerly, and John slipped a pair of handcuffs on Asisi's wrists, "This is the kind of prize the government gives to a 'maus water' —a blusterer like Asisi."

The assembled natives were clearly flabbergasted and seemed to hold their breath a full minute, then let it out in one loud exhalation. Asisi, taken by surprise, didn't utter a word. John was well aware that the natives greatly admired a slick stratagem; thus he felt that they would admire what he had done. The bridge building would be resumed to the satisfaction of all concerned.

Asisi wasn't put into the jail, however. In John's opinion it would be an unwise move, for Asisi could easily become a martyr in the eyes of the natives. Even if he jailed Asisi, he could not force the natives to sell him the hardwood logs if they did not want to. Actually, Asisi was not breaking any law, and John was never one to take the law into his own hands.

So John ordered the removal of the handcuffs from Asisi's wrists and let him go with the greatest insult that one can give to a native, "Asisi—Rabisman."

While on leave in Australia, John received news that Asisi had committed suicide by jumping from a tall hardwood tree, smashing his skull on a giant rock outcrop. John was deeply distressed. His conscience troubled him since he had brought about the loss of face that caused Asisi's death. It was no use telling himself that had Asisi continued to gain influence and fluster people, an entire roadbuilding project, which the people themselves eagerly wanted, might have been lost. I should report that this tale was told me by a storyteller of the darkest jungle, and the dark jungle covers a multitude of stories.

In hope of acquiring a Kiap with the abilities and character of the two previous ones, Liklik and I happily set up housekeeping anew.

My conviction that the collection of Kuru specimens would proceed smoothly with no hindrance happened to be correct. Toward the second week of our arrival we obtained, beyond all expectations, over two dozen blood samples from Kuru subjects. Kuru victims came to Okapa one by one, ungrudgingly, staggering or carried on primitive native stretchers. Underlying this success was Ape-kono's and Sinoko's proficient motivation. I observed strictly all instructions given to me by Gray Anderson. Blood samples were carefully labeled and stored, first in the cold compartment of the refrigerator, thus protecting them from hemolysis (destruction of the red blood corpuscles). After a day or two, I separated the serum and stored it in the freezer. This procedure was incomprehensible to my helping hands, Sinoko and Liklik. In their eyes I was an odd character—obviously "long long," or crazy.

I saw the Kuru sufferers when making my rounds day after day. They were always the same, lying on the ground of a canegrass shed filled with smoke. Their faces were more ghastly than a black death mask, so farcical as to be almost idiotically useless. Day after day I walked sad-eyed among those forlorn people while Sinoko took temperatures and gave injections of penicillin: "shots in the dark."

"What is that?" I asked myself one late evening, perplexed. There, on the ground, was a mother of four children, helpless, with a fixed, idiotic grin. She lay, sullen, shut inside herself for days. Except for the shallow rise and fall of her chest and the occasional twitch of her limbs, she was not moving. On her right was a marasmic baby clinging weakly with his tiny hands to his mother's breast. On the other side was a girl about eleven years of age, sitting cross-legged on the dirty ground. She was holding on her lap a feebly crying infant and trying hard to feed it by spitting premasticated sugar cane into the infant's mouth. Her brother, a few years younger than she, was delousing his mother, now living a vegetable existence in a limbo between life and death. He crushed the ominous vermin between his thumb and index fingers by the dozens and flung them into his mouth. I could see them running over the doomed woman's neck, over her belly, down to her groin, under the soiled grass skirt. In Liklik's opinion, this was a bad omen. It was the first sign of approaching death. When the body temperature begins to drop and blood circulation slacks off, according to him, the lice thick in the hair and on the back of the neck feel the human warmth fading and desperately try to abandon what he calls the "louse box" behind the head.

I stood, motionless, watching Nature's signal of endless sleep. Most young doctors—like obedient servants of Christianity and technology—are inclined to do a great deal more than nothing. With the help of mechanical devices, they often keep the patient's inert body functioning for the sake of granting a few more weeks of life.

But seeing this moribund figure, a mother of four, decline into a state worse than vegetable, I stood waiting for her to die. For Kuru victims, temporary improvement could be more shattering than a quick exit. I bent down, gently unclenching the infant's koala bear-like hands from its mother's breast, and picked up a baby now almost in extremis. I pressed its tiny body to my chest and carried it to Sinoko's wife for expert motherly care.

Pushing through the still chillness, I halted short, for I felt the baby's body suddenly turn flaccid, lifeless, and weightless. A momentary glimpse told me the truth. Tearfully I quoted from the memory of my early youth one of Goethe's ballads, the Erlkonig "Das Kind war tod!"

Liklik's judgment in the matter of the "louse box" proved to be correct. The woman, now mother of three, passed away only a few hours after I left.

Upon entry into John's former office cum courtroom, having been summoned by Liklik and Sinoko, I observed the woman's stark body on the home-made office desk. Liklik joyfully announced that there was no objection from her husband to my looking at her "brain box." As recompense, I would have to pay carriers to take her body home, where she would be buried in her family ground. In addition, I had to give her a blanket to keep her "warm." Both Liklik and Sinoko were looking at me with their faces flushed with success and inducement, as if telling me, "She is all yours. Go ahead, chum!"

Thus, under the light of two hurricane lamps, with flakes of dust and chaff showering from the thatched roof, the first autopsy of a Kuru victim's brain was initiated.

I was no stranger to the protocol for the removal and fixing of brains. It was a straightforward procedure. The first step is the incision of the scalp, from ear to ear over the vertex. The second step consists of peeling the scalp back, one flap to the front and the other to the back of the neck. It took Sinoko and Liklik close to one hour to make the horizontal saw cut around the skull, from forehead to occiput, for it had to be performed with a single hacksaw blade that Liklik found in John's workshop. When the tedious job of sawing off the top of the cranium was completed, I removed the dura mater from around the skull. Gently lifting a fold of membrane with forceps, I slit it with the tip of my scalpel, parting the membrane and revealing the brain itself. The living cerebral cortex was still pulsating, perhaps only in my imagination, and was slightly blueish. Under the lamplight its surface glistened with a clear sheen.

I then removed the brain by cutting the cranial nerves and, by gently lifting the frontal lobes, the optic nerve. Finally the cervical spinal cord was cut and the whole brain and cerebellum, falling backward out of the skull, was in my hands.

I looked with veneration at this vulnerable gel-like substance, laced with delicate arteries and veins. I imagined the billions of neurons with their multiple dendritic branchings under the serous protective covering. Here, I believed, somehow, lay a perilous virus. And as I watched, red blood gradually cleared off the grooves of the sulci, making the brain look dismally gray.

At last the precious Kuru brain was put into a "Gypsona" container filled with glycerin. The common rule for fixing brain was to use formalin-saline solution. This one, however, had to be preserved in glycerin and refrigerated, as instructed by Gray Anderson, for it was to be used not in histological, but in virus isolation work, using a method that involved the inoculation of chick embryo membranes as well as the intracerebral inoculation of suckling and adult mice. To my still unskilled mind, all this was just scientific gobbledegook.

My two valuable assistants were now engaged in "plastic surgery," stuffing the empty cranium with cottonwool and conjoining the two flaps of the scalp.

For no obvious reason I felt tired and while rinsing my hands, viscid from the mixture of glycerine and blood, slightly faint and trembling. Humbled, I seated myself on a rickety bench. Here, in the bush courtroom, now an improvised morgue, in the early morning hours, it seemed somehow right that I sequestered myself with a corpse. I lit one of the twisted-tobacco rolled-in-a-newspaper cigars. It tasted more of newsprint than of tobacco, but the bitter smoke revitalized me. The tip cast a pinkish glow on the rigid figure of the woman before me. I pondered. How many mothers like this one were dying of Kuru, together with their unborn babies and nursing infants who, though not immediate victims of Kuru, were dying from starvation? Did these foresaken womenfolk not accept the practice of transferring their infants to another nursing mother? This I was determined to find out.

What I found, through reliable informants and Apekono himself, depressed me terribly. It was difficult to
believe. The motherless nuclear family was now a common domestic unit. Men longingly recalled the time, not
long past, when a man could find three or four wives to
work in his gardens and care for his pigs and children.
Today a polygamist was almost a rarity because of the
acute shortage of woman. Hence child marriage became
a common practice. In these days it was difficult to find
an adult man who was not affected by the loss of immediate kin as a result of Kuru. One man lost his mother, his
half-sister, two wives, and one son. Another man, from
the same village, had lost three wives and two daughters.
There were more men like these, Apekono informed me.

Men who lost their wives found themselves responsible for the care of several young children, performing
the dual role of mother and father to their families. They
had to carry out not only the traditional heavy work, fenc-
ing and furrowing, but also dig the ground, plant crops,
weed, harvest, cook the food, and feed their children. In
some instances, there was a Kuru-incapacitated wife as
well. If a father was fortunate enough to have a daughter
as his firstborn, she would compensate for the lack of an
adult female laborer in the family, carrying home tremendous loads of garden produce and firewood each evening
and cooking for the family, until she married at twelve or
thirteen and went to live with her husband.

One morning I was invited by Apekono to visit his
"poroman" (friend), a man of the Komira clan named
Taka. We found him in the garden digging sweet potato
and placing them in a "bilum," a string bag made from
bark fibers. After the customary greeting, a standing embrace in which each man held the other's scrotum, Apekono looked askance at the bilum half filled with pota-

toes, jesting at the woman's task Taka was performing.
Taka, took a step backward androse out of the shallow
furrow to deflect Apekono's ridicule lightly by acting the
jester, swaying his hips like a well-padded woman. I
could read nothing in his still and self-contained face.

His eyes, however, were bright points of humiliation
in the shadow of his brows. He was embarrassed, I guess,
by his inappropriate behavior, performing a woman's
task. As if wanting to draw attention from his unmanly
act, winking at Apekono, he pointed at a shelter in the corner of the garden.

Downhill, in the far corner, a rough shelter had been
made to retire to when the sun was high. A small fire
burned in front of this refuge, sending out a thin, hazy
plume of smoke. Inside I could see a young woman sitting on the ground. Her arms were trembling. Her fingers were clasped on her knees as though to brace herself
to maintain equilibrium and arrest her involuntary quiv-
er. Turning her head briefly to look at Apekono and me,
her mouth opened in a hideous empty grin and her whole
body shuddered. She tried to speak. The muffled sound
of her voice echoed the lifeless appearance of her eyes,
like the eyes of a snared wallaby. The lines of prostration
on her mummery face ran from her nose to the corner of
her mouth. She suddenly looked like an old woman.

Then, from the shelter, a rough lean-to of grass and
cane, I heard the feeble cry of an infant. He was lying on
the foliage, sodden by urine and feces. With no hesitation
Taka picked up the crying infant. With the palm of his
hand he wiped the yellowish fetid mucus from the infant's buttocks. He rubbed it off on his bare thigh and
handed the child to his wife.

She treated her infant to a typical display of lavish
affection. Extending her trembling arms slowly in a cus-

tomary gesture of concern, palms upwards, her fingers opening and closing, she eagerly embosomed the small body. Her gesture of accepting the small infant was a graphic accomplishment of uninhibited endearment. Now holding it on her lap she was attempting to force the nipple of her weakened and wasted breast into the infant's mouth. Meeting with no success she lifted the child like a vacillating platter, one trembling hand under its buttocks and the other supporting its neck. Then, bending down, she rained resounding kisses between its legs, stopping only when Taka lifted the child from her lap.

Unwrapping a banana leaf bundle, Taka selected some pieces of sugar cane and put them into his beetle-nut-stained mouth with a hunk of pig fat. When the mixture was thoroughly masticated, he spat it into the infant's mouth, repeating this at short intervals. Finally, he returned the child to his wife's lap. Adding some cooked sweet potatoes to the open-leaf bundle, he put it down beside her. Apart from an occasional shudder, she sat there stiff and still, as always with Kuru's victims.

I squatted beside Apekono. While I listened to them, trying to follow their unemotional recital, I became galled and reacted strongly to the flat tone of their voices. I expected more positive concern, more personal involvement, more essential sympathy, and the lack of these alienated me. Taka's voice was matter of fact as he told Apekono what had happened since he last saw him.

Until recently he had two daughters of marriageable age and a wife of robust health. All went well in his household. Meals were cooked and gardens and pigs were well attended. Then the first daughter got married and went to live with her husband. The second died of Kuru in her teens. His wife became pregnant, and after the birth of the child it became apparent that she also had Kuru. Her condition deteriorated rapidly and Taka began to accompany her to their gardens each day. As her walk became an erratic stagger and she was no longer capable of carrying the newborn child in the net bag hanging from her head, Taka had to carry it. His brother's wives, from whom he might expect help, were unwilling to take the child, for fosterage was not accepted among Fore women. Many Kuru mothers preferred death for their children, rather than the uncertain care of a foster mother.

I looked at Taka. His face was in profile. His broad shoulders, the curve of his back, even his heavily lined face seemed to be relaxed, confirming my impression that his wife's moribund condition and the helpless state of the child did not move him.

The gardens crept silently away, while my thoughts drifted to the natives' attitudes as revealed by the whole pattern of their lives. Their apparent indifference to pain, disease, and death, for instance.

Kuru, for example, is met with a fatalistic attitude, by which the victims and their relatives accept the fatal disease. Victims know positively that they are going to die, since they have observed the terminal incapacitating stages of the disease in many others, and yet they discuss their lethal disease freely and without apparent anxiety. Doomed persons will laugh at their own clumsiness, their inability to get food into their mouths, their own stumbling gait and falls. Kinsmen will join them.

Furthermore, the natives' ritual keening, the cries that were to me a genuine show of emotion, now appeared to be some form of conventionalized expression.

But how mistaken one could be....

I was unprepared for what I saw in Taka's face and the meaning of his words when he suddenly turned to me. I immediately saw the intensity of his eyes, the anxi-

ety-ridden demand that showed on his face. His inarticu-
late struggle seemed even harder in contrast with his
fluency of just a moment ago. He told me simply that his
wife must not die, phrasing his words imperatively, "This
woman cannot die," as though the command might help
to prevent its happening. He added hurriedly that he did
not want to lose her, that his feeling for her, touching his
hand to her stomach, killed him inside. His beseeching
eyes were filled with genuine emotion.

I had never seen a man like him before; nor had I
heard a comparable emotional outburst from any other
Highlander. I wanted to respond in a way that he could
understand, but was drained by my own helplessness,
unable to find the words of comfort and reassurance. So
with *mea culpa* on my lips, I rose. Turning away I went
across the gardens, my mind crowded with thoughts,
without a glance back, even at Taka.

On my way to Okapa I retrieved, little by little, all my
lost feelings. Now that Taka had reassured me of what I
had doubted, I was relieved and strangely lightened. It
was this, more than anything else, that made me realize
that the native's silent immobility did not indicate what
would appear to be incredible callousness. Their apparent detachment from the problem was not a sign of lack
of concern or decreased love. Simply, their behavior suggested that they exhibited considerable emotional maturity in relation to illness and death. When looking at certain death, they neither bowed to it or snapped their fingers in its face.

I also realized now that apart from Kuru death, a
considerable number of people were murdered in repri-
sal for having worked or been suspected of working Kuru
magic. Also, a Kuru mother was unable to take care of her
child through infancy. When the mother died, the child

usually died too, of starvation, since no other nursing woman would care for the suckling infant. All this appeared to me as passive genocide of the Fore people.

As the mist began to collect in the mountains, a plan formed in my mind. It matured upon my return to slumbering Okapa. I would seek John Gunther's assistance in assigning an anthropologist to the Fore region. Not just an anthropologist, but *the* anthropologist, one knowledgeable in applying his or her trade in practical fields.

Time was fleeting—hours, days, and weeks. The day was approaching for my return journey to Kainantu, together with my precious specimens, the blood sera and the brain.

For the last few days I remained mostly in the house writing of the days' events and reviewing the Kuru case histories.

As I reviewed the case analysis, I couldn't escape the feeling of sore disappointment. The use of a variety of therapeutic agents, such as sulfadimidine, antibiotics, liver extracts, and vitamin B complex effected no change, and deterioration progressed unhindered whether or not patients received these drugs.

Though Kuru ran an afebrile course from onset to terminal stage, I was not convinced that my presumption that it had an infectious etiology was wrong. I was not especially concerned about the medical belief that an elevated temperature and fever were a sign of infection; that infection always begins with the presence of a foreign substance of infection—viral or bacterial.

Finally I drafted a concise report to Gunther of my present activities, together with a strong request for an anthropologist to evaluate the social effect of Kuru upon the Fore people. It seemed to me that the contemporary medical and social scientists should avoid being trapped in the straightjacket of their secluded worlds; rather than being distinct entities, they must merge to form symbiotic relationships with other disciplines in order to arrive at a satisfactory "explanation" for their respective points of view.

As it happened, my report to the Director never left the house at Okapa, for Providence answered my prayer in the form of Charles Julius, the government anthropologist who suddenly appeared on my doorstep.

I knew him only by name. Meeting him now in person, I had the impression that he was a foppish type. He was tall and handsome, wearing a tailored powder-blue canvas safari jacket with a matching pair of imported weave trousers and a pair of soft calf beige shoes—all of which made him look quite expensive and remarkably out of place in these unkempt surroundings. His wavy hair, graying at the temples, was meticulously groomed as if it had been set. His face of fair complexion seemed the kind that wins the eye, but not so much the mind. In short, he appeared to me to be every inch gentility.

Shaking my club-fingered hand with his well-shaped one, he greeted me cordially in a soft-spoken voice, saying, "I know too well that an unbidden guest is never welcome, but I had no alternative, since I received an urgent request from the Department of Native Affairs and Doctor Scragg. I have come to study sorcery among the Fore, with special reference to Kuru."

I smiled as one does when feeling like a master of hospitality, and welcomed him, asking him to be seated and to feel at home.

The evening breeze was erratic and strong. While my guest delivered the latest "news bulletin" of recent events in the Administration with headline news of John Gunther's unexpected appointment as Assistant Administrator, and Roy Scragg, completely unknown to me, as new Director of Public Health, my nose caught an appetizing vapor from the kitchen. For a moment I wondered fretfully if Liklik, who lately had acquired a fondness for the art of cookery, was showing proper respect for the sheep's brain brought here from the freezer at Goroka. I went to the kitchen, where my eyes perceived a startling sight. The last remaining sheep's brain, rolled in bread crumbs, was in a frying pan and a sliced portion of priceless Kuru brain was ready for its turn. My voice, now harshly self-conscious, broke into a fortissimo in German, *"Donnerwetter, verdamt nochmal!"* Registering this, a bewildered Liklik abruptly stopped his "hideous crime." Agitated, I rinsed the sliced brain and placed it back into the glycerin-filled container.

Finally the food was ready. It was served by an unwincing Liklik with his head held high. The welcome dinner consisted of an entree of breadcrumbed brain sprinkled with fresh shallots, brown rice, and a main dish of wild pigeons braised in fatty pandanus oil. Natives liked pandanus oil because it tastes very much like pork fat, of which they are fond. From the sound of the smacking lips of our guest, I guessed he genuinely enjoyed it.

The following hours were taken up with talk, during which Charles Julius repeatedly brought the conversation around to the question of Kuru.

He said that he was in a responsible position. As a government officer and trained anthropologist he would be investigating something of first-rate anthropologic scientific importance—something that had never before been investigated. His chatter went on and on. His voice was brisk and unemotional, a good chairman's voice.

Annoyed by his excessive use of the word "I," on a splenetic impulse I said scornfully, "You seem very warm

about Kuru. You talk as if the whole thing had been arranged for your anthropological benefit. What about the
potential depopulation of the Fore tribe?"

"You may not agree with my point of view," he said
with a smooth pretense of impartiality, "But you must
realize, Doctor, exactly what is at stake. There is nothing
known about this form of sorcery except a fairly wide
belief in its existence. As a trained observer I am going to
find out! Don't you see what a challenge it is for social
science? In the deepest part of my mind I don't believe in
sorcery, but if it is true—my God, what a book I'll write
about it!"

"Your observations merely for the sake of a book?" I
added, "To put in a book like a schoolboy sticking in foreign stamps?"

"That is the crude and vulgar abuse of an illiterate
mind," said Julius with no malice.

Remembering my father's advice, "Better to lose
your fortune than your manners," I said no more. Excus-
ing myself, I left the house.

The cluster of stars seemed to balance on the crest of
the opposite hill, and the air throbbed with the sound of
bamboo flutes in the valley. A light breeze blew. The air
was chilly, and so was I. I could not help feeling a chill
inside me as well. I felt like a heel for my blustering. Why
did I swear at Liklik? Surely he had had good intentions.
One sheep brain was insufficient for two "masters." Why
not supplement it with an extra brain—"marinated" in
sweet oil? Why not, indeed?

And why was I so rude and inconsiderate of civility
toward Charles Julius? He was my guest and colleague,
a research worker like myself. And, after all, he was a
trained observer, unlike myself; a simple young man who
knew very little and believed a lot. I should have shut up,

I sat very still, listening to the distant beat of the drums. The chilled feeling faded, and I forgot the day's unpleasant episode.

Charles Julius now appeared to be an irrepressible and flamboyant mogul of the anthropological field. In less than one week he produced a lengthy report of over ten thousand words, though he made no actual observations in the field. His procedure followed no method that I knew. He used "armchair" reasoning, spending long days expertly interviewing relatives of the Kuru sufferers and elderly clansmen. His sound account of the anthropological background of native thought in relation to Kuru and other types of sorceries practiced in the Fore region was read by me with profound thought. I was particularly intrigued by his reference to ritual cannibalism.

"Though it was until recently the custom for all Fore groups to practice ritual cannibalism involving the eating of their own dead kindred, the somewhat elaborate kinship and other rules governing this practice differed slightly from area to area...."

This, to me, was a new item of information. But why had my trustworthy informants withheld it from me in the past? And how could I reconcile it with my own experience? Not long ago in a remote hamlet I had encountered a group of adolescent males masticating small pieces of dark, smelly, fleshy substance. My enquiry revealed that they were chewing the flesh of a recently deceased great warrior. I requested to see the body, and found it placed on a sugar-cane-covered bamboo platform. Decay had already set in. The dissection of the pectoral, deltoid, gluteal, bicep, and quadricep muscles was performed with superb skill. I wondered if the most skillful anatomist would be capable, using only a primitive bamboo knife, of performing this task with such dexterity. Small portions of the dissected parts were handed to the youths. At that time I could not interpret the significance of the rite as a form of ritual cannibalism. It appeared to me that they ate a small portion of radical muscles in order to acquire vital qualities of the dead warrior in hunting, using bow and arrows, and warfare.

In the Gimi and Atigina areas, according to the information obtained by Julius, only females and young uninitiated males had the right and duty to eat dead relatives. In certain other Fore areas, however, it appeared that the duty of eating specified portions of the bodies of dead relatives extended to males and females in the kinship groups concerned. In Julius' report there was no reference to the significance of ritual cannibalism, nor did he mention anything about eating dead Kuru victims. This I placed into my agenda for investigation in the time to come.

I was most disappointed that the information on the subject of cannibalism came from an outsider and not from my informants. But I was amused to learn later that it was I who was at fault, not they.

One evening my informants came to me to repeat all that had been said to "Master Savvy," as they had nick-named Charles Julius. With bubbles of laughter they repeated the entire conversation in pidgin English with an exact imitation of the inflections of Julius' voice and even his gestures. It was incredibly amusing and ended with, "This master tink savvy planty." When finally satisfied with the corroboration of the new facts, I asked them, "Why did you not tell me about the eating of dead relatives?" I got the reply," Because you never asked us about it."

I should have known better the habit of the natives of never furnishing information except by continuous ques-

tioning. And then, if bored, they would likely say anything that came into their heads, just to silence your questions. It was not a deliberate withholding of information,
except in the case of tribal secret matters taboo to outsiders. Rather it reveals the innate contempt for white man's
understanding of what concerns their lives, their laws,
their beliefs, their natural history. "White man, he no
savvy," so why should they be plagued by queries of why
and wherefore that occupy inquisitive Western minds?

Later, I was told that, since the absence of John Colman, the bodies of young Kuru victims had been cut into
small portions and eaten—in the Fore minds, as a prophylaxis against Kuru.

I returned to Kainantu safely with the specimens for
Anderson in Melbourne, taking two Kuru sufferers as
well. They were pleasant looking elderly females in an
advanced stage of Kuru, able to walk only with support
and mostly sitting and smiling soundlessly. They were,
as usual, not mentally lacking, but had a speech impedi-
ment that made them difficult to understand.

While at Okapa I remembered reading about "sway-
back" disease in lambs, clinically akin to Kuru. It was believed to be caused by a primary copper deficiency, although other dietary factors could play a role. The lambs,
if affected early in life, died from anorexia, or absence of
appetite, and if affected later in life, died under symptoms
of ataxia. Speculating that Kuru might be a disease of
primary copper deficiency, I brought the two patients
with the intention of supplementing them with copper
sulfate and rich dietary intake.

I did not believe that my trial, if successful, would
stop the belief in Kuru sorcery, for it was a deep-rooted
belief that was a long way from eradication. Trying to
explain to the Fore that Kuru was not sorcery, but that the

person was sick, was to no avail. After much argument, the native would say, "All right, you say she is sick. Put her in the hospital and cure her." The Kuru patient is put in the hospital where she dies, and the native comments, "You, Doctor, savvy plenty and can do all sorts of things we can't, but you just don't understand sorcery of Kuru. If she had been sick you would have cured her, but she died. Therefore it was sorcery." In the case of the two Kuru females, if cured, the native would simply say, "Ah, well, you had the luck of recovering the Asaina, or Kuru-inducing charm." It is therefore almost impossible to find a convincing answer to the natives' arguments. I was painfully aware of the long road to go in eradicating the belief in sorcery.

I nevertheless continued my experimentation with bright anticipation. Days passed in the month of March, nineteen fifty-seven, with a dazzling combination of light and air and moving clouds in the Highlands. I always enjoyed this time of year, the beginning of the dry season.

In the mornings I would walk along the government road, cherishing everything within the landscape; the green shades of cultivated earth in the small garden plots, wet with dew, gradually dehydrating under the consuming sun, the dark green heaps of sweet potato leaves, and the lighter, emerald standards of the rows of corn testifying to human care, symbols of the larger promise men seek in everything they do.

During one of those early morning strolls I had a deep and silent premonition, a feeling difficult to explain, lacking definite shape. The silence seemed like a temporary lull, the kind of pause in which events move closer. I tried to arrest the feeling, turning my mind to the road, and climbed the hillside to the hospital. Here I found awaiting me a radiogram relayed from Goroka. It stated that Doctor Scragg was on a familiarization tour and would be visiting me the next day at noon.

The Acting Director of the Public Health Department, Dr. Scragg, was tall, with a balding head and a permanently sour expression. He had a slow way of speaking with frequent hawking of his throat. His tendency to avoid eye contact reminded me of the social dictum that not looking one straight in the eye spells aggression and fear and causes mistrust of the man's sincerity.

I was pleased by his genuine interest in the two Kuru cases, who were by now in their second week of copper sulfate and rich dietary therapy, with no sign of progress. His reasoning for the lack of results from the copper sulfate treatment was that sufficient copper intake during a two-week period may not restore a central nervous system that is already severely damaged. He proposed supplementing copper to early cases of Kuru.

We spoke for about an hour in strained formalities, addressing one another by surname with the appellation of "doctor." In spite of our mutual interest in Kuru and unanimity in exchange of information, there was no real exchange of feelings. With an estranged, "See you soon," and with no handshake, he left for Port Moresby.

For some unexplained reason, I was concerned at the prospect of him occupying the Director's position. I suppose it is because I am prejudiced against people who shun one's gaze. I was determined to conduct myself with all the manners of urbanity and at least try to keep my resentment toward the Director, in the interim, to myself. I hoped he would do the same.

On the fourth day after Scragg's visit I received the feverishly awaited letter from Anderson in Melbourne, which I opened with foreboding. It was most disappointing, advising me that no infectious agent was isolated from the brain and that the sera contained no Murray Valley encephalitis virus. He also informed me that he intended to join me in my Kuru research at Okapa shortly. This cheered my sunken mood.

With an open mind and only the slightest preconceived notions of what I was going to do and how I would continue the Kuru research, a few significant events took place. Mick Foley, a most competent administrative officer, old-timer, and close friend, returned from his leave. His rather airy colleague, Harry West, was transferred to Goroka. In addition, a young Kiap by the name of Jack Baker was transferred from one of the most remote New Guinea regions to take charge of the Fore region.

After only a few day's acquaintance, Baker impressed me as the right man for the Fore people. He was also from the set of John MacArthur and John Colman; of independent spirit, sharp humor, and humanistic approach. Within a few days I saw clearly that he loved the natives. His warm approach to the people was easily seen, as was his love for the green island. I felt good in finding one who was at home with the natives. His physical appearance was the antithesis of both Johns, the previous Kiaps of Fore. He was much shorter and rather beefy, with a premature "beer belly."

Unlike me, a Baltic Australian who required much humoring—by myself and others—Jack possessed the characteristic feature of the true Australian. He enjoyed life and expected others to do likewise, while avoiding all possible clashes. He always had a cheerful grin. Nothing was ever too much trouble for him; nothing seemed to upset him. His oft repeated "no worries" and "no sweat' portrayed him as a carefree, happy Jack, the "easy-going" Kiap who did not "kalabus," or jail people indiscriminantly. I looked forward to working with him in Okapa.

The date was set for our trip to Okapa, Jack's first and my fourth. The fourteenth day of March was the intended date.

The day before our departure, while finalizing the essential supplies to be taken along, my preoccupation was interrupted by a peculiar visitor. At first glance he looked like a hippie, though shorn of beard and long hair, who had rebelled and run off to the Stone Age world. He wore much-worn shorts, an unbottoned brownish-plaid shirt revealing a dirty T-shirt, and tattered sneakers. He was tall and lean, and one of those people whose age was difficult to guess, looking boyish with a soot-black crew-cut unevenly trimmed, as if done by himself. He was just plain shabby. He was a well-built man with a remarkably shaped head, curiously piercing eyes, and ears that stood out from his head. It gave him the surprised, alert air of someone taking in all aspects of new subjects with thirst.

Everything he possessed spoke of his being peripatetic. Even standing still, he seemed to be on the move, with top tilted forward, in the breathless posture of someone who never had time enough to get where he had to be.

When I met him at the front of my house, my first thought was that he was one of those globetrotters, a kind of "freelance anthropologist" looking for a fertile hunting ground for whimsical studies; constantly scrutinizing, depriving people of privacy, watching every moment and manner day and night—what, how, and when one eats, sleeps, posture while urinating, frequency of sexual intercourse and copulating positions, the shape of breasts, their muscular tonus, and so on.

As it turned out, I was far astray in my assumption. I guessed him to be from America, a nation of strange mixtures of blood. This time, I happened to be correct. Judging from his surname of Gajdusek, with the letter "s" pronounced as "sh," he was of Slavic parentage, though his first name, Carleton, sounded more Anglo-American.

He told me that prior to his visit to the New Guinea Highlands he had been working with Sir MacFarlane Burnet in Melbourne, where he had successfully developed the autoimmune complement fixation test; to me, this was just more jargon. While at the Walter and Eliza Hall Institute of Medical Research, between periods of laboratory work in immunology and virology, he initiated studies on child development and disease patterns with Australian aboriginals and the New Guinean population. At the present he was on his way home via New Guinea to follow up on his previously launched studies.

He then informed me that he had heard of Kuru in Port Moresby from the Acting Director, Roy Scragg. I felt muddled. Why not from Sir Mac (Gajdusek's tag for Sir MacFarlane), who knew about Kuru, having learned about it from me over a year ago? This question I kept to myself, at least for the time being.

I responded to his enquiry about Kuru and my preliminary studies with an invitation to the hospital. The Kuru-stricken women were lying on homemade wooden beds. They were ready for the early morning journey back home, where they would soon be resting in the hills under the blanket of thick earth of their hamlets.

As we moved toward the doomed women, they both tried to get up, but their efforts were in vain. And when my American guest, Carleton Gajdusek, tried to help one of them stand for neurological tests, she displayed an exaggerated emotionalism with uproarious, foolish laughter that he, later, termed pathological laughter. Neither woman could obtain her equilibrium unassisted.

I was machine-gunned by his numerous questions. I had barely answered one when another would be asked.

There seemed to be a no-doubt unintended impatience in his voice.

My suggestion that he accompany us the following day to Okapa and my assurance that he would be in a position to observe several dozen Kuru victims of different sex, age, and phases of the disease was met with shining, eager eyes full of enthusiasm.

Pioneers Against
the Dreaded Scourge

That night, as I lay in bed listening to my American guest's gentle breathing and occasional heavy thump as he shifted position, I thought deeply. Why, I wondered, had I brought him to Okapa? Would he be one of those self-centered "glory grabbers," hunting for medical oddities; one who, equipped with a budget of valuable information, writes a scientific paper or book with no concern for the people involved, thus acquiring a lofty reputation and academic awards? Was he a politically intoxicated scientist lacking a code of scientific ethics? One of those who set the rules of ethics, yet would not think of following them; speaking truths they do not believe, yet expecting others to obey the rules, believe the truths, and admire and respect their social and academic status?

Or, again, was he one of the scientifically minded medicos detached from usual want of rewards, looking for neither human studies without any chauvinistic and professional jealousy, conducting research with due regard for all scientific and public interest; who loses himself in the sheer delight of inspired research, with passion for pure, unperverted science, the science that is so close to humanity, and that, though subject to fad and error, is constantly corrected by its contact with the immediate?

I held out hope that science would be on Gajdusek's side, and vice versa. I felt he was a man with eyes sharp

229

enough to penetrate the obscurity of the obvious, and guts enough to know that no scourge is incurable. Not long ago pernicious anemia was as enigmatic as Kuru, and just as invariably fatal. But medical science solved that riddle. Now and then a malignant tumor that was surely fatal suddenly begins to get smaller and finally fades away altogether, spontaneously and without treatment. There lies a clue to the cancer mystery: As sure as tomorrow's sunrise, some unknown threadbare researcher sweating in a cubbyhole of a laboratory will trick the human body into telling its cancer-curing secret. So with diabetes. Not long ago the control of severe diabetes also seemed hopeless. Then Banting—an unknown ex-farmboy laughed at by prestigious professors—found insulin. What actually is an incurable disease? It is merely one that doctors know little or nothing about.

In my groggy mind I saw our peculiar visitor, sprung from the land of inventions, as a curious researcher who would fight for these doomed people, with me steering our successful research against the Kuru spell in the right direction.

The lack of equipment very much restricted our research work. Fortunately, however, there were a number of studies that could be carried out with only minor gear. And as long as Gajdusek had paper, pencil, and a typewriter, he was satisfied. The daylight hours were normally spent outdoors. Our scintillant guest kept busy with the ample demands of his case histories, laboratory work, ethnological studies, and letter typing. I performed the clinical examination of Kuru patients and monitored their medication as clinical trials. Although Gajdusek had little faith in the medication for Kuru victims, he did not discourage the practice, regarding it as a followup requiring clinical investigation procedures.

The nighttime hours were spent in the house, mostly crowded with youngsters enthralled by our American visitor. They called him "Docta America," and later just "Coutun." They were as curious as kittens and became his affectionate companions and valuable informants. Here, in our one-room setting, long hours were spent studying village census books, writing case histories, and listening to "Coutun." His voice was musical and deep; it could thunder or woo at will, with fascinating vocalization. Apart from its usual role, the dining table was also used for desk work and microscopy, for patient examinations, for lumbar punctures, and for autopsies. On several occasions it was laid with enamel plates and wash basins containing Kuru brain and viscera. There were also specimen bottles with tissues fixed in alcohol, together with bottles of rum and lime cordial. At that time, I guess from being light-headed with the initial emotional impetus of the research that had overtaken us, we ignored the potential danger of exposure to Kuru specimens. We were blind to the fear of contracting the disease if it should prove to be contagious. There was a desperate need for more space—that we knew full well.

I soon learned more about my unforeseen scholastic visitor. He was three years younger than I; born in nineteen hundred and twenty-three in Yonkers, New York. Even in his boyhood he had wanted to be a scientist. His experience with William Youden, the mathematician and physical chemist, led him to discover that an education in mathematics, physics, and chemistry was the basis for the biology of the future. Upon completion of study of these three scientific disciplines at the University of Rochester, the teenager Gajdusek entered Harvard Medical School, from which he graduated. Thereafter he trained in clinical pediatrics as a postgraduate, also working in virology under the guidance of John Enders, the Nobel laureate, at Harvard. At the age of twenty-eight he was drafted into the military and stationed at the Walter Reed Army Medical Service Graduate School at Washington, as a research virologist. Under direction of Joseph Smadel, Chief of the Department of Virus and Rickettsial Diseases, young Gajdusek gained valuable experience in pursuing laboratory and field research, and presenting scientific results.

Since boyhood he had traveled extensively, first with his parents in Europe and thereafter to all corners of the globe to work on rabies, plague, arbovirus infections, scurvy, and epidemiological problems in exotic and isolated populations. He had close associations with world-renowned scientists, as well as with the ignoble everyman. Observing him, one could not say that his attraction to children as a pediatrician was merely a deep interest in clinical pediatrics. He was attracted to them with a passion as great as his love for science. "Children fascinate me, and their medical problems seem to offer more challenge than adult medicine," he often said.

To me he appeared eccentric, so I was of course prepared for eccentricity. He gave the feeling of being a winner, and by degrees became the principal figure of my interest, apart from Kuru. Paraphrasing his own remark regarding me, "His enthusiasm and American extravagance match my own well." He had a habit, however, of being rather rude, short on courtesy. For example, he addressed Jack and me by our surnames without titles of Mister or Doctor. At first this passed barely noticed, but gradually it played on my nerves. It afflicted Jack's nerves as well, judging by his neatly trimmed moustache, which twitched with a compulsive tic everytime his surname was pronounced by the Yankee's lip. To be addressed by one's family name without prefix is regarded by Australians as impudent if not barbaric. No Australian answers happily to a person calling him by surname. Whether meeting on the roadside or in the halls of Parliament, one would be addressed by first name within a few minutes, even if a complete stranger. To me the habit was reminiscent of culturally domineering prigs expecting a flunky to run at the snap of the fingers and the cry of "Hey you." I let the matter hang for a while, but was left with anger at my incompetency to wean him from his ill-mannered demeanor. It was my suppressed desire to work within an informal, family-like clime; to be a complement to a team with *esprit de corps*, and not just a flunky.

I do not need my notes to recall this particular day—the 20th of March, the fifth day after our arrival. It rained harder than we'd seen before. The place was drenched; there was not a dry niche in which to stand. The effect was cheerless. Okapa looked like a dark, pathless marsh—shallow, encumbered, extinct. It was late, but not yet midnight. I sat listening to the dull twofold sound of the rain with its heavy drops beating against the windows and the rat-tat-tat of the typewriter. Jack was in the process of opening a can of meat as a "nightcap" for his dog, whom he had named Kuru. My American peer was engrossed in typing, surrounded by half a dozen small boys curious about the machine, an old battered portable Olympia. His typing was loud and fast, like his talk, and that particular night he was completely absorbed in his task. His eyes were darkly circled and his clean-shaven face clearly showed the emotions of reasoning and arguing. Abruptly the sound of rat-tat-tat ceased and, turning toward Jack, he asked for a Milo drink. "Oh, my, can such things happen?" my mind exclaimed. For the first time he had used Jack's first name. Still I felt cautious—couldn't it be just a slip of the tongue? I was anxious to be certain.

And then it came. I heard my baptismal name as he asked me to read and sign several typed pages, "if you wouldn't mind." I was now sure; the way had been paved to trusted friendship and toward a Troika—Kuru research was initiated with Carleton holding the team reins.

That rainy night I spent reading Carleton's two lengthy letters, written four days apart. Both were addressed to Drs. Burnet (Sir Mac), Anderson, and Wood, all of Melbourne. I leafed idly through the pages, reading passages at random. Then I began to slowly read them again, from the beginning.

The letters were not merely matter-of-fact correspondence and epistolary rapport with his peers. They were a precise treatise for scholarly journals. His persistent use of "we" impressed me. It served to characterize his humility. Most segments of the letters shunned the use of "I." "We shall do our best to secure a whole brain.... We can undertake anything you desire...." and so forth.

His description of the Kuru cases was graphic. In the introduction, for instance, regarding his first Kuru patients seen in Kainantu, he wrote, "When I saw them they were no longer ambulatory and the tremors, athetoid (spasmodic) movements, and blurred speech all point to a chronic neurological disorder unassociated with any acute infectious disease at onset, or even in the months or years before onset, which was dramatic enough to be recalled by reliable informants in their community. They were rational, but articulation of speech was very poor. Silly smiles, with grimacing, were prominent. Fixed and pained faces and slow, clumsy, voluntary motion (apparently in an attempt to overcome tremors and athetoid movement) were prominent also. They were carried to our Jeep and managed to sit through the rough four-hour drive here...."

Being a pediatrician, he paid close attention to childhood cases that ended fatally. He noted, "one child, a boy of about seven, had been carried here; he is obviously unlikely to survive for long, can no longer walk, has hardly distinguishable speech, and urinates and defecates in the house (although he is not dribbling or incontinent). As with all cases, he has to be fed now, having lost the ability to bring food to his mouth. It is hard to believe that he is a recent case—a boy previously of normal intelligence and physical development—but multiple reliable informants testify that he was walking, running, and playing normally only three months ago...."

And there were eight other graphic accounts of Kuru children. For example, "Today, a ten-year-old girl, intelligent and cooperative, was brought in in her second month, having marked tremors of unstability that appeared with slight athetoid movements. Seven of her close relatives had had Kuru. Another child admitted yesterday, a girl of seven years, that she had lost her father's two siblings and mother to Kuru."

In his writing was also a complete medical account of our preliminary physical and laboratory findings, consisting of routine neurological examinations, cerebrofluid dynamics, and repeated hematological and urine examinations. The underlying motive of his "treatise" was to persuade his Australian associates to admit a case or two of Kuru to a high-grade hospital for "further accurate chemical, encephalographic, and X-ray studies, and serial neurological observation with good neuropathology on autopsy material." Or for one of them to promptly observe the disease *in situ*.

When I had finished reading, I had unearthed another nugget of knowledge about this new friend. He was a skilled writer. He could stir the dullest person, instill incentive, prod, or create sympathy. He could tackle any subject, develop it artistically, and ride into a finale that sometimes resembled a short story climax. That night I slept the most peaceful sleep of a man who has suddenly been relieved of a huge burden.

I wish I could say "Our first objective was...," but there were a multitude of them. They were all beginnings, with no sight of prompt endings. They were all of importance, not to be overlooked. With an old adage in mind, "Setting out well is a quarter of the journey," we laid a broad course for our operations.

In no time, through the assistance of a small grant from the Public Health Department and Jack's direction, special buildings of native material were erected. One structure would house the patients and another would serve as a laboratory. In Carleton's opinion, quoting Louis Pasteur, "Without laboratory, men of science are soldiers without arms." It was not a million-dollar research laboratory of rich endowment that housed unlimited animals, reagents, and technical paraphenalia. It was rather a simple bush material structure with a thatched roof and bamboo mat floor. It had neither running water nor electric power, but did contain one microscope, a host of laboratory reagents, and essential equipment. In addition, it had Carleton, who made up for what we lacked by his country grit and stubborness. Within this four-walled modest space we would perform clinical examinations, lumbar punctures, and autopsies. Here we carried out numerous hematological examinations, which included erythrocyte and leukocyte counts and differential counts from stained thin films, hemoglobin determinations, estimations of the erythrocytes sedimentation rates, examinations of the urine, including pH, specific gravity, sugar, and albumin determinations, and microscopical examination of urine sediment, cerebrospinal fluid examinations, including cell counts and determination of the total protein, sugar, and chlorine contents. It was now appropriate to call Okapa a Kuru research center.

In the course of less than three weeks we managed to undertake a six-day patrol to the fringe of the South Fore region. John Colman's Patrol Report indicated that this was a little-known region, uncontrolled at its extremity. Tribal wars, bow-and-arrow murders, raids, and cannibalism were still rather frequent. To Carleton and me, the purpose of this patrol was to determine the southern extent of the incidence of Kuru. To Jack it was also a familiarization with his new "parish"—its terrain and people.

The patrol was the most trying experience in my seven years in the mountainous jungles. Most of the climb of about 7000 feet was such that we had to ascend hand over hand. Once attaining the ridge, we then had to descend to 3000 feet, and then climb another ridge of about 6000 feet; like a yoyo, straight up and down for long, strenuous hours. There we encountered the major environmental hazard—the swampy sago country. Here we all suffered badly from leeches, which were extremely numerous and aggressive. Every member of our party also developed bleeding legs and feet each day from the trek. Another hazard was afforded by wild bees. In cutting tracks, especially on hills and slopes above the sago palm elevation, we often penetrated tree stumps and old logs that housed hives of native bees. Thrice I was severely stung. Mosquitoes were also a problem, as were swarms of other native Diptera, each species with its own particular time of day to swarm our camp.

The final hazard was the long, razor-sharp elephant grass. Try as we did to avoid contact, when we lightly brushed against it the sharp edges would cause deep cuts.

In the lower jungles, the problem became a vine with reverse-hooked thorns. Along the frond rib, on the underside, was a row of strong, curved needle-like hooks that fastened strongly on clothing and grabbed at skin. This often stopped us on the trail and hindered our clearing. It was this "wait-a-while" vine and similar fern fronds that had to be cleared away most meticulously. We were pretty well scratched up by these two species, making us potential victims of yaws, for these scratches could serve as portals to yaw spirochetes, carried by flies.

In spite of all the discomforting features on the trails, we succeeded in accomplishing our goal. The geographical data helped us to produce a comprehensive map of the Kuru boundaries. We learned the prevalence of the disease and the estimated total population of the area. We also saw more than forty cases of Kuru.

Our six-day trek provided an opportunity to observe even more pictorial parables of Carleton, the crewcut maverick. His strength and endurance were outstanding. Upon our arrival in a village after the most strenuous "thrills," soaked to the skin, numbed and short-winded, Jack and I would have to rest for a while. Carleton, however, would immediately commence to interview the villagers and collect blood specimens. There was a smack of fanaticism in the way he collected blood from every willing person, including infants, regardless of sex or age. Although I had to go along with his "folly," I did not dare bleed infants and toddlers. Being inexperienced, I feared hitting the femoral artery instead of the vein.

Carleton was under the spell of the muse of writing. Whenever a new mode of thought gripped his heart, he would have to stop and write it down. He wrote in notebooks or on any scrap of paper with great pleasure and eagerness.

Another obsession for Carleton was photography. In one of the villages where a little girl had died of Kuru, we were allowed to attend the funeral. The father and his two wives sat around the body and lamented their loss. Carleton, as usual, took many photographs, and feared the villagers might not be pleased about this. However, the contrary appeared to be the case. I was told that in order to detect the Kuru sorcerer, the clan made use of a banana leaf containing water. This acted as a mirror, and by peering into it one was able to see the person responsible. The natives had the idea that Carleton's camera was able to do this because the lens was seen to have reflections, believing that the culprit would soon be indicated as Carleton photographed the dead child. Although this did not turn out to be the case, the people persisted in their belief that he could help them with his camera. When an old man had killed a pig that later disappeared, he approached Sinoko, who accompanied us, and asked him whether it was possible for Carleton to discover the thief "photographically." This, too, had to be declined.

By now I was convinced that Carleton was gripped by Kuru's mystery. While Jack took a census of the people, Carleton spent long, laborious hours correcting family case histories. He noted names and tried to determine relationships; who was married to whom, what their parents were called, how many children they had, how many were still alive, and how many family members had died of Kuru.

As with most other peoples in the New Guinea Highlands, there was no time measure among natives in the Kuru region. They had no calendar, which is not surprising since they lived in a region without winter or summer, and even the rainy and dry seasons were variable in duration and occurrence. It follows therefore that they did not keep track of their chronological ages. There was no way to learn even approximately how old they were. However, adults in the community did have a very accurate memory of genealogical lineages and of the sequence of births in their community. Thus, although they could not state the age of anyone, they could consistently order all inhabitants of their villages in a time-of-birth sequence. This accurate knowledge in any village permitted Carleton the construction of a crude time scale, which he called the "amnesis technique." By this technique he was able to estimate the ages of people rather accurately. He lined up all the children and adults of the village according to order of birth and would then refer all events to the time sequence they represented by such statements as, "Before A (or B, C, D, and so on) was born," or, "A few days after E was born," or "When F was as big as A is now."

A similar technique was used later in investigation of "prehistoric" events of Kuru by use of the time scale based upon estimation and significant events.

Every night, without exception, under the dim light of kerosene lanterns, sitting on the galvanized iron patrol box, he collated, classified, and studied the collected data. I do not know when he slept; I assume there was no time for it. The source of his dynamic energy and restlessness inrtigued me.

He was interested in everything. His scientific interest was essentially holistic. His mind always tried to enlarge the smallest picture. He had a remarkable faculty for putting everything out of his mind that did not suit him. His memory worked like a burning furnace—it was purged of what he did not wish to keep.

We differed fundamentally in that he doubted anything that diverged one jot from what had been published, whereas I was all agog about the new factors in such stories. This led to a few arguments, all on the warm but friendly side. In a way they were good for me, since he would often introduce a new opinion that had never occurred to me. As for altering his set opinion on any subject, I was not conceited enough to value my own powers of persuasion.

It was also good for me to cultivate the phraseology and analogies that I learned from him. I knew how to express my reasoning and opinions, but he spoke as though he were tearing up a dictionary that no one needed anymore. His words spilled as if he had forty thousand more and no need to economize.

There were days when he was in a listening mood, and days when he wanted to do all the talking himself. I respected these moods, and if he chose to sit in silence with a cup of Milo, that was welcome too, for then I could meditate without interruption. From this patrol onward I grew to depend on his scientific knowledge, which heralded the correct approach to research and its evaluation.

On our return we hurriedly shipped blood and cerebrospinal fluid that had been collected on our trip and from earlier deposits at the Kuru research center, to Melbourne and the National Institutes of Health in the United States. Beyond my regular duties, I now also functioned as a courier. Depending on weather and road conditions, I had to drive to Kainantu to dispatch specimens and mail, returning with provisions, various drugs, and the mail.

One misty late afternoon I returned from Kainantu with a long-awaited mailbag. Most of the correspondence was addressed to Carleton. He went through it silently, reading avidly and occasionaly nodding or grunting with satisfaction. Then, with a frown, he handed me one of the letters. It was from Melbourne, signed by Sir Mac himself, with an enclosed copy of his letter to Scragg.

The letter was not in the style of a silver-tongued politician. It was urbane, straightforward, and of approximately two hundred words. In the letter to Scragg, he indicated that both of us were "working very hard on Kuru investigation." After thanking Carleton for his three "extremely interesting" reports and "invaluable" help to me, he rather bluntly asked Carleton when he intended leaving "Australian New Guinea." He ended the letter by expressing his desire to see the whole Kuru research become an "Australian affair." I passed Sir Mac's note to Jack and quietly left the house.

I yearned for solitude. My mind was oppressed. I needed a place of retreat where I could clear the dregs of my thoughts. I chose the outhouse, called in pidgin English "haus pekpek." It was a six-by-six-feet weatherboard structure of nondescript exterior and strange interior: a dungeon full of shelves stacked with old newspapers and magazines. Along the front wall was a bench-high box with the vital and purposeful hole in the middle.

I sat on the aperture, my guts heaving and bubbling as my mind tumbled from one thought to another. Hard as I tried, I couldn't understand the motives behind Sir Mac's menacing attitude with regard to Carleton. Was he hoodwinked by his cocky superiority, or was he under the influence of chauvinism tinged with xenophobia?

To me there is no room for chauvinism in medicine. My intellectual training had led me to believe strongly that fruitful research is achieved only by those with no practical purpose in view. An investigator must be free and unshackled. Truth, I was taught, is the primary importance of all research, no matter how sharply this truth may conflict with social and political conditions.

While I troubled over Sir Mac's messages to Carleton and Scragg, and viewed the outlook for future Kuru research, the echo of immortal words came to me. They were the words of the world renowned German surgeon and discoverer, Alfred Sauerbruch—"Every true scientist desires to serve his nation. His work, however, cannot be completed if it is merely a service to his nation."

My anxiety and distress, without doubt, far exceeded that of Carleton. His extensive experience in research and political squabbles, I presume, helped him to control it. Unlike me, he knew how to respond to pressure tactics.

He "counterattacked" Sir Mac with his usual profusive, information-laden letter. He urged, once again, that Sir Mac send someone from his Institute to join us in the Kuru research. In his view, there was enough work for researchers of all different scientific disciplines to keep them busy for decades. He stressed that he was unconcerned with where the support for the work came from, or what nationality was behind it. "Here on Kuru research," he wrote, "we could immediately use a dozen workers—epidemiologists, microbiologists, and pathologists; two dozen would not hurt or exhaust the problem, and the quicker they arrive, the better....The problem of medical investigation is an open field, and one that to me has always been noncompetitive." He then expressed thanks for Sir Mac's frankness and rebutted it, saying, "I should like to remain in Australian New Guinea until I have exhausted what little I can contribute to this Kuru problem on the spot....I therefore consider it a duty both to Kuru patients and to my intellectual curiosity to stick to it for a month or longer, as the matter works out."

At the same time he wrote to Smadel, his fervent supporter and friend in need, giving him a detailed report of our current activities and events. He also wrote to Gunther, advising him of the progress of the Kuru investigation and cordially inviting him to briefly visit the

Kuru Research Center, and to Scragg, accounting fully for our doings and future plans, requesting, on my behalf, permission for me to accompany one or two Kuru patients to Port Moresby for clinical demonstration.

With the letters ready and waiting to be dispatched, a message in the form of a radiogram arrived. It was from Scragg, addressed to Carleton, requesting that further investigation on Kuru be stopped "accordingly on ethical grounds." It informed him also of Doctor Anderson's arrival from Melbourne and suggested a rendezvous with him at Goroka "to discuss problems."

In Jack's opinion it was "a piece of bastardy." To me it was an affront to medical science—the harshest insult of all. And here, once more, Carleton revealed his stubbornness and unshakable determination. He decided not to coo like a pigeon to please anyone's whims; not to retreat a single inch, but to roar like a lion to please himself. Jack and I admired his guts and resolute standpoint. So we stuck with him.

That afternoon Carleton asked Jack to transmit his reply to Scragg, which read: "Intensive investigation uninterruptible. Will remain at work with patients to whom we are responsible....Will discuss plans with Anderson at Okapa...."

The prospects for Kuru research once again had a bright outlook, at least so it seemed at the time. Carleton dismissed from his mind the "spats in the mail" and continued working more vigorously than before. In addition, Scragg had approved our request to take two Kuru patients to Port Moresby.

I left for Port Moresby accompanying the two women with the exotic names of Manto and Asomea. They were classical cases of the advanced, but not the late or near-terminal, stages of Kuru. They had marked ataxia with an awkward placement of the feet, and a swaying and weaving gait; they also had to brace themselves with a stick while standing or walking.

We had promised the local population that we would have the women back soon, a promise we had to keep at any cost, for the Fore people were most resistant to having a death occur outside the local village setting.

My opinion differed from Carleton's. He felt that the brief visit to Port Moresby was, as he put it, a "farce." True, it was an expensive trip by chartered plane. In addition, our two patients were neglected and snubbed by the hospital nursing staff, and my scholarly colleagues, besides being bewildered, proved to be devoid of constructive ideas. In spite of these shortcomings, however, the trip was worthwhile on the whole. It emphasized the importance of Kuru research, helped to enlist several collaborators, and, on the lighter side, gave me the opportunity to see long-lost friends.

John Gunther, Assistant Administrator, witnessing first-hand two Kuru patients, shortly afterward wrote to Carleton. In his letter he expressed his sincere thanks for Carleton's detailed account of the Kuru investigations and for his intense interest and energy as reported by me, and concluded by saying that, "Kuru is the most interesting medical epidemiological problem of my generation." He also secured specialists from the Public Health Department for our research. I knew them all. They were most diligent workers in their respective fields and had genial dispositions. For example, Bill Smythe, apart from being a competent pathologist, was an expert on Melanesian languages as well. In Okapa he would work on Fore's language and grammar, and concentrate on those linguistic-anthropological studies that would be of most help to our genealogical research.

Lucy Hamilton, another health worker assigned to us, was a very skilled nutritionist, specializing in tropical environments. Her assignment was to investigate peculiar eating habits, and the nature of any unknown plants consumed. She was of immense assistance in determining chronic poisoning. Then there was Charles Campbell, a specialist-physician. I held him in great esteem not only for his superb diagnostic abilities, but also for his close and warm identification with the natives. It bore not a trace of the paternalism that I abhorred in white–native relationships. A brief visit to Okapa was arranged so that he could consult with us on these Kuru cases. Beyond that, Gunther's recommendations—that an entomologist determine the rodent ectoparasites, and for one permanent medical assistant—were also more than welcome.

The reunion with my old friend Alex Price, Director of the Public Health Laboratory, was most cordial and of great significance. Without coaxing, he enthusiastically performed liver function and blood copper level tests on two Kuru patients. Although no abnormality was found, he extended his offer to all Kuru patients, along with controls for trace metal determination. He believed researchers must explore all avenues—in Carleton's words —grasp at every straw that might lead to the cause. I was told that a heavy metallic toxicity—such as that from copper, mercury, arsenate, and manganese in certain forms of chronic poisoning, could produce neurological tremors that closely paralleled Kuru's symptomology.

Every evening of my sojourn in Port Moresby was spent in Clarissa de Derka's invigorating company. I was lavishly entertained by her amiable mother with delicious Hungarian dishes and Tokay. I also learned of the current squabblings among upper echelon staff and of the gossip and conflicts over the Kuru investigation.

On one such refreshing evening, Clarissa introduced me to the recently appointed Director of Medical Services. He was of average height and well built. He had an air of grace that belied his age, and a firm handshake that stopped just short of bonecrushing. His carefully modulated voice and grooming conspired to present the cultivated image of the mythical Esculapius, rather than the more common medico. His surname was Abbot. After a few brief hours of social intercourse, I found him to be a person who defies description. He refused to be categorized, pigeonholed, or summed up in a single neat phrase. He had none of the qualities of Scragg, his peer. He proved to be warm and reasonable, even in disagreement. Terry Abbot emerged as a generous man, a man of integrity and, in the best sense of the word, simplicity.

I was informed by Clarissa that he was highly qualified in tropical medicine and had earned many postgraduate degrees. He was Australian, but most of his life had been spent abroad, mainly in England and Burma. Later that evening, tranquilized by Tokay, I poured my heart out to him. In this catharsis, I reestablished a clear vision of my future in the Service. He listened to my outpourings with sympathetic understanding. Puffing at his pipe, he implied in an awkward and rather roundabout way that I had little future. Unless I submitted myself to Scragg's wishes, becoming "a Scragg man," I would be "dumped." He freely admitted the deplorable state of morale in the Medical Service, and condemned, without reservation, a current attempt to "dump" the foreign doctors on whom the Service had depended for almost a decade. Terry Abbot grew into an intimate friend of Carleton and me, and an ardent stalwart of Kuru research.

I was also in discord with Carleton about Gray Anderson's visit to Okapa. It was not entirely true, as he claimed, that this was just "a half-hour political visit—designed mostly to smooth over controversies with the Administration." Anderson, accompanied by Scragg, arrived at Kainantu the first week of May. I found him an affable, unpretentious, serene, and cordial gentleman. His soft voice and refined manners at first made him seem a benign mortician, but this was misleading. After a few hours of discussion, I discovered that he had all the conviction of the keen researcher, a scientist cast in the old mold. I felt that his slightly languid manner concealed an extremely hard-working, highly disciplined man; a steely manager who knew his field of virology. He was resolutely cool and laconic, though less so than Sir Mac. Despite this, I must admit that his whole being inspired me.

He regarded Carleton as a good scientist—in his definition, a scientist who understands the science, who deals with a disease problem meticulously, step by step, without shortcuts or incomplete data for quick publication. He had great respect for Carleton's unfaltering optimism and matchless pliancy. Carleton's hyperbolism and somewhat boyish emotionalism, however, were foreign to his nature. As he expressed it, "They don't lower my estimation of Carleton, but he is not exactly welcome to my chummy fold." My question as to why Sir Mac had concealed from Carleton all the knowledge of Kuru that he had gained from me over a year ago was met with a shrug of the shoulders and the brief remark "It is, I reckon, one of Sir Mac's secretive trends."

Gray Anderson looked upon Sir Mac, his principal, as one of the most outstanding Australian scientists and an extraordinarily able man. In Anderson's opinion, he was a rarity, a scientist who could write clearly and engagingly and who was always far more interested in ideas than people. He had additional intellectual gifts.

His mind was analytical and creative. His talent was for originating and constructing something of his own, as well as for improving or removing the fault of what was already begun by other scientists.

One of Sir Mac's shortcomings, according to Anderson, was his notion that the Walter and Eliza Hall Institute was his own possession—a sort of personal secretariat. This shortcoming was aggravated by his own two-sided character—one pragmatic and the other moral. No one ever knew which side was to prevail in particular circumstancees. In Anderson's phrase, Sir Mac was "emotionally simple and intellectually complex."

The meeting between Carleton and Anderson took place the next day at Okapa. It was not, as I had anticipated, a confrontation of two pansophic minds. Instead it turned out to be a friendly meeting; a sort of casual get-together. There were no harsh words spoken, nor any belittling of personalities. It was more of a scientific than a political discussion, including a review of the probable diagnoses of Kuru and physical examinations of seventeen patients in all phases of the disease.

Together with Carleton we returned to Kainantu at nightfall. Here, at my home, gainful discussions between Anderson and Carleton were resumed. I gave Anderson high marks for his smooth handling of the swirl of diverse viewpoints and personalities. His knowledge of medical science was perhaps less broad than Carleton's, but not significantly so.

Many important points emerged from their discussions. But the essential triumph of Anderson's visit was the establishment of future undertakings in Kuru research. On his departure Anderson told me in private that he had written Sir Mac recommending that Carleton and I continue Kuru research at Okapa. He would make a formal report to the Administration and assured me that the Hall Institute would do whatever it could to assist.

He was as good as his word. Less than a month after his return to Melbourne, we had received many letters full of suggestions, as well as laboratory supplies. His exertive influence mellowed Sir Mac, whose last letter to Carleton was most approbatory, with best wishes to me. Moreover, his personal microbiological technician, Lois Larkin, was allowed to come to Okapa. Technicians of her caliber were hard to come by, but Sir Mac placed her at our disposal, though for only one month, to assist us in any possible way. Later, on her return to Melbourne, she became our valuable assistant in coordinating the receipt and handling of many Kuru specimens, sending them safely to their respective destinations.

September was drawing to an end, but nearly seven months of exhaustive study and an additional three months of intensive dietary research by Lucy Hamilton had netted not a single hint as to what might be "poisoning" the Fore. Lucy's extensive lists of all the food and native products showed not a single sign of dietary deficiency. Our studies of all toxic and possibly toxic medicinal herbs, minerals, and plants revealed no trace of increased or special exposure in the Kuru patients. Our experimental approaches, such as removing patients from all contact with native products for months, did nothing to halt the progression of their illness.

Patients in all stages of illness, particularly those in the early phases, had been placed on a variety of therapeutic regimens in an attempt to determine whether any of the drugs employed could influence the course of the disease. High doses of sulfas and broad-spectrum antibiotics had no effect, nor did fish liver oil, crude liver extract given parenterally, thiamine, other components of the vitamin B complex, folic acid, and many multivitamin products and therapeutic doses of ferrous sulfate and gluconate given without noticeable change in the patients' conditions. Other drugs used included antihistamines, anticonvulsants, cortisone, and testosterone administered in full therapeutic doses. British anti-lewisite, used to treat heavy metal poisoning, was also given. The disease, however, remained unchanged or progressed.

From a research standpoint, however, we had accomplished much. Hundreds of sterile blood specimens were collected from Kuru sufferers and their relatives. A great portion of these were sent to the notable Australian hematologists, Roy Simmons and Cyril Curtain of Melbourne, for blood group genetic and serum protein abnormality studies. The remainder of the blood was forwarded to the National Institutes of Health (NIH) in America, to be stored for future hematological studies.

By now we had scoured more than half of the Fore population, and the total number of active Kuru patients reached 200. A great number of autopsies were done. In principle, the law requires a delay of twenty-four hours before an autopsy is performed. To Carleton this was a sheer nuisance. He felt that the visceral decay and the spongy brain might impair the histology and neuropathology workup. All our autopsies were therefore done immediately after death and brains were obtained less than one hour postmortem. We worked quickly, sawing the skull, cutting the body, and sewing it up again with big stitches, dressings, and bands of leukoplast.

There was a highly dramatic conflict between immediate pity for the poor victim's remains and another, higher pity that wants to know, to discover, to learn, in order to alleviate future such great tragedies. In less than four months we performed a dozen autopsies. Three brains, together with tissue specimens, minus complete spinal cords, were sent to Graeme Robertson, a neurologist at Melbourne University. The rest were sent to Joe Smadel at NIH, who assigned a senior neuropathologist, Igor Klatzo, to full-time histological work on them.

Over the course of the last two months, certain significant happenings had taken place. Roy Scragg, still acting Director, wrote asking whether Carleton would like to receive financial aid for his assistance in Kuru research "without any strings attached." The letter ended by saying "I wish to place on record the appreciation of this Department and the Administration of the excellent work you are doing on our behalf...." It was a winning streak, and the end of political squabbles. From a painful burr under the Australian Administration's saddle, Carleton had become a welcome assailant against Kuru. At the time I did not anticipate that this triumph could only be tentative and ambiguous.

In mid-September an Australian government film unit arrived at Okapa. In four days we shot hundreds of feet of black-and-white film on Kuru. Despite some shortcomings—it showed nothing of Kuru in its native village setting, for example—the film turned out to be a great addition to Kuru documentation.

An unexpected three-day visit by Alex Sinclair, Director of Psychiatry of the Royal Melbourne Hospital, was most welcome. After seeing a few dozen Kuru victims, he was as baffled as we were. He fully agreed that such a neurological degeneration could not be a psychosis or hysterical phenomenon, although many things in early cases led one to think so.

Then shortly after his departure came news of a neuropathology report from Australia and another from the United States. Robertson's Australian report revealed that neuropathological changes in the Kuru brain were "surprisingly slight," and most marked in the cerebellum, the control center of balance and physical stability. On the contrary, Klatzo's US report showed "striking changes" in the cerebellum. His impression was that the widespread involvement of various structures did not fit any of the known hereditary degenerative patterns. Toxic causation of the condition appeared to be most likely. Furthermore, Klatzo noted that it seemed to resemble Creutzfeldt-Jacob disease. This illness, Carleton explained to me, was first reported in the early twenties by two German physicians, Hans Creutzfeldt and Alfons Jacob. It was a fatal subacute presenile brain disease occurring mostly in middle-aged persons. The predominant clinical symptoms were ataxia, severe dementia, and somnolence. It was quite rare. Klatzo's findings meant little at the time, but later proved to be astute and vital.

There was no question of the significance of the findings. It was the first breakthrough in our six months of research. Carleton was bubbling with excitement, inflated with plans and schoolboy enthusiasm. Despite his initial euphoria over the news, I had a more sober response. The autopsies had revealed much about the brain pathology involved, but they did not throw the slightest light on the cause. What dispirited me most was that all this did nothing to keep people from dying.

I watched them die in numbers, often whole rows of them. I was surrounded by bodies that were on the brink of death or even technically dead; a grim picture. It was a terrible fate.

One would imagine that I would have gotten used to its effect on me; that I would have adjusted myself to the *fait accompli* philosophy, just as the Fore had. Instead it bit deeper and deeper into me. I had to turn my face from

Kuru victims' kinfolk to hide from them my knowledge that this was a merciless presage of death. There was no remedy for this dreadful scourge. Was it an invisible miasma that killed these people? Was it an unknown epidemic influence of an atmospheric-cosmic-telluric nature, all pervading, inexorable, sneaking into them, poisoning them, killing them? If this was indeed a miasma of atmospheric-cosmic-telluric nature, why did it not pervade the neighboring tribes?

If Kuru proved to result from genetic predisposition, the Fore were doomed beyond all hope. Naturally it would be a challenge to medical science, which would have much to learn from it; it would be one of the most curious genetic situations to be found in a human population, but a tragic problem for the Fore people. I had the need—probably idiotic—to trick the legacy of genetics.

I was certain that Carleton shared my sentiment. He, as I, was anxious to see these people live to enjoy their mode of life. Yet, with an immense lack of tact, I continued to bother him about it.

With every passing day, I discovered in myself a growing, free-floating anxiety. I became impatient. I felt that a seven-month intensive study of Kuru's frustrating problems was enough for now. I felt a desire to call a halt to our field studies. The slow progress of research and the endless day-to-day investigative inquiries made me irritable and quarrelsome. In my view we had reached a point of diminishing returns and, like me, the Fore had reached the limit of their patience and tolerance. While I looked for the Kuru study to be finished, Carleton saw it as only beginning. If not for him, whose patience seemed boundless, I would have quit. He was ever more convinced that Kuru was one of the most important problems in existence in the medical field. It had all the earmarks of a disease that would provide real insights into the causes of all chronic degenerative neurological diseases.

In spite of our rather frequent disagreements and sharp exchanges, we continued to work well together. Carleton sensed my moodiness and tried to dispel it with a touch of levity and encouragement. He gave no heed to my unpardonable "spats" and regarded them as family squabbles. Then things began to happen all at once, moving so fast that it is impossible to accurately record all events in their chronological succession.

Two graphic papers—preliminary scientific reports on Kuru—were finished. It took Carleton two weeks, round the clock to write and rewrite them. No doubt—he had a stylistic touch and literary knack that is rare in an academic medical scientist. My part in the writing was minimal, though I had provided much relevant data.

Although we were able to report certain intriguing successes in our studies, we had ruefully to admit that our work had not yet identified the likely causes of Kuru. During one of Carleton's nocturnal typing marathons, I imagined I could read his mind. In my fancy I saw the course of his thoughts arrested, as the water of a frozen river. Cut across the surface, and the workings of his intelligence were revealed; below, less visible, was the idea of imminent success, strongly colored by an exaltation of pride; under that again, more clearly visible, was a third level of thought, tinged with a disagreeable element. "It was 'he' who first discovered Kuru—not me—he was the first." And at bottom, obscure and suppressed, "Don't mention 'his' part in it." Was this real, this fourfold layer of thoughts that flowed through Carleton's mind?

Which of these supposed layers of thought would take possession of his mind, I pondered. But deep inside I felt that none would do so! Not with his inborn integrity.

Not only did he record my initial observations of
Kuru, he made me coauthor of that first paper and senior
author of the second. When I thanked him, he simply
said, "It is you I must thank. It is you who started all this
and got me going along this course."

Now Carleton cooked up vast plans. He intended to
obtain more blood specimens, more urine for metabolic
studies, and more autopsies with complete spinal cords,
and to survey every nook and corner of Fore and beyond.

By now he and Jack were ready to cross the Lamari
River into Kukukuku territory and travel down the Papuan coast. They anticipated being away for over two
months, trying to spot differences in ethnological pattern
or ecology that might account for the absence of Kuru
across the river. I couldn't accompany them for various
reasons, the dominant one being a ruptured knee cartilage. I was crippled, but still ambulatory. I could stay on
my feet without falling over; I could limp about, drag
myself up to the hills; drive to Kainantu; but these were
my physical limits.

During Carleton's absence I had my hands full trying
to cover medicine at Kainantu and spend as much time at
Okapa as possible. There was a constant need for cajolery
and bribery to ensure that new cases would turn up and
that terminal patients would not be whisked away to the
village. Carleton's insistent cry, "We need more autopsies and in a hurry" was not a simple request to meet. The
Fore were a proud people with their own ideas. Although
they conceded that we could cure their yaws and pneumonia, they had decided that their Kuru sorcery was in-
vincible, just too strong for us. Despite their understandable "hands off" attitude, they were still tolerant of our investigative mien. To humor our skepticism of Kuru sorcery, they reluctantly let us, keep some of the patients.

By good luck I succeeded in fulfilling Carleton's wish, performing three autopsies on young Kuru victims, two girls and a boy, in just over a week. The families of the victims were "handsomely" rewarded with blankets and tomahawks, and the carriers, who took themhome, with a few sticks of twist tobacco. The relatives appeared to take as much interest in the reward as in the death, to which they had long ago resigned themselves.

The autopsy on the boy was the most dramatic scene I have ever experienced. Late one night, while packing bleeding venules and essential medical supplies to be delivered to Carleton, Liklik rushed into the house. In an urgent voice he told me that Ereio, the boy, "dai pinis."

The last time I had seen Ereio was two days before. He was in his early teens, couldn't talk, but could at times cry and mumble. He had already stopped eating and drinking. He had bed sores over both hips and starting over his sacrum. Yet he was amazingly alert, answering with his eyes, and even vocalizing rumbling complaints about flies moving into his mouth when his mother failed to fan them off. To predict his death was difficult, although I had expected him to die any day.

Now there he was, forsaken on the bamboo-plaited bench in our laboratory-cum-morgue building. His body was still warm, and rigor mortis had not yet set in. Taking a firm grip of my scalpel and bending over the lifeless body, I made a swift incision to the vertex of the scalp, from ear to ear. At just that instant the boy's eyes fluttered. and with a sudden motion he raised his head. I saw his dark lucid eyes, immobile, not even blinking, looking *at* me—not past me, or through me, or around me. He looked directly into my eyes! His mouth opened twice, dry pale lips, paper frail. A serous red liquid trickled down his inert face.

I stood in a daze of wild horror, gazing at him. At that moment the entire universe was the body of the boy. A certain ineffable force—real and deep—passed between us. A moment of high emotion. As I wavered over what I had done, my vision darkened, and for a timeless moment everything seemed to slip away. By now the boy's head seemed wrapped in a veil of blood, tearing me out of my stupor. All at once he trembled, then lay his head still, as though going to sleep. He was not yet dead. Technically he was still living. Although his pulse couldn't be felt, his pupils were nearly as big as peas constricted by my flashlight. Moreover, hopeless as he was, he possessed a certain ineffable aura, as though a few struggling cells still emitted some spiritual radiance.

Liklik, recovered by now from the commotion, meticulously sponged blood from the boy's face and stitched the incision with surprising authority. With my thoughts asea, I sat and smoked. An image floated before my yielding consciousness, amid an atmosphere of steel and enamel trays. On one tray sat several strange objects, gray as overdone meatloaves, misshapen as lumps of children's clay. Removed from their skulls, severed from their spinal cords, the gray lumps were human brains.

I jerked awake, but the image persisted. The girls', Atona and Isoisi's, brains were here, and others would come—they would not lack company. Only the brain of Ereio had a chance of residing within its skull for a little longer, but eventually it would be sealed in formalin, ready for slicing. At last I snapped out of my trance, feeling no remorse, only a peculiar sensation that trickled sweat down my back and through to the swarming mystery beyond.

Back at home, in order to gain a few minutes sleep, I searched for some happy memory. It took me a long time to dredge one up, and it was brief. A woman who held my head against her warm breast, rocking me and humming gently. That was not a long time ago, and it hadn't worked out. She had left me for good.

The next morning it was difficult to think of anything except the eyes of the boy. They came unbidden into my consciousness. Ereio's life lasted two days and two nights longer. Time congealed in his wide, staring eyes. And for many long years I could not erase that boy from my damned memory. He was there, always there, before my eyes. The other corpses I have forgotten, or could forget them when I wanted to. That one, never.

During the next few months, much of my time was swallowed up by entertaining visitors. Some were memorable, some as transient as the clouds. It was my pleasure to entertain three distinguished Australian personalities—Professors Eccles (a neurophysiologist from Canberra, and President of the Australian Academy of Science), Suderland (a neuroanatomist from Melbourne and Secretary of the Australian Academy of Science), and Robson from the University of Adelaide. I found all three most informal, pleasant, and relaxing; pure in mind and speech, and appreciative.

After witnessing twelve cases of Kuru, including one advanced case in the natural village environment, and studying hundreds of records of our case histories, they unanimously agreed that this was the most important neurological discovery in decades. They thought that the entire neurological world had in Kuru "its choicest and most promising problem." The professorial delegation was beside itself with enthusiasm.

They read copies of our manuscripts in stunned silence. To them it was a devastating problem. Eccles remarked, "No more exact, more classical, and surely no such heart-rending human scientific work has ever been read by me." They strongly urged that we name Kuru the "Gajdusek-Zigas syndrome." Like the tongue of vanity, the suggestion was pleasing, but we declined.

The three leaders in medicine and neurology in Australia were carried away by the probabilities and possibilities involved in Kuru and, no doubt, were pondering the etiology and physiobiochemical basis of the disease. The three-day "convocation" may well be remembered as one of the first sessions dealing with future studies of the complex research of Kuru.

In their concise report addressed to the Minister of the External Territories, with copies to Gunther, Scragg, Carleton, and me, they stated that our work was "wholly admirable and worthy of the greatest praise." They also confirmed that Kuru was a unique neurological condition well worth continued and intensive investigation. But by far their most important point was a recommendation for an expert Australian clinical team to be sent to Okapa for a period of approximately two months.

Only a few weeks had passed since the three eminent Australian savants had returned home. An even shorter time had elapsed since Kuru became front page news. One morning the radio news announced "Territory doctor finds new killer disease...." And suddenly, the next day, the local tabloid dramatically reported, "An Administrative medical officer...watched Kainantu children eating their dead father...found a new killer disease...." They called me a brave, dynamic, and excitable medico. This pitiless publicity made my blood curdle.

Then, a few days later, the Australian press responded in print, with headlines that may have set a new standard for journalistic sophistry. Kuru was dubbed "Dance of Death," "Laughing Death," "Mystery Disease Kills

Cannibals," and other hideous misnomers. The overseas press followed suit with identical distorted, well-padded accounts and balderdash. The lay press made a farce of the pathetic plight of the Fore people and presented a much garbled account of the Kuru investigations

We were both embarrassed by the global publicity. Carleton mistrusted all journalists. He found the publicity and misquoting of facts we had supplied to others a most embarrassing matter. In his words, "Research cannot be documented blow-by-blow for the lay press; the very thought of an effort in that direction could stifle successful enquiry." To our horror copies of our manuscripts marked "confidential and not for release"—originals that had been submitted to medical journals—had been released in Port Moresby to the press and radio. In brief, we found the publicity that broke to be appalling. Newspaper clippings poured in—all nonsense and awful.

A *Time* magazine reporter, the only one to visit Okapa, impressed me as sincere and intelligent. He was disturbed by the mournful scene of sullen staggering victims facing a ruthless, lingering death. He took many photos of doomed children and adults and scrupulously wrote down all information given by me. Later, I enjoyed our evening discussions on various topics. One of these was the news media. It was pleasing to hear his candid comment in response to my enquiry, "Why is it that newspaper men show so little responsibility in giving the details of medical discoveries and research?"

"One problem, of course," he retorted, "is that the newspaper or magazine as a form for conveying news *ipso facto* is inadequate. The newswriter is expected to compress the essentials of a story. Fortunately, this standard is gradually changing, but reporters still compose their first paragraph in a way that will command attention."

He admitted that this kind of reporting could be misleading and lethal. "It is a problem," he continued, "especially in the case of medicine, where the headline writer
will try to focus on and direct attention to the 'catch the
eye' aspects of the story." In his view, a reporter dealing
with medical news should stick to the essential issue,
namely, what is the disease, what are its causes, what is
the cure, and so on. Regrettably, he said, the majority of
the press tends to depart from that approach.

We both agreed that the sensational "proclama-
tions," whether from reporters or academicians, have one
thing in common: the profound simplemindedness of
their interpretations often involving falsifying facts and
uniform, boldfaced, and arrogant ignorance.

Time carried a two-column, well-balanced account of
the story on Kuru. On return from his "cross-island" marathon, Carleton was most pleased with their coverage.

In mid-December, the Australian vanguard team in
the persons of Donald Simpson, neurosurgeon, and
Harry Lander, toxicologist, both from Adelaide, arrived.

Being, as we were, near amateurs in neurological
pedantry, Donald supplied a good deal of neurological
training. In his well-meant and polite way, he corrected
our neurological errors and pointed out blunders and
oversights. We were most pleased to see that we were not
as far afield in our observations as we might have been.

He was an excellent teacher. During the autopsy of
a female middleaged Kuru victim, I had the privilege of
assisting. When the top of the cranium had been sawn off,
Donald motioned me closer. As if the brain was his own
creation, he commenced his "lecture."

"Now, here is the dura matter...and underneath it...
here...." He pointed with the handle of his scalpel, careful not to touch the surface of the brain. "Here we have

the Sylvian fissure with its two branches... here, the fissure of Rolando...deep under the temporal lobe, the Island of Reil." "The speech center?" I asked. He nodded and continued, "Broca's area in the frontal lobe...and here is Wernicke's area..." And so he continued specifying sections of the brain. Finally, the disjointed brain was put into formalin.

Resuming work with his scalpel, he attacked the cadaver, already three-quarters demolished. With minute care, he finished: Most of the internal organs were removed, cut into lumps, and placed in various jars and containers. Then, rolling the body onto its belly, he made a quick incision along the spine, from the cervix of the neck down to the sacrum. With the help of retractors and the scalpel, he separated the vinaceous flesh from the spinal column. He then cut off thornlike structures and, through the long slit in the spinal canal, extracted the spinal cord. It was whole and intact. "Incredible. The best work I have ever seen," I thought to myself. A year later, as luck would have it, it was my honor to sit one evening in the company of Donald and his intellectual wife in their cozy homestead in the Adelaide hills.

After two weeks of comprehensive neurological examination of over two dozen "Kuru menagerie," the first members of the "Australian team," excited and impressed, departed for Adelaide. The brain, complete with spinal cord, went along with them.

At long last, our two papers on Kuru were published. One in the *New England Journal of Medicine* and the other in the *Medical Journal of Australia*. The publications covered all aspects of the disease—historical background, clinical pictures, laboratory and pathological findings, therapeutic trials, differential diagnosis, prognosis, and finally, hypothetical etiology.

From the moment the first publication appeared, this dreaded scourge attracted the wonder, curiosity, sympathy, and imagination of the lay and scientific world. It became an issue of immense theoretical importance in social and medical science, and stirred up a few political issues as well. The editorial in the *Medical Journal of Australia*, the voice of Australian medicine, expressed displeasure at not having all Kuru studies "exclusively" in Australian hands. This was stated clearly in the article, "...some regret may be felt that work... should be diverted overseas, when it could have been done at least as effectively by Australian investigators." Of course, that "animus" irked us a little; especially me, after Carleton's observation, "For some reason you do not seem to count to them as an Australian." It appeared to us that some Australian nabobs ignored Kuru collaborators, both American and Australian. They looked upon them not as co-workers seeking knowledge, but as competitors. This to me was an unpardonable breach, not only of good taste, but of medical ethics. One fragment of conversation overheard at the Goroka Hotel remains in my memory.

"...What ya reckon, mate, about these two foreign chaps? One, I hear, is from one of those rich American Foundations. They went up to the area where there is a tribe of Kanakas, the only one in the world they say that's subject to laughing sickness. These Kanakas get ill, but other tribes all around them don't. So, I hear, this Yank comes along and snap, he's got it—they must have more or fewer convolusions in their brains. He's put a standard order on the brain of every Kanaka that dies. If he offers enough, there'll be plenty of stiffs." The "mate" replied, "I bloody couldn't care less about this laughing sickness—it'll make a few Maumau less."

And so, once more, another yule was nigh, with another chapter in the Kuru adventure about to begin.

Meandering Pathways
of Kuru Research

On preparing to write this final chapter, it struck me that the best form in which to cast it would be that of a volume of annals. I cannot indeed remember the exact dates, but the course of events that occurred in the second or third year, or thereafter, I recollect with the utmost precision. By laying before the reader the more important facts, I feel that he or she will form a much more accurate and faithful notion of the aspects of the social organization of medical science; some of its human costs, passions, frailties and gaieties, frustrations, and achievements.

It was 1958, a year of great significance for Kuru research. Carleton had postponed his departure to the US, where all the facilities needed for biochemical and other Kuru studies would be provided by Joe Smadel. He was determined to stay until the rest of the Australian team from Adelaide arrived. He wanted to see for himself how well and elaborately equipped they were. We both hoped that the "team" would bring extensive laboratory facilities for stepping up "bedside" clinical investigations.

The trio, Professors Robson, Cleland, and Rhodes, the last a physician from Port Moresby, arrived at Okapa on the first day of the new year. To our disappointment, they did not bring the high-powered laboratory we had hoped for. They came, in fact, only to check family histories, calculate statistical probabilities for genetic etiology, study toxic agarics, and, for some obscure reason, collect further blood samples. Actually, we had already done all these things, compiling extensive family tree data in both our case files and in the massive volumes and card files of epidemiological data, most of which were already published.

It is often a foolish mistake to praise someone to outsiders. You may believe that you are creating a favorable impression, but the effect is sometimes the reverse. Such was the case with our visitors' reaction to my admiration for Carleton. What I meant as praise for him, whom I knew as well as myself, caused prejudice against him from the onset. To them, especially to Robson, Carleton appeared an irritating nuisance.

The differences between Robson and Carleton were extraordinary, though they shared some characteristics. Both were articulate, persuasive, and poised, but where Robson was rather icily formal, Carleton exuded warmth and casualness. He was frank and witty, and reasonably generous to his opponent. Robson, as I was told by Donald Simpson, had a reputation for being hawkish, but not brilliant, "...Perhaps brilliant is not the word to describe his mind, but he is very precise and disciplined." This was another trait Robson had in common with Carleton.

In style and appearance Robson's two associates could hardly have differed more. Cleland was elegant, urbane, and diligent, with a glint of mischief in his eyes. The slightly pudgy Rhodes, on the shady side of forty, was an opportunistic-appearing, playboy type. This grand old professor never made a start on his intended project, the study of botanical environment. He came down suddenly with uremia and had to be flown to Australia for hospitalization, where he later died of prostate cancer.

On my return to Okapa I found Carleton prepared for his departure home. The voluminous Kuru data were already en route to the National Institutes of Health. An almost complete copy file of all case records was left with me. He took only a few accessories and his faithfully kept journal, an intensely personal document—part travelog, part anthropological field notes, and part confessional.

Our *adieu* was pure and simple. I shook his hand and looked him in the eye in the manner of men who don't know whether they would ever meet again. I resigned myself to waiting for his return. Waiting—that was what I hated most. Waiting for day, waiting for night, waiting for good weather....

Soon he was in the laboratory, where the scientist works, peers, probes, sweats, and argues, ransacking endless libraries of scientific reports, those drab documents that can suddenly become as exciting as a bursting mortar bomb. His departure gave me poignant pause. I felt a strange and intolerable sensation of being lost, and peered into the mirror of recent events. Those ten months with Carleton had been an outlandish seesaw of hope, despair, frustration, and fizzled-out pseudo-success. I had learned more in a year than I had in thirteen years of medical studies. With all his being, he invented, cooked up idiotic schemes, and devised newfangled ways to snuff out the evil spell of Kuru. I owed a great deal to Carleton. If I paid my debt by introducing him to Kuru, it was a cheap payment indeed. That an eccentric scholar from an outside world should come to mean so much to me seemed to emphasize poignantly my loneliness.

Although Robson's and Rhodes' medical acumen was widely recognized, they had never been inland and understood nothing of this type of field research. Crippled though I was by the torn cartilage in my knee, I did my utmost to assist in their investigations. I took them to the nearby villages, to the Kuru victims' relatives, where they rechecked our collected family tree data. I collected blood samples for them and gave our case files, left by Carleton, to Robson. It was satisfying indeed to find later that Robson obtained the very same family trees that we had recorded. It was important to have an independent check as proof that the Fore natives were reliable informants on case anamneses and family backgrounds.

My respect for Robson was great. I felt he had it all: good looks, the common touch, and a sense of humor when needed. What's more, he injected a marvelous dose of Scottish blood and common sense into the Adelaide team. He was most sympathetic and fraternal toward me. Without being asked, he made arrangements with his friend, an orthopedic surgeon in Australia, to operate on my injured knee. He urged me to submit a dissertation for a Doctor of Medicine degree, which in Australia, as in Britain, is a recognition of seniority. I saw him as my ally and, disappointingly, as Carleton's opponent.

In my observation Robson did not know a great deal about hereditary diseases. Though he had obviously read a great deal on genealogy, my impression was that his knowledge in that area was not as deep as his knowledge of clinical medicine. As he studied our family tree files, he often paused and looked into space when a thought had struck him. He would then fidget a little and write or say something, the logic of which would not be immediately clear to me, for his approach was not deductive. He did not closely study all the facts in order to draw a sound conclusion as to a possible genetic basis for Kuru. Instead he focused on what he thought would support his thesis.

The Adelaide team seemed to be planning to rush out a few reports on Kuru in order to get the "Australians" into print. As I suspected, two papers entitled "A Possible Genetic Basis for Kuru" were dashed off, one of which was presented at the Tenth International Congress of Genetics in Canada. What intrigued me most was that the senior author of both papers was not Robson, but Bennett, a Professor of Genetics at the University of Adelaide who was unheard of by Carleton or me.

Bennett summed up the genetic studies by stating, "The analysis of the records suggests that Kuru may have a genetic basis." I must admit the hypothesis favoring genetic susceptibility was rather attractive. However, the validity of the genetic hypothesis was much in doubt. It is well known that many a scientist has fallen into deplorable error by basing findings solely on statistics. On a large scale there is nothing wrong with the use of statistics. It is the basis of many important sciences; but one may prove anything with figures.

Bennett and Robson's hypothesis arose from graphs, curves, and figures. Their statements stemmed mostly from sentimental hope and emotional blindness, rather than from genetically based "hard data." I eagerly awaited the critical appraisal of Bennett's theorem by other reputable geneticists. I hoped it would be totally discredited, thus allowing for a serious investigation into the fundamental central nervous system mystery of Kuru victims.

In the meantime, I had no idea that the days ahead would be so hectic and problem-filled. Carleton's correspondence was becoming voluminous. Not a week went by without a letter from him. They were well-stuffed envelopes containing closely typed pages of his activities and Kuru research progress, together with copies of his letters to various officials. Many of his letters also contained urgent calls for more blood and urine specimens, brain, pituitaries, spinal cords, and, most baffling, eyes.

I had to leave Okapa and make my base of operations at Kainantu. Here, once again, I ran the hospital, this time restraining two outbreaks of disease: dysentery among nearby villages, and anthrax among the natives' treasure —their pigs.

Before leaving Okapa I picked up a small group of Kuru patients at all stages of the disease. Together with their close relatives I brought them to the Kainantu hospital. Here they were no longer guinea pigs, and were free from repeated lumbar punctures, bleedings, and painful shots of crude liver, cortisone, and many types of hormones. They became merely urine "donors," which was collected around the clock for metabolic studies. A few were candidates for a full autopsy, including eyes.

During this bustling time I discovered illness in myself, being plagued by troublesome psychiatric symptoms—anxiety, delusion, insomnia, and nocturnal perspiration. Every day was the same. My thoughts were in the clouds, my spirit was in confusion, and nothingness claimed my soul. I grew apathetic. I knew that if I stayed, the newly detected illness would become grave and possibly end in complete mental collapse. The only hope for a complete recovery was to take a sabbatical leave.

At last I reached a decision. I would return all Kuru patients to their respective villages, where they could die in peace, and rest in graves within their hamlets. I would take a break and accept Carleton's proposition to join him in the US, the nation I had read and heard so much about.

Though my heart was heavy with grief at leaving, I felt satisfied that I was not running away. I would return and be sound again. I would battle to see knowledge win over the unknown and humanity win over mortal disease. With dauntless resolution and an open mind I took off for the US, positive that I would like my sojourn there.

It took me several weeks, however, to adjust. In the beginning, New York—the largest city in the Western hemisphere—was a constant irritation to me. It appeared as a vast amorphous body with hundreds of eyes and ears and the patter of many tongues, both rough and smooth. I was beset by the multitude, which no one could number, of all nations and kindreds, moving like a vast ocean. The traffic seemed insane. Big hunks of steel and chrome roared, whipping by sidewalks like bullets and stopping like grumbling dinosaurs at designated red lights. Pedestrian crossing zones scared me. Subways terrified me. Constant sirens grated like a drill on a rotten tooth. Everything was distinctly different from my former life. For almost a decade I had led the common life of a primitive community member—so unlike this one.

I do not know how it happened, but by degrees I became a part of this metropolitan community. I began to enjoy walking in my neighborhood and adjusted to the 24-hour jostling streets, the manners, the traffic, the numerically numbered streets, and the skyscrapers. Everything began to look less seedy, after the low-pressure New Guinea Highlands, than it had in the beginning.

I was also greatly impressed with the capital, Washington DC. It was a most amiable city, with inner landscapes and urban meadows, without alleys of urban terror. The majority of the population was black, and I felt right at home. There was also plenty of greenery to keep this diverse ethnic recipe from exploding. And so of all places, this city became a temporary base, for which I had a close and warm feeling. To me it was a city of science and art. The souls of its inhabitants seemed imperturable; even their thoughts were shiny and new. A beauty and knowledge, ingenuity and virtue, weakness of body, and strength of spirit were united in these people.

And when I commenced my work at the National Institutes of Health, part of the United States Department of Health, Education, and Welfare, my slow-speed psyche began to unlink; I was eventually able to work until the early hours of the morning analyzing the lengthy laboratory and genetic data on Kuru. I felt that I could at last unwind from the tension that had accumulated in the last year or so from political polemics in Kuru research. I slept much better, my state of mind was easier, and I gratefully gave a paean to Carleton, and, most of all, to Joe Smadel for giving me the opportunity to make this move.

The NIH is based on over three hundred rolling acres in Bethesda, Maryland, a Washington suburb. Most of its more than eleven thousand full-time employees worked on what is appropriately called "the campus." I knew that the NIH did more and better biomedical research than any place else. There have been few biomedical advances in which the NIH has not played some role.

NIH scientists, or its grantees working in the US or abroad, developed the first artificial heart valve, the first heart-lung machine for the first successful open-heart surgery, and a cure for choriocarcinoma, a rare but once-fatal cancer that arises from the placenta. They also found that an inadequate absorption of vitamin B-12 caused pernicious anemia. More than fifty scientists supported by the NIH have won Nobel prizes. It is an institution totally dedicated to research, where one is not distracted by the duties and obligations of a university. "In the most poetic sense," as phrased by one of the NIH scientists, "it is a place where the search for reality goes on, where we seek to understand the universe of biology and find the knowledge most needed for tomorrow's world."

So there I was, a jungle physician, enveloped in the aura of medical science, working harmoniously with other scientists. I began to feel that some exotic foreign bug was eating away the ridiculous sense of inferiority I had brought here. And of course the NIH was an excellent work retreat; quiet, with everything at one's disposal. There was a concentration of scientific competence and collaboration. When one had ideas relating to a problem that required another expert's help, you had simply to walk down the hall, and if somebody liked your idea, they would work with you. What struck me most was the absence of psychic pressure. I was left alone to do what I wanted to do, when I wanted to do it. In a particular instance, I learned that Carleton's friend, the director of a virus laboratory at Alabama State, was going to conduct an international, five-week course on advanced laboratory procedures in virology. Being an abecedarian of that field, I was all agog at the forthcoming course.

My request for five weeks' leave without pay was approved with no questions asked by my immediate superior Joe Smadel. In fact, I was advised that my absence would be regarded as study leave, thus entitling me to stay on the payroll. I was also given a round-trip airline ticket to Alabama, together with a check for three hundred dollars as an advance *per diem* payment. I accepted it with a growing sense of bedazzlement mixed with embarrassment. My five-months' stay in the US ultimately enriched not only my knowledge of medical science but, above all, my self confidence—essential for my future struggle against Kuru and political polemics.

Through participation in numerous international medical conferences and symposia on neurology, I was cheered to learn about new treatments of some neurological disorders. I was discouraged to learn, however, that there was no widespread agreement among neuroscientists on the criteria to be used in determining the cause of

Kuru. Research had shown that the course of Kuru was definite and inevitably fatal, but its etiology and treatment remained elusive. All medical scientists knew that many years of intensive work would be required before a solution to Kuru—called by some "the great unknown" and "the feebleness of science"—would be obtained.

Eventually, the time arrived for my departure from this marvelous place. My sadness at leaving those who had extended their friendship so generously was brightened by an unexpected letter from Professor Robson of Adelaide. It was an informal and genial letter. Addressing me by my first name with "my dear," he expressed his regret for the "trouble" in the Kuru investigation, much of which he felt sure had been caused by "poor communication and an unfortunate series of misunderstandings all around." He stressed that he and Bennett were anxious to continue the genealogical studies in order to prove or disprove the hypothesis that Bennett had produced.

The tone of his letter fully implied that he expected me back soon and that I would be in charge of all Kuru investigations. He thought that I was "the ideal person for this...with sufficient authority and experience to supervise all research activity in order to ensure that nothing is done that might destroy the confidence and trust of the Fore people...." I was pleased to hear that, "the work on Kuru is so urgent and so important that there is really no room for personal squabbles." I took no notice, however, of his remark about my spending a fortnight in Adelaide to discuss future plans. His mention of an opportunity for me to receive an honorary MD degree from the University of Adelaide was also ambiguous. He did not specify what "pendent factors" were required. The news of Scragg's appointment as Director of Public Health was equally perplexing, and I suspected political juggling.

As it happened, Joe Smadel tragically passed away after my departure, leaving behind a monument of devotees. Now, a quarter of a century later, I try to fix the essential qualities of this grand man—intelligence, integrity, dedication, and justice. But perhaps the quality that best describes this American, almost uniquely among his contemporaries, is "magnanimity," in the sense of nobility of mind. Beyond doubt he was a thinker who, according to his beliefs, explored all that can be explored and quietly worshiped the inexplorable. He was one who wore seven-league boots of the mind, covering as much distance in two steps as ordinary mortals cover in a day.

It was now 1959, the year of the boar, according to the Chinese zodiac. It is also the year my fond hopes for harmonious work in Kuru research faded away under a cynical mockery of the principles of medical ethics. During the first week of my homecoming I encountered a baffling official letter. Written on behalf of the newly appointed Director of the Department of Public Health, Roy Scragg, it requested me to proceed to Adelaide "to undertake a short period of duty with the University." It also contained the rather blunt statement that "Robson's work is of greater immediate importance than Gajdusek's.... and the decision to defer Gajdusek's return stands." What irked me most was the "order" to keep the Robson-Gajdusek comments confidential, since these would have to be taken up with Gajdusek at the ministerial level. Believing the letter to be a prank, I wired headquarters for confirmation. By return cable I was requested to proceed immediately to Adelaide for a two-week conference, where I would be met by Professor Bennett.

Apart from weary strangers and sultry air, I was met by no one. I was not angered; I was not even upset. I felt only a sense of pity for the official, incompetent bureau-

cratic machine. It was through the help of my former
tutor of "neuroautopsy," Donald Simpson, that I finally
came across my supposed host, Professor Bennett.

Our meeting took place in the hotel lobby. He deeply
regretted not having been able to meet me at the airport,
supposedly because of a misunderstanding in my department. Shaking his hand, I found that it lacked all warmth.
It was like a wet cloth, cold and clammy. I dropped it as
one would a burning coal. He looked to me more like a
garden gnome than an academician. After our brief verbal exchange about the next day's conference, I was left
with the impression that he was a fastidious man. For
some reason I had no respect for him. There was a trace
of the weird that told me I should mistrust his sincerity.

The conference, pathetic in memory, was a farce. Except for Bennett, the chairman, there was no room for anyone in that oligarchic fraternity. In an awkward and rather roundabout way, he praised my important discovery,
which, in his view, presented a unique genetic model in
the Fore population. Thus, he implied, the region should
be seriously considered for a eugenic policy. He grace-
lessly chided Carleton for not supporting his views, and
then asked whether I would hand over the remaining
Kuru specimens and all data collected by Carleton and
me. He craftily implied that by doing so I would obtain
recognition from the University of Adelaide and secure
my position as director of Kuru research. All I need do
was disassociate from "Gajdusek and his collaborators."

This was the most blatant piece of bribery I had ever
seen. His ill-mannered address and offensive overture
stunned me. I felt stricken by emotional dysphoria at the
thought of selling out one's friend. Somehow, though, I
managed to control my paternally inherited Teutonic
temper and simply corrected him on points of fact.

Carleton and I did make available to the Adelaide team all our genealogical and other data, and many Kuru blood specimens, four brains, and viscera were all put at their disposal. These were explicitly documented in Bennett and Robson's paper, "Observations on Kuru—A Possible Genetic Basis," published in the *Australian Annal of Medicine*, wherein they expressed "grateful acknowledgment" to us for freely giving "unique information and experiences." I assured Bennett that his and Robson's studies would be my first and foremost consideration, though other lines of research proposed by Gajdusek could and should be pursued simultaneously. I also stipulated to Bennett that Robson, at that time in the US visiting the NIH, be in full accord with this arrangement. Bennett, in characterisic fashion, emitted a labial consonant and gave me a quick suspicious glance that indicated something had clicked in his mind, and said nothing. So ended the Adelaide conference. I was more than bruised by it, but remained optimistic and loyal to Carleton.

I spent the next few days, while waiting for my reentry permit to New Guinea, in Melbourne and Sydney. In Melbourne I paid a visit to the Walter and Eliza Hall Institute. This reputable establishment of medical research, Sir Mac's domain of the past 15 years, did not meet my expectations. Initially it seemed a spacious brick structure; a no-nonsense, no-frills, no-serenity edifice. The members of the Institute seemed totally aloof; there was something intimidating about them that prevented me from opening up in my usual way. They seemed never to abandon their natural inhibitions, staying on guard, scrutinizing their surroundings, giving nothing of themselves.

Only now did I understand what Carleton Gajdusek meant in his journal-travelog when he wrote, "Eric French and Gray Anderson at the Hall Institute...are easily bullied and pushed about, to a degree, by those few 'Australians,' such as Sir Mac....Herein lies the major factor accounting for their 'plight' at the Hall Institute." Evidently the grand master of Australian medical science, Sir Mac, was a man of strong opinions. Ambitious, perhaps flattered by people of social standing, he used the reputation he had achieved here and abroad to exert authority among his professional colleagues at the Hall Institute.

At Gray Anderson's cozy, carefree home, in the company of his amiable wife and his colleague, Eric French, I saw Gray's face develop the fatherly softness that I had seen before. Both Gray and Eric were receptive to my story of the Adelaide conference, and as bemused as I by Bennett's pressure tactics. Surprisingly, I learned that Sir Mac had decided to close the Institute to direct association with Kuru work. He thought the disease would turn out to be almost, or wholly, of a genetic nature.

Strangest of all was my visit to the Commonwealth Serum Laboratories. The moment I opened the door, Roy Simmons, our valuable and close collaborator, began to snigger, turning toward the window. I was surprised and somewhat taken aback by his unexpected manner. I asked for an explanation, and after trying to evade the question, he finally explained. He had received a call from Bennett in Adelaide informing him that I had disassociated myself from Carleton and joined the "Adelaide group," and enquiring whether he would follow suit. I would continue the collection of blood samples and send them to him for family studies on the Kuru people. Moreover, in Roy's words, Bennett was "contemplating the introduction of a eugenic policy on Fore natives."

Cyril Curtain, another one of our collaborators, had received a similar proposition from Bennett. Roy asked Cyril to write immediately to Carleton and tell him about "the strange setup." After my succinct, precise account of the Adelaide "conference," Roy exclaimed, "The contemptible squirt!"

My final stopover was Sydney. Here I saw Jim McAuley, my confidant, who greeted me with an ecstatic welcome. I felt completely at home in his simple brick house bursting with Australian intellects. I was petted and pampered without ulterior motive.

His piano performance of Fantasiestück lulled me into a tranquil calm, like that produced by a fine wine, stimulating the better self. I was allured by a lively recital of his poems, particularly those on New Guinea. They revealed his passionate attachment to the "barbarous" people of nature, lacking all advantages of civilization; he felt attached to these people as by a kind of umbilical cord.

I still remember the passages of one of his telling poems:

> The mountains speak, the doors of spirits open,
> And men are shaken by obscure trances.
> We in that land begin our rule in courage,
> The seal of peace gives warrant to intrusion;
> But then our grin of emptiness breaks the skin,
> Formless dishonor spreads its proud confusion.

Those lines incited and persuaded me to will against Bennett's intent to place the entire Kuru population under strict quarantine, prohibiting migration of tribal members from their own ethnic area, returning to their homeland all those who had already been recruited as laborers elsewhere. In Jim's words this "Draconian measure" would be the cruelest of all possible actions. He was convinced that John Gunther, the Assistant Administrator, would condemn such a "devil's advocate." I was assured by Jim that he would, if necessary, block any such measures through his trusted political wirepullers.

My homecoming to Kainantu had to be postponed for a few days when I was informed by Terry Abbott that Scragg wished to see me to discuss a "reorganization." When I remarked to Terry that this sounded a bit ominous, he showed me the letter. In it, Scragg altered our mutually agreed upon plans for work in the Fore region. Originally it was agreed that Carleton and I would continue to work in the area. Because of the latest information from the University of Adelaide, however, Scragg felt that Bennett and Robson's hypothesis that Kuru was determined genetically should take priority over the American approach. For this reason a request would be made to the Minister to have Carleton's return deferred for at least eight months. By that time, it was hoped, the studies done by the Bennett team would be nearing finality.

The meeting took place not in Scragg's office, but for some obscure reason, in John Gunther's chambers. For the first five minutes or so the latest development in the Kuru research project was discussed. But to my disappointment, Scragg was rather disinterested and the subject was dropped. Roy Scragg then stressed the importance of the Adelaide team proceeding to the Territory without further delay, with all members being stationed at Okapa. I would be responsible for the team's accommodation and their welfare. He asked John Gunther to recommend to the Minister the formation of a committee to discuss the policy in relation to the control of Kuru research. As a pretext for the postponement of Carleton's return, I was to submit a written statement that no accommodation was available for Gajdusek at Okapa. He then tried to invoke the support of Bennett's eugenic program.

When I protested his proposals, he simply smirked. And the faster I advanced arguments against his policy relating to Carleton and eugenics, the more he smirked.

As it dawned on me that I was in fact struggling for the right to proper research, I became more vocal. Scragg seemed highly pleased at the turn of events. John Gunther, who took no part in the conversation, continued to maintain silence. Had he, as a third party and policymaker, taken conciliatory steps, some of the heat of confrontation might have been avoided.

An exchange developed with charges and counter-charges made on both sides. Scragg had finally said that now as in the past I had acted in a cowardly way toward "controlling Gajdusek." I contained my anger with difficulty. He dared to judge and accuse me of cowardice. Why and how was I to "control" Gajdusek, the genuine researcher? My impulse was to charge Scragg, choke him, blind him. A man like that had no right to judge others.

I took a deep breath to control my anger. It was important not to hate him. I concentrated all efforts to silence my hatred, for contempt was all he deserved. I had no further desire to speak or listen. I was weary, as after a battle. He then smiled a curious, ironic smile, the meaning of which I was soon to understand. I exhaled loudly, stood up, opened the door, and left.

I left for Kainantu that day with jangling nerves and contracted diaphragm. The tension was eased somewhat, however, by the arrival of Reo Fortune, a lecturer of social anthropology from the University of Cambridge. I knew him by reputation as the author of several books on New Guinea, two of which, *Manus Religion* and *Sorcerers of Dobu*, were best known. He was a tall man, not young, with a brisk yet gentle manner. His eyes, as he introduced himself, were friendly and his handclasp warm.

It was a pleasant surprise to discover that he had once been the husband of Margaret Mead, whom I esteemed highly. I had met her in the US and later in New Guinea during her frequent visits to Pere village on Manus Island. To me she was the personality and giantess of anthropology. She was of noble mind; a deep, unabusive thinker. Through her I was guided and influenced in certain factors in the art of anthropological observation.

Reo Fortune, New Zealand-born psychologist and anthropologist, proved to be one of the most enlightening visitors I had met in a long time. We talked nonstop for two weeks on many topics of mutual interest. Learning about his work on Freud and Rivers' theories of dreams, I questioned him about Freudian analysis, to which he exclaimed happily, "That's one of my favorite examples!" "The New Guinea natives," he continued, "used dream analysis in almost the same way Freud did. The patient who came to the witch doctor would describe the dreams that troubled him. Then, though he didn't have to lie down, he'd be asked to free associate about his dream. Finally, the witch doctor would give his own interpretation of what was wrong. There is no more difference between the New Guinea technique and Freud's than between the styles of Freudian and Jungian analyses."

In his view, there are two ways of viewing the world of things, events, and persons: the natural and the supernatural. Witchcraft is the art or craft of the wise, since the word witch is allied to "wit"—to know. The magic art is a living reality, and is still popularly used as a practical means of succeeding in any critical human understanding. When one says that Hippocrates is the father of medicine because he separated medicine from magic and philosophy, and the natural from the supernatural, it doesn't mean that magic and philosophy ceased to exist. In fact they continued side by side with scientific medicine.

I paid close attention to his final remark, "Let witch doctors take their place in the Council of Equals, in which seats will also be allocated to sociologists, psychiatrists, and representatives of the ill and healthy."

Reo Fortune eagerly accompanied me to the villages where Kuru cases had been reported. The Kuru phenomenon engulfed his mind, and one particular case disheartened us both. It was over two years ago that I had first seen Teirari. She came to my door with a load of bananas, corn, and kumu, a spinach-like green vegetable. Although she had brought far too much for my needs, I took the lot, hoping to secure a future source of supply. From then onward, Teirari became my vegetable vendor.

Teirari was the complete antithesis of her playmates, who were timid and full of the wide-eyed hesitancy typical of small girls. Teirari could not be ignored. She may have been twelve years old; it was difficult to tell precisely. She had reached the age, in any event, when it was easier to find children attractive; no longer with a perpetually runny nose or prone to defecating on an adult.

She was Apekono's favorite daughter, and he treated her more like a boy than a girl. Being slim, with undeveloped breasts, she was easily mistaken for a boy. Her behavior also resembled that of a boy. She was quite at home in my kitchen, joining the boys in conversation, never content to merely listen. No boy tolerated such a manner from other girls, but Teirari was an exception. Unlike other village girls, she was usually in the company of a band of boys and, like them, spent most of her days in unsupervised games along the ridge.

Apekono's deep affection for his daughter, whom he indulged outrageously, contained an element of sadness. With his first two wives Apekono had had only two children, both girls. He, like other men, envied those whose wives produced several sons. Although children were much desired, it was ultimately the males who assured the continuity of the patrilineal group and, moreover, were less prone to Kuru sorcery than females. Without a son, Apekono apparently turned to Teirari as a surrogate.

I liked seeing Teirari, seeing her father in her, perhaps as he saw himself, with her alert and direct eyes. These had an unusual shine, a gleam that flickered and varied in intensity with every change of expression, matching every mood, altering as rapidly as the movements of her body. She was not a beauty, but her face was arresting, making you want to smile along with the flash of her white, even teeth and to feel concern when she was serious. More than once she had come to my house when I was alone, something that no other girl would have been forward enough to do. She sat beside me on the floor, her gestures almost imperious and assertive, rather than fluttering in shy and giggling embarrassment like so many children her age. In many ways she appeared as open with me as she was with others; at least she was more relaxed with me than were any of her friends. She was always willing to talk and to part with information on the Kuru cases. She was by no means the best of informants, but I learned a great deal from her. And what was learned was not gained from formal interviews; rather, it was given when she entered my room unannounced in the evening and silently watched me until I was ready to talk. It was a natural part of the relationship we had developed.

I now recognized Teirari, as pathetic as she was, as soon as I saw her, this time in her village. She was standing under a breadfruit tree bracing herself with a stick, no longer the cheerful, boyish girl whom I knew so well. Before me was a mature woman, with firm breasts and slim thighs, smooth and shiny as dark-hued silk. Alas, the face on that alluring body was that of a simpleton, betokening her lifelessness. Her quick-changing, mobile expression had become hardened far beyond her years. The muscles of her legs were taut and poised, as if ready for flight.

It took her a moment to register my identity, at which point she began to tremble with emotion. She was like a wire through which passed a current too powerful to bear. Her speech was slurred and incoherent, and her lips began to wobble as she called my name. I held her shaking shoulders and talked to her softly, calling her name over and over. Her trembling ceased and she became perfectly still. I studied her eyes for some clue to her feelings, but could find none. Her eyes were as expressionless as those behind the milky film of cataracts. I let her shoulders go, and with the help of a stick she started to walk toward her hut with a characteristic Kuru-swaying gait.

Although I had witnessed hundreds of pitiable cases of Kuru, I had never felt the personal involvement that I now experienced. I felt so helpless, so emptied by distress that my eyes filled with tears. Reo Fortune, hearing my story and seeing Teirari's plight, was thoroughly roused.

I knew well that, as a classic case of advanced Kuru, Teirari was doomed. Yet for a brief moment I hoped for the impossible. Could she perhaps be one of the Kuru "recoveries" observed by Carleton and me? Five young females, they had allegedly been typical advanced Kuru cases whose progressive symptoms had ceased. All five, like Teirari, were in close contact with other Kuru victims, and being of emotional, somewhat hysterical temperament, had developed what was obviously a hysterical mimicry of Kuru. Teirari, unlike those "recoveries," however, was of most stolid disposition. This expectation, unlikely though it was, provided me with a kind of hope.

With goodbyes and thanks for his hospitality to Carrol Gannon, the newly appointed "liklik doctor," or medical assistant, at Okapa, we took off for Kainantu.

Fortune's eventual findings were derived from a study of 150 sibships, in each of which there was a contemporary case of Kuru. Over fifty percent of those siblings were born to Kuru-free patients. His figures thus differed somewhat from those previously discussed by Bennett. From a statistical point of view, no uniform pattern of pedigrees was found. The population genetics picture of Kuru may indeed suggest a genetic basis, but according to Fortune's understanding of this tragic situation, there was definite need for more supportive evidence before accepting Bennett's genetic hypothesis.

In Kainantu, after a farewell party for Jack Baker to celebrate his forthcoming marriage to Lois Larkin in Australia, I rushed home with fuddled brain and jubilant heart to "audit" Scragg's letter addressed to me. His next letter was predictably a statement of fact, typical of orders, terse, unsympathetic, and impersonal. His first sentence was open and shut, "Following your visit and further discussions with the Assistant Administrator and Professor Bennett, it has been decided to withdraw you from the Australian group." He went on to say that my place in Kuru research would be taken by two doctors. Consequently, I would resume my duties again as Medical Officer in the Kainantu subdistrict. There I would assist the Adelaide team in logistics and, time permitting, be of some help to Carleton Gajdusek in his future undertakings. One specific sentence caught my attention. It read, "...we are in the process of contacting Dr. Gajdusek and advising him that he can proceed to the Territory in early April." That is to say, two months from the present date, and not eight months, as earlier intended. This unexpected change, I discovered later, was the result of a parliamentary inquiry by the opposition. Far from being distressing, what Scragg wrote made me feel cooly sure of myself. It also eased my mind about Carleton. And I now felt like a soldier who after a long wait has finally received his orders, with nothing to do but carry them out.

In order not to miss the opportunity afforded by the now-existing truce, I left hastily for Mt. Hagen, the head-quarters of the Highland district. I had received a tip-off from my devoted friend Leo Petrauskas, District Medical Officer, about a few cases of Kuru observed in the Western Highlands. All three were adult males with newly observed neurological disorders that were particularly interesting. The clinical similarity to Kuru was so striking —with progressive ataxia, incoordination, tremors, and dysarthria—that a comparison of those cases with Kuru seemed essential. The uniform fatality of the Kuru syndrome, however, contrasted sharply with the progress of these three patients. Though evidently advancing, their conditions were already of many years' duration, and so lengthy a course had never been encountered in Kuru. Also, unlike with Kuru, I was not able to elicit any sorcery system associated with the disease. On the other hand, individual patients did offer elaborate supernatural explanations for their symptoms. One, for example, gave the following reason for his disorder: The patient's father was killed by an enemy group. The patient, then a young boy, was reared by his father's murderers. When he noted the onset of tremors as an adolescent, he reasoned that his dead father was angry with him for having lived in peace with his murderers. The spirit of his father was thus wreaking vengeance upon the nonavenging son.

My brief contact with these patients was such that it did not permit a detailed clinical and epidemiological study, which I left to Carleton. On seeing the cases on his return, he would undoubtedly be thrilled and initiate an intensive study on this new discovery.

Apart from a few consolations, the remaining months of that year consisted of a perpetual battle of ludicrous pettiness. The Kuru research tussle involved the Public Health Department—led by the Director, Roy Scragg, and Professor Bennett of Adelaide—and Carleton Gajdusek and me. The degree of pettiness was extreme and unusual for medical science. It was more like something from a Monty Python script than a confrontation between leading men of medicine.

While I was in the process of transferring Kuru patients with their guardians to the Kainantu hospital, a newly established Kuru research center, the two new doctors of the Adelaide team were settling down at Okapa. Andrew Gray from England and Clive Auricht and his wife from Adelaide appeared to be of pleasant disposition. Their main task, as directed by Bennett, was to collect genealogies. The Rockefeller grant, which Bennett received through Carleton's help, would be used to pay for transport and salaries. Both doctors were well acquainted with the squabbles and political bickerings between the higher powers and Carleton, and they felt somewhat guilty by their association with the "prosecutors." Bennett shamelessly warned them not to associate or work with Carleton or share data with him in any way. When learning from me of the postponement of Carleton's arrival for three months, and his intention to not reside at Okapa, they seemed relieved.

Finally came the memorable day in the month of June. The old campaigner Carleton Gajdusek was back, bright and sunny. He was greeted by the Fore youngsters with glinting eyes and rolling laughter.

During his stopover in Port Moresby, A "peace conference" had been set up between John Gunther, Scragg, and Carleton. Andrew Gray, Director of the Australian

Kuru research team, was also present. After thrashing out matters of Bennett and Scragg's "immense concern" as to what he might do, areas in which he was interested, where he intended to work, and other mind-numbing points, Carleton decided he would go easy and plan accordingly.

Carleton was amply aware of being *persona non grata* to Gunther and Scragg, yet he bore no ill will toward them. On this disappointment, he said, "They are both mild men with whom I should like to be friends, and with whom I have no argument or complaint other than the despair at our misunderstandings. They are small men, rather of politics and manipulative 'services' than of ideas, for creativity is not of concern to them. Theirs is rather to order people or things about so as to reflect credit on themselves." This was perhaps true of Scragg, but not of Gunther. Yes, he might have been temporarily infected by the Bennett and Scragg's views, but, in the end, he would be swayed more by reasoned logic than by flowery rhetoric. Gradually, I was sure, he would either lessen his praise for the magnificent role of his countrymen in that theater of science, or conveniently choose to ignore it.

There came an echo of an earlier time, over two years ago, when Carleton was concerned about two female Kuru victims in Kainantu hospital. This time it happened to be a young man with Kuru-like symptoms, brought by me from Mt. Hagen. Seeing him he exclaimed, "Incredible! Let's go for further investigation!"

A day before we left for the Western Highlands, Andrew Gray arrived at Kainantu to decode a "secret" radiogram he had received from the Public Health Department. Confused and deeply embarrassed, he ran back to Okapa, omitting to tell us the contents of the message. Shortly afterward we learned that the disgraceful message had instructed Gray to closely follow our patrol to the Western Highlands and to check the Kuru-like cases reported by me to Scragg.

Within three days, through the superb help of Keith Wilson, the local Medical Officer, we managed to register two dozen cases with tremor syndromes. There was no indication that Kuru incidence was as prevalent as in its Okapa-centered focus, some two hundred miles away. Moreover, all cases seen were found to be of many year's duration and not as fatal as Kuru. To Wilson and me this new discovery was of little significance. To Carleton, however, the implication of those discovered neurological disorders was great. Some of these new syndromes, in his opinion, could be clinical variants of Kuru and related to it in pathogenesis.

On our return to Kainantu, Carleton dashed off a paper entitled "New Tremor Syndromes" to the authoritative British medical journal, *The Lancet*. To obviate criticism and resentment by his jealous hosts in Port Moresby, he listed Wilson and me as coauthors, with his name placed at the bottom of the list.

The second and the last "peace conference" took place in the middle of August on neutral grounds in the house of Carrol Gannon, which we had built in Okapa not long ago. The caucus comprised three high-caliber academics, Sir Ronald Fisher from Cambridge, and the two professors Robson and Bennett, followed by Andrew Gray, Carleton Gajdusek, and me, as observer-cum-chauffeur.

As might be expected, Carleton spoke openly and fully, hiding nothing of his hopes, ideas, plans, and impressions about Kuru. He disturbed the erudite trio to the extent that they objected to his every conceivable effort in Kuru research—even to his sitting in an obscure area of the Kuru region and observing. When the discussions led by Bennett became intense, Carleton asked whether they really wanted us to do anything on Kuru or to simply "get out of the way." This resulted in a bold call for the withdrawal of Carleton and all his collaborators—fully, unequivocally, and completely—from Kuru work. Bennett even offered to write Carleton's scientific colleagues, explaining that he could no longer work on Kuru. The Adelaide team, he said, would take over at this point.

I could hardly believe what I had heard. My head was heavy on my shoulders, like a separate burden not my own. I couldn't understand the mentality of the man, and could see no reason for him to make such a move. It was my first experience with the type of mind that lies behind religious and political bigotry, that fears and hates and mistrusts the "stranger," the one who holds opposing ideas as different, and therefore evil. I was appalled.

Late that night the small talk over dinner ran in curious circles, as if they were trying in turn to probe Carleton's spirit and feeling. They had found exactly where he stood without greatly committing themselves. He was on one side, they on another.

On Bennett's subject of eugenic policy, Sir Ronald maintained an expression of cold indifference and carefully restrained from taking an interest in it. Robson said nothing, except for an occasional rather surly interjection. Carleton, his face impassive in the lamplight, sat quietly. There was a stillborn silence that caused me great discomfort. As children at a circus enthralled by acrobats on the trapeze will shut their eyes against a moment of peril, so I from time to time kept my eyes on my plate, and never thought of conversation. It was a miserable evening, I decided, and on a splenetic impulse excused myself and left the table.

It drizzled all the way on the three-hour return trip to Kainantu. The land rover glided down the mountains, curve upon curve, serpentine after serpentine. "What a monotonous and frozen stretch—you must be tired," Bennett said to me.

Tired! I thought. Monotonous! Couldn't he see that I was quivering all over? Didn't he understand what was going on in me? Couldn't he feel his "frozen" picture of this mountainous world thawing and moving and talking; the rain, the wet rocks, and the road talking? Didn't he know that it might be one of my last journeys on this "monotonous" stretch if his senseless plan of quarantining the whole of the Fore tribes is implemented? Didn't he have any idea what it means to the Fore people—the enslavement? To live under government standing rule, to become subject to the inconstant, unknown, arbitrary will of the white man, subject to limitation of their freedom and negation of human existence? Didn't he notice that I scarcely spoke because my heart was swelling so, feeling only one thing again and again? Kuru.

Shortly after the atrocious event at Okapa, Carleton left for Washington to raise funds for a new laboratory at Kainantu and for proper study of some of the Kuru specimens already collected.

Since all of our houses and land in Okapa had been taken by the government and the Adelaide team, a new Kuru research center was established at Kainantu hospital. As intended by Carleton, we would be involved in biochemical and metabolic studies, specimen collection, patient observation, and an ethnoenvironmental type of program. Meanwhile, we began to study six Kuru and two Western Highlands tremor patients at Kainantu. These studies had thus far included the collection of 24 - hour urine specimens under various conditions and

blood specimens from Kuru victims, their families, and
control groups. We anticipated having some ten patients
at one time for study, replacing them with others when
one group returned to their village. "The important
thing," Carleton said, "is that we are original and that we
advance in our thinking and approach, not stagnate in the
same procedure."

Carleton's youngsters and I, in Kainantu, were looking forward to his return in a few weeks. To our bitter
disappointment, our anticipation was dashed by Scragg.
In his official letter he informed Carleton that the Minister
had agreed to the Administrator's recommendation for
the formation of a committee of six members, including
Sir Macfarlane and Scragg. The main objective of the
committee would be to set up an administrative policy in
relation to Kuru. Carleton was asked to attend its first
meeting in Australia. Finally he implied cunningly that
though he didn't think it possible... "it could be that the
committee would recommend that you (Carleton) not be
permitted to return to the Territory for an indefinite
period." This was rephrased somewhat in a second letter
written only two days later. He said his reason for writing
again was that he feared that others reading the first letter
might misunderstand; the implication of this being that
although the committee may recommend Carleton's ex-
clusion from the Territory as a whole, it supposedly applied only to the Kuru area of the Territory. Odd, how
very odd....

Tidings received from my trusted friend Clarissa
recompensed all acrimonies of that discouraging year. It
appeared in black and white in the medical journal *The
Lancet,* presented by American veterinary pathologist,
William Hadlow. While engaged in intensive research on
scrapie in sheep in England, Hadlow called attention to

Kuru as well. He revealed a striking similarity between the neuropathology, clinical symptoms, and epidemiology of Kuru in men and scrapie in sheep.

Scrapie, I learned later, is a fatal brain disease of sheep and rarely of goats, with the principal symptoms of disturbance of gait, which is wide-based, and a high stepping movement of the forelimbs. There is a severe ataxia and the animals reel like drunken humans; the coarse tremor or trembling is accentuated by excitement. Like Kuru, scrapie usually ends fatally within six months of onset, or rarely, within a year. The affected sheep rub and scratch their hindquarters or flanks against fixed objects. This behavior led to the name "scrapie."

Scrapie had been known in Europe for more than two centuries, and more recently in North America, Australia, and Iceland. The cause of scrapie had long been disputed. For a century, investigators considered scrapie to be hereditary. Only in the recent past had the view that it is a naturally infectious disease gained ground, supported by studies of experimental transmission. More and more researchers began to believe it was caused by a slow-acting infectious agent, probably a virus.

Hadlow and his colleagues, Eklund and Kennedy, successfully transmitted scrapie to mice and goats by intracerebral, peripheral, and oral routes. The neuropathological features of scrapie, Hadlow noted, were remarkably parallel to those that characterize Kuru. The "soap-bubble" vacules, as he termed them, in the cerebellar cortex of scrapie were similar to those "plaque-like bodies" seen in Kuru.

William Hadlow's proficiently presented paper did not merely enumerate interesting similarities between scrapie and Kuru, but more importantly indicated an intriguing analogy of the experimental investigation of scrapie. Thus, he urged, "... it may be profitable, in view of veterinary experience with scrapie, to examine the possibility of the experimental induction of Kuru in laboratory primates." Although I realized it was unwise to draw too close a comparison between animal and human diseases, I hoped that in scrapie we had an experimental tool with which to probe the unknown origin of Kuru. Hadlow's astute observation nourished my spirit with hope and unmingled joy.

The new year 1960 began with encouraging news from Carleton. He had received a valid visa for travel to and from New Guinea. It was granted in Washington by the Australian embassy, which had been authorized to do so from Canberra by telegram, I assume as a result of political pressure from some quarters. He suggested that we not broadcast this fact to our Adelaide colleagues in view of the current "hot climate." He urged me to continue with the laboratory building. All essential laboratory equipment, including a deep freeze and an incubator, were already on their way to Kainantu.

But Carleton's most stimulating news was that he was very impressed with the scrapie conference in Washington, in which William Hadlow and other British investigators participated. He discussed the analogy of Kuru with Hadlow extensively, and planned the inoculation of monkeys and chimpanzees. This depended on obtaining good frozen autopsy material directly from New Guinea. In the meantime, in the event I get another fresh Kuru autopsy, I was to obtain sterile bits of cerebellum, place them in sterile buffered glycerin, and forward them to him immediately. It was indeed alleviating news, and was followed immediately by another welcome fact. Roy Scragg surprisingly became somewhat mellow, pliable, and cooperative. In a letter to me he not only approved the building of a laboratory on hospital grounds, but was also in full accord with the plan to keep a small group of Kuru patients at Kainantu for further study. By the same token he rebuked Andrew Gray for his opposition to Kuru patients being taken to Kainantu and for his anti-autopsy stand. He stated that "Doctor Gray was an officer of this administration and no longer an actual member of the Adelaide team as such." He pointed out that there had been no direction from him that Gray cease all cooperation, nor did he believe such a direction had come from the Adelaide group. If it had, it would be, as he expressed it, "an unreasonable Adelaide demand." He ended his pleasant letter by saying that he had always valued my service and would have welcomed a compromise, rather than Gajdusek's extended absence from New Guinea.

In the course of that genial respite, Carleton returned to New Guinea. During his two-month sojourn my contacts with him were few and far between, since he spent most of his time touring different parts of New Guinea.

Okapa, for a time, was virtually deserted of officials. Clive Auricht and his wife departed for Adelaide, Andrew Gray left on vacation, and the Patrol Officer and Medical Assistant were transferred. To keep law and order, a native Police Corporal took charge. In the meantime, Bennett was vigorously campaigning for his insane idea of building an "immense wall" around the Kuru region. In spite of opposition from the select "Kuru committee" and the reluctance of Robson and Scragg, Bennett to my disgust was gradually overcoming resistance.

Then, just after Carleton's temporary departure from New Guinea, the administration of the Territory of New Guinea announced its astonishing plan to prevent introducing the Kuru gene elsewhere by prohibiting emigration from the Fore tribal area. To my utter surprise Carleton did not protest such a snap decision. He was no doubt completely in favor of free migration and egress from the area, and regarded Bennett's scheme, completely without precedent, as lunacy. His noncommittal attitude, however, confused me. Was he simply confident that Bennett's plan would fall flat? Or did he feel certain that it did not jeopardize his collection of frozen specimens? If the latter was true, then we spoke two tongues—his the language of self-centered science and mine the language of humanism. Our answers to the question would thus be very different.

The calmer portion of my mind insisted that such an asinine decision could never come to pass; that the unthinkable would not possibly be allowed to happen. But it was a fact that for the past week or so major changes had been occurring in Fore life. Coastal labor from the Kuru region had been stopped, and many of those outside the region had been brought back. A young Patrol Officer was moved to Okapa, and seemed excited at taking part in the "immense wall" erection.

Consequently, I was assigned to special duties—the duties of a gendarme. My main task was to trot around the island tracking down all inhabitants of the Kuru region and deliver them home. What happened next would be an electrocardiographer's joy; it caused my heart to flutter as though it were a captured bird. Shortly after my urgent call to tell Jim McAuley about this somber turn of events, Bennett's eugenic policy was besieged in the press. Australian headlines such as "Concentration Camp in New Guinea," appeared everywhere. A prominent medical scientist wrote, "This is obviously a severe restriction to be imposed on a whole tribe....The study of the disease is to be continued in the hope of finding another remedy...."

Two noble scientists wrote in a letter to the editor in *Lancet*, "The negative evidence for the genetic etiology of Kuru is considerable and has not been stressed....On the other hand Fore society presents such a clear-cut possibility for an environmental etiology resulting from a toxin, virus, or deficiency...."

Before the year was out, to the relief of all concerned, the quarantine project was abandoned. I wondered who was responsible for such a courageous deed. Was it John Gunther who, finally regaining his inborn logic, had ignored Bennett's suggestion? Twenty years later while on the subject of Bennett's eugenics plan of the past, he curtly said, "Let's forget that little squirt and his policy...."

From 1961 to 1963 the tension and feudings of the past eased. Things were working out well for Carleton, but circumstances beyond my control had reduced my involvement in Kuru investigations. I remained in close contact, however, with Carleton and the various studies.

Meanwhile, there had been an influx of newcomers that began with the arrival of a potbellied and overbearing Kiap by the name of Brightwell, followed by an experienced Medical Assistant to act as an aide to Andrew Gray. Other arrivals included several traders buying coffee beans and selling junk, an agricultural officer teaching the natives coffee cultivation, Lutheran mission lay workers building an up-to-date hospital, two nurses taking care of Kuru orphans, and a family of three from the American World Mission, hunting for potential converts.

For Kuru research, there was a single medical student, studying as a "Rockefeller Kuru Fellow" from the Adelaide team who collected further Kuru genealogies, and an American anthropological duo, Robert and Shirley Glasse, studying the social effects of Kuru, Fore medicine and sorcery, and cannibalism.

The last entrant to join the agglomeration of new faces was a young doctor from Adelaide, Michael Alpers, and his wife and baby daughter. He was actually with the Public Health Department as a researcher rather than with the medical service at Okapa, and devoted himself entirely to Kuru investigation. Unlike Carleton, Michael Alpers was a taciturn type with a philosophy of listen, look, and be silent. He was a supremely confident yet self-effacing man, gracious in manner, polite in speech, but implacably stubborn. In later years, when he became Director of the Institute of Medical Research of New Guinea, he coolly presented his views during many conferences, without once losing his temper or raising his voice. And no matter how heated the forums became, he did not budge a millimeter from his position. "He is a gentleman with a rod of iron in his back," said one of his associates. I found this to be true. He tended to announce or intone rather than speak. What he had to say, however, was knowledgeable as well as forthright.

Despite the difference in their temperaments, Michael and Carleton fit each other well. Carleton had absolute confidence and trust in Michael. He revealed most of his pet ideas, suspicions, and leads to him without regret. And Carleton's belief that Michael would dig up valuable data on Kuru epidemiology turned out to be accurate.

Not by scientific speculation, but through his care and thoroughness of epidemiological surveillance, Michael Alpers observed that the whole of Fore society had undergone a great upheaval. In contrast to other tribes, the Fore had shown an unusual degree of cooperation with the administration and the missions. They had also welcomed and quickly embraced most aspects of civilization. With the disappearance of intervillage warfare, it was possible to reside in unfortified hamlets. In addition, the former practice of males living communally in the men's house, with females and uninitiated boys sleeping in small separate huts, had been completely abandoned. Each family unit now formed a separate household.

Young men, as they obtained increasing wealth from their coffee plots, became more and more independent of their elders and turned to the administration for authority and guidance. They were no longer taught the secrets of their elders; the lore of their ancestors was regarded as superseded; the young men belittled the significance and importance of the traditional rites of passage and though they continued to be performed, the painful and embarrassing details were now omitted.

Another important change was an increase in the population's mobility. With local feuding now reduced mainly to debate, and the administration providing assurances of safe conduct, it was common for small parties to travel to the large centers of Goroka and Kainantu. As a result, more wives were gradually obtained from distant areas, despite the fear that most outside women had of living in the Kuru region for fear of the disease. Alpers' observations were substantiated by Carleton in their joint comprehensive scientific paper. One of the most striking changes they confirmed was the progressive decline in Kuru mortality and incidence. Among children, the reduction had been particularly remarkable. Despite this, however, Kuru remained a uniformly fatal disease and its general clinical picture had not changed. Suggestions by Alpers and Gajdusek that the changes in Kuru mortality might be directly related to sociocultural and environmental factors required further investigation. Too, an excellent preliminary account of the social effects of Kuru and cannibalism, with reference to similar recent changes, was also given by Robert and Shirley Glasse.

It is always difficult to be sure whether accounts given by native informants are true or not. Not all information came from direct observation, and informants tended to color their accounts to startle the interviewer or to hide facts if they saw an advantage in doing so. This was a serious problem for investigators. However, it was clear that many Fore practices in the areas of health, medical care, traditional remedies, and the complex taboos of diet associated with initiation, menstruation, and childbirth were undergoing gradual but definite change. The abolition of child marriage and a reduction in the number of polygamous marriages were also reported by the Glasses.

One practice that disappeared completely was the endocannibalism of close relatives as a rite of mourning. This had prevailed throughout the Kuru region before the coming of the administration. Robert Glasse traced the route of the spread of cannibalistic practices from the north, beginning at the turn of this century. The rules governing consumption of Kuru victims were basically the same as those that applied to cannibalism generally. However, people were originally hesitant to eat the victims. Uncertain of the cause of death, they feared the possibility of infection. This deterred many cannibals from eating Kuru victims, particularly the men. As the sorcery ideology for Kuru developed and was disseminated, though, the fear of contagion waned. If Kuru was caused by sorcerers, it was unlikely that eating the victims would transmit Kuru to the cannibal. Since those who ate Kuru victims rarely developed Kuru immediately, this belief won and the practice became more popular.

Glasse's conclusion was that the disposal of dead Kuru victims may conceivably be significant in the spread of the disease. The validity of his assertion that Kuru was new, however, with the first cases reported only forty years ago, was seriously in doubt. The accuracy and availability of data from four to five decades ago was hard to evaluate, and informants over sixty years old were few and rarely dependable.

While all these investigations were in progress, Carleton was hunting for autopsy candidates. There were many terminal cases of Kuru in the scattered villages. However, one could wait for weeks on a "terminal" patient, and without the necessary logistic support, keeping the specimens under refrigeration was sheer vexation.

The year was nearly at an end, and a winning year it was. Through the fortune and help of Paul Brown, Carleton's new recruit from NIH, pathological specimens of three autopsies were successfully obtained. All arrived in liquid nitrogen at NIH for the experiment suggested four years earlier by William Hadlow.

The year 1966 is recorded in medical Kuru history as the year of Eureka. Kuru was shown to be transmissible; the first chronic disease to be a "slow virus infection"—an inexorable, wasting process caused by an agent that could incubate undetected in a victim's brain for years. That revelation brought about medical considerations that had importance for all medicine and microbiology. For neurology, especially, it provided considerable new insight into the range of progressive neurological disorders of the central nervous system.

When the great breakthrough came, it was not from medicine, but from science and the scientist, Carleton Gajdusek, who must certainly be given the lion's share of credit for defining the disease and for carrying out the successful experiments on chimpanzees. One of the most notable "shareholders" in that credit is microbiologist Joe Gibbs, long time protégé of Joe Smadel and Carleton's mainstay for years. He was of small build, and his bespectacled face revealed little of the fighter that he was. Rather, he had the benign look of a good Quaker. When one came to know him, he modestly characterized himself as a man without great gifts, but with a faculty for diligence, tenacity, and absolute consistency in thought and action. Credit also belongs to Michael Alpers, who by now had become Carleton's close collaborator at NIH. And not least, to William Hadlow for suggesting the experimental induction of Kuru in laboratory primates.

Scrapie became the prototype for a new classification of disease known as the "slow virus infection." For the first time, a long surveillance of chimpanzees inoculated with the agent of Kuru had been carried out. This trial was expensive, protracted, tedious, and nerve-frazzling. In spite of past negative findings in the search for a Kuru pathogen, particularly a virus, Gajdusek, Gibbs, and Alpers continued the experiments. Tirelessly they produced suspensions of brain and visceral tissue specimens obtained from Kuru victims. They inoculated test animals intracerebrally, primarily chimpanzees.

Their laboratory, in a red brick building at NIH, was far too small and full of books, files, specimens, and scientific paraphernalia. But, after all, Galileo saw the mechanism of the universe while locked in a dungeon, and if Fleming's laboratory had been air-conditioned, he would never have discovered the secret of penicillin mold. The fatal disease we fought was to some outsiders minor, posing no real threat to white people; those we were trying to save were unimportant, a small isolated group of thirty thousand or so cannibalistic brutes. Yet among the comrades in that red brick building there was a humane understanding—never openly expressed or advertised.

The initial intracerebral inoculation of Kuru brain suspension material from eleven different Kuru patients was carried out on fifteen chimpanzees. Every week, month after month, their progress was watched with profound anxiety, but revealed no sign of Kuru. During the months of observation, however, several inoculated chimpanzees died of acute infection, though none had developed symptoms suggestive of Kuru.

Nobody knew better than Carleton Gajdusek that medical research is a steady progress toward a final unveiling of the panacea. Progress is made in spurts, sometimes disappearing up blind alleys, knocking itself breathless against unexpected obstacles, then rushing forth from inspiration that comes in the middle of the night. It is more of a creative process than a scientific one. So Gajdusek coaxed his two coworkers to inoculate more chimpanzees and, this time, other species of mammals and birds as well.

Finally, after an exceedingly long observation, two inoculated chimpanzees began to develop Kuru-like symptoms—slight lassitude, ataxia, and progressive tremor. In less than six months both reached the terminal stage and were killed for neurohistological studies. Thereafter, the many other inoculated chimpanzees came down with neurological disease. Among the species inoculated, only chimpanzees were affected, and all of the chimpanzees regularly manifested clinical syndromes remarkably similar to Kuru in humans, with neuropathological lesions identical to those seen in Kuru victims. Later, the disease was serially transmitted from chimpanzee to chimpanzee. An average symptomatic incubation period in the affected animals was just over twenty months, and the duration of clinical disease occurred by this route in the primates.

In the years that followed, an attempt was also made to inoculate chimpanzees and spider and squirrel monkey with brain material obtained by biopsy and autopsy from other chronic degenerative diseases of the central nervous system. In addition to Kuru, those included Creutzfeld-Jacob disease or presenile dementia, clinically akin to Kuru, multiple sclerosis, Parkinson's disease, and others. No neurologic illness developed in the animals except Creutzfeld-Jacob disease. Chimpanzees and monkeys developed the disease after they were inoculated with brain tissue from fourteen different patients from several countries. The clinical signs and brain lesions in the animals were very similar to those found in humans.

Often in science successful experiments cannot be easily reproduced. Never, however, have experiments succeeded so prettily and so progressively. Our research continued those rare rewards for the researcher whose bane and usual experience is a succession of experiments that are negative, go haywire, or contradict each other. Gajdusek, Gibbs, and Alpers were like happy boys telling each other, "We have got the virus, we have got it!"

In view of this remarkable success in veterinary virology, Carleton Gajdusek launched an intensive program aimed at exploring the possibility that slow viruses produce other progressive neurological diseases. For transmission experiments he and his loyal scientific workers used monkeys and other small laboratory animals in lieu of chimpanzees. The transmissibility of Kuru was elucidated, but the source of infection remained obscure. Clarification was needed. Gajdusek and Alpers then took it upon themselves to provide that clarification.

Leaving Gibbs and David Asher, a calm, soft-spoken young doctor, to perform the experiments on the animals, Gajdusek and Alpers crisscrossed the Kuru region. They laboriously hunted the field data for an ecological elucidation, with full collaboration from the Fore natives. Unfortunately this cooperative spirit was not shared by Richard Hornabrook, a neurologist and Director of the newly established Institute of Human Biology at Goroka. Hornabrook was a doctor with ever-lurking weaknesses —professional pride and jealousy, frustration over indifference to him by colleagues or the world, and a weakness for honors and status. He had little true devotion to humanity or medical science, and sought to share accomplishments, while contributing nothing of himself.

The former Kuru office with all its files was locked, and Hornabrook provided Gajdusek and Alpers with no information on recent Kuru patients. There was not a sign of collaboration, nor was there the slightest offer of help, facilities, or interest in what they were doing. Obviously there was no friendship lost between the three. Hornabrook treated Gajdusek and Alpers as dangerous competitors. He revealed nothing to them, yet wanted to keep close tabs on their activities. He had been doing all he could to tie Gajdusek and Alpers' hands, preventing their access to any data he could keep them from, and doing all he could to thwart their efforts. More annoying, however, were his recurring attempts to forestall their access to the village population register, which they had used freely over the years as an established procedure.

Gajdusek and Alpers made an ideal team. Both were clear-witted, methodical scientists. Despite obstructions interposed by Hornabrook, they successfully collected and evaluated the relevant facts, and together built convincing equations based on the data in hand. It wasn't long before one of their theories of Kuru etiology was accepted by most medical scientists.

Various hypotheses had been put forward to explain the etiology of Kuru. In Alpers' words, the list of possibilities "read like the players' repertoire in Hamlet: genetic, infectious, sociological, behavioral, toxic, endocrine, nutritional, immunologic." Of the many threads, the one to which Gajdusek and Alpers clung was cannibalism. By fitting together the causal links, they formed the most plausible hypothesis of the mode of Kuru transmission.

Fore women and children, the overwhelming majority of Kuru victims, practiced cannibalism only as a mourning rite. Traditionally, the women performed their preparations using their hands and sharp bamboo blades. The men participated to a much lesser degree. Throughout this process, the younger children were constantly close to their mothers. Subsequently, the Kuru virus infected its prey by contamination through openings in the skin or mucosal tissues such as eyes, nose, mouth, and, in some cases, the ever-present open wounds of jungle sores. According to Gajdusek, the actual consumption of the internal organs, such as the brain, which was primarily practiced by women, was not the single etiologic factor.

Moreover, their statistics bore this out. Since government intervention had brought an end to ritual cannibalism, Kuru incidence had dramatically declined. No one born in the village since cannibalism ceased ever developed the disease, though it continued to affect those born earlier. Over the course of ten years, the incidence of Kuru fell significantly, and in some villages virtually ceased.

Gajdusek and Alpers' analogy between cannibalism and Kuru infection, and their notion that Kuru would burn itself out in a decade or so raised skepticism in some academic quarters. Certain scholars produced an anecdotal speculation that the most likely cause of the spread of Kuru was the ritual handling of skulls by women, allegedly once a widespread custom in New Guinea. Another, rather absurdly, stated that cannibalism in any form had never existed anywhere as a regular custom. In fact, according to this scholar, cannibalism was a myth used by the West to justify colonialism and slavery.

More rational thinkers merely posed questions: Is Kuru like other diseases that strike and retreat for no apparent reason? Is Kuru primarily the result of infection that is influenced by inherited differences? And, lastly, is Kuru vanishing slowly with time and will it eventually disappear from the Fore region, or could it recur in a wave -like pattern similar to that of influenza, its resurgences being separated by long intervals of varying duration?

* * *

The last months of 1976 were closing in. It was the time of year when the King of Sweden awards the Nobel Prizes. Much rhetoric is accorded the Nobel prize, the most prestigious and revered honor in the world. Along with a hefty stipend and a gold medal, the prize brings instant fame, flooding winners with speaking invitations, job offers, book contracts, honorary degrees, and even sperm bank proffers. As the time of announcement approaches each fall, many contenders are so afflicted with Nobel fever they literally jump everytime the phone rings.

Carleton Gajdusek's groundbreaking discovery of the virgin territory of these new viruses had earned him the sobriquet "father of human slow virus infection," and in the month of October he won an even greater honor— the Nobel prize in medicine. This was shared with another scientist from a different area of medicine. Indeed, it was the most luminous event of that year, the seventy-fifth anniversary of the first award inaugurated by Nobel.

Whispers of cynicism were heard from some academicians about Gajdusek's Nobel award. It was greeted with disbelief and inquiry. Why was it not shared with Joe Gibbs, who played a key role in the research of Kuru? Or William Hadlow, whose astute analogy between Kuru and scrapie was the resultant factor of successful experimentation with chimpanzees? Whether Gibbs or Hadlow earned the right to share Gajdusek's Nobel prize is arguable, and even a few star-struck Nobelists wondered about their omission.

KURU—the laugh that brings death

From A. E. STEPHENS

PORT MORESBY, Today.—If you giggle in Kainantu, that climatically perfect Eastern Highlands retreat for New Guinea settlers, the chances are that you will be dead within eight months.

Territory Doctor Finds New Killer Disease

An Administration medical officer who four weeks ago watched Kainantu children eating their dead father has found a new killer disease which so far has baffled science.

The officer, Dr. V. Zigas, arrived in Port Moresby this week with two patients from the primitive Forea group of people who live 35 miles south of Kainantu on the fringe of the Kukukuku country.

SUNDAY TELEGRAPH, NOVEMBER 3, 1957   5

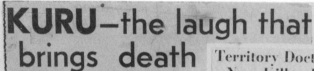

Native "laughing death" palsy genetic, specialist says

PORT MORESBY, Sat. — Evidence on the "laughing death" palsy among New Guinea natives pointed to a genetic factor, an American specialist, Dr. Carleton Gajdusek, said today.

Laughing death

Cannibalism could cause the disease

It took almost 20 years before qualified observers became interested in kuru. The Walter and Elizabeth Hall Institute, of Melbourne, Victoria, took the first steps in 1956 to make a serious study of the apparently fatal disease. Dr V. Zigas was the first to send blood and brain specimens to the laboratories of the institute to find out if a virus caused the ailment. In 1966 the American virologist, Dr Carleton Gajdusek, risked getting the disease when he went into the heart of the area to make investigations.

TIME
THE WEEKLY NEWSMAG ZINE

MEDICINE

The Laughing Death

In the eastern highlands of New Guinea, sudden bursts of maniacal laughter shrilled through the walls of many a circular, windowless grass hut, echoing through the surrounding jungle. Sometimes, instead of the roaring laughter, there might be a fit of giggling. When a tribesman looked into such a hut, he saw no cause for merriment. The laughter was lying ill, exhausted by his pitiless fits. Too soon an expressionless mask. He had no idea that he had laughed, let alone why. New Guinea's Fore (pronounced foray) tribe was affected by a deadly foe. It was kuru, the laughing death, a creeping horror hitherto unknown to medicine.

Mystery Disease Kills Cannibals

PORT MORESBY, Tuesday (A.A.P.-Reuter).—An unidentified fatal form of palsy is spreading among a cannibal tribe in central New Guinea.

Two women victims have been brought to Port Moresby where they are awaiting examination by Dr. G. C. Anderson, virologist of Melbourne's Walter and Eliza Hall Institute.

Dr. Vincent Zigas, district medical officer at Kainantu, likened Parkinson's disease to the disease for five years until it affected the central nervous system in some respects.

It occurred mainly in the age group between seven and 60 and was especially prevalent among young women.

Dr. Zigas, a somewhat less commonly prevalent palsy, had died, and none had the disease. It almost invariably killed its victims in seven to (10) months. "They lose go into a coma and die," he said.

Sunday Telegraph

A new clue to the Laughing Death

TIME In the eastern highlands of New Guinea sudden bursts of maniacal laughter shrilled through the walls of many a circular, windowless grass hut, echoing through the surrounding jungle.

KEY TO "LAUGH" DISEASE
A.A.P.-Reuter

Cannibals stricken

Disease Detectives ZIGAS & FAZEKAS
After giggles and guffaws, creeping horror.

Nobel winner educates 21 from Pacific

WASHINGTON, AAP — Dr Carleton Gajdusek, who won a Nobel Prize for his work with brain disease in Papua New Guinea developed a deep affection for the area and its people during the 20 years he spent there doing research.

Epilog

Many times, along thousands of miles of mountainous jungle through the country of so-called Stone Age people, during almost three decades spent on the track of Kuru's story, I have pondered:

"Will Kuru's drama dribble away, its significance perish, and the medical world be left only with a flat monotonous iteration of facts?"

Judging from the emerging literature of recent years, both in the popular and scientific presses, Kuru's adventure is not over by a long shot. The end cannot be told in this book, for the saga continues today.

New vistas in the study of degenerative neurological disorders are unfolding, with great activity in laboratories around the world. Remaining in Papua New Guinea, Michael Alpers keeps vigilance on Kuru cases that still occur now in adults only and in inconsiderable numbers.

Carleton Gajdusek, a skinny youth before he broke into fame, grew stout, yet is still vibrant and witty in conversation, and dignified in demeanor. He remains actively engaged in research on the still-unsolved problems of slow viruses. He feels duty bound by love occasionally to spend a week or so among the Fore people, and visits them regularly.

Furthermore, the "post-Kuru era" presents an auspicious occasion. Despite every effort in the past, the transmissible agent of Kuru, Creutzfeldt-Jacob disease, or scrapie has never been convincingly visualized nor characterized. Recently, however, a young professor of neurology at the University of California, brilliantly persuasive and a disciple of Hadlow, by the name of Stanley Prusiner, found the key to this closed door. After many years of studies, using thousands of laboratory animals and enormous patience, he has at last evinced the chemical structure of the scrapie agent.

What is past is prolog.

Index